DATE DUE

OCT 1 0 1986			
GAYLORD			PRINTED IN U.S.A.

The Thalassocracies

The Thalassocracies

Studies in Chronography II

Molly Miller

State University of New York Press
Albany

PUBLISHED BY STATE UNIVERSITY OF NEW YORK PRESS
THURLOW TERRACE, ALBANY, NEW YORK 12201

© 1971 BY THE RESEARCH FOUNDATION
OF STATE UNIVERSITY OF NEW YORK

ALL RIGHTS RESERVED

ISBN 0–87395–062–3 (clothbound)
ISBN 0–87395–162–X (microfiche)
LIBRARY OF CONGRESS CATALOG CARD NUMBER 77–91204

PRINTED IN THE UNITED STATES OF AMERICA

CONTENTS

PART 2 THE ANTE-HISTORIOGRAPHIC THALASSOCRACIES

PART 3. GENERAL HISTORIOGRAPHY OF THE
THALASSOCRACIES

TABLES

ABBREVIATIONS

aA: annus Abrahae, year of Abraham
AJA: *American Journal of Archaeology*
CAH: *Cambridge Ancient History*
CQ: *Classical Quarterly*
Jac: F. Jacoby, *Fragmente der Griechischen Historiker*
JHS: *Journal of Hellenic Studies*

THE PROBLEM

IN DISCUSSING THE Sicilian colony dates,[1] we considered what they were, how they were arrived at, and what they mean—in other words, the textual problems, the chronographic problems, and the historiographic and historical problems. Throughout the enquiry we were able to make use of the archaeological evidence, largely because a colony (in spite of occasional constitutional complications, as at Zankle and Rhegion) includes a physical entity which can be checked by archaeology. Thalassocracy on the other hand is at best a political entity, and at its most difficult it is merely a historiographic creation: consequently in the present study we shall have much to discuss about written sources, and little contribution from archaeology, or (with some exceptions) from original oral information. The primary problem is the definition of the term 'thalassocracy,' and within that problem the constancy of the definition and of its historical application in the historiographic tradition.

Accordingly, this enquiry is divided into two major parts: the thalassocracies of the historical period from the 530s onwards, about which we can safely assume that the memory was fresh in the time of Herodotus and the earliest local historians, so that there will be a large element of *information* in the historiographic tradition; and the thalassocracies of the ante-historiographic period, from the fall of Troy to the 530s, where there will certainly be a large element of *construction* in the historiographic tradition. From the historical part we hope to derive a definition of 'thalassocracy' which will help us to interpret the ante-historiographic part.

Thalassocracy as a concept of local historiography, sea-power in more or less local waters, has always been known to scholarship from Herodotus' remarks (III 122) on Polykrates of Samos and Minos of

[1] *The Sicilian Colony Dates*, M. Miller (Albany: State University of New York Press, 1970).

1

Crete, and from entries on a number of thalassocrats in Jerome's translation of the Eusebian *Canons*.[2]

As a concept unifying a treatment of Universal History however, thalassocracy was unknown to modern scholarship before the publication of the Armenian translation of the Eusebian *Chronographia*,[3] which contains the decayed relics of the list of Thalassocracies quoted from Diodorus in (it is supposed) the lost seventh book of his *History*. The list claims to be a Register of thalassocrat powers from the fall of Troy to the Persian wars: the text is so badly damaged, and the relation of its figures to those in Jerome and the Armenian *Canons* is so dubious, that the importance of thalassocracy as a concept of Universal History has largely been ignored. Study has concentrated on those aspects of the list which can be treated as though the Register were nothing more than an adding together of supposed events from local histories.[4]

But the notion of thalassocracy as a continuing entity through time, passing from state to state as empire passes from one individual to another, is quite different from the notion that at various times important states also commanded their seas. It is a notion which not only powerfully affects the conception of how history moved from Troy to the Persian Wars, but also presupposes, or provides, new notions in political geography: the eastern Mediterranean is now, apparently, imagined as so small that it was necessarily commanded by some single power throughout a considerable historical period. Such suppositions naturally act back upon the view taken of the historical data (whether recent information, archives, or tradition) and upon the constructions on them.

The Greek bias in historiography was institutional; and one of the questions we have to ask of the Register of Thalassocracies is whether it represents an attempt by some historian before Diodorus to break away from the established tradition of histories of states, of the tracing

---

[2] *Eusebii Pamphili Chronici Canones*, ed. I. K. Fotheringham (Oxford 1923).
[3] *Die griechischen Christlichen Schriftsteller der erstem drei Jahrhunderte* Vol. 20: *Eusebius Werke V, Die Chronik* herausgg. von Dr. Josef Karst (Leipzig 1911).
[4] Winckler in *Der Alte Orient* Vol. 7 part 2 (1905) sought a political foundation for the concept; Aly in *Rheinisches Museum* 66 (1911) 585 ff. thought only of an historiographic origin. See also: Myres in JHS 26 (1906) 84 ff.; Fotheringham in JHS 27 (1907) 75 ff.; Myres ibidem 123 ff.; A. R. Burn JHS 47 (1927) 165 ff.

of genealogies and so forth, and a movement towards what we should regard as a more modern bias—the tracing out of process and movement. If there is any such element at all in thalassocratic history, then all the detailed problems must be handled within an awareness that the Register of Thalassocracies marks a stage in the development of Universal History in the great tradition—though with doctrines opposed to some of those of Thucydides.

PART 1

THE HISTORICAL THALASSOCRACIES

WHEN THE LIST of thalassocracies was first published, before Diodorus copied it, the learned world of the time might have reservations in mind, or revisions to make, on many of the earlier entries, but would most probably regard the last five thalassocrats as historical. The first of the five was Samos at the time of the tyrant Polykrates, of whom Herodotus reported that he was the first known Greek for whom thalassocracy was a policy (leaving aside Minos of Knossos and any earlier ruler of the sea): in the post-heroic age Polykrates was the first, and he had great hopes of becoming ruler of Ionia and the islands. In these remarks we have the germ of a definition of 'thalassocracy', and we examine the historical thalassocracies of the Register mainly from the point of view of discovering whether these Herodotean remarks apply to them all.

A. The Texts
i. the Diodoran Register
The first of the two volumes of the Eusebian *Chronika* is the *Chronographia*, which contains the fragile remains of the Register of Thalassocracies quoted from Diodorus. Karst's translation of the surviving Armenian version of the historical portion of the Register is:

    13. Samier   *Jahre* ⟨ ⟩
    14. Lakedmonier Jahre 2
    15. Naxier   *Jahre 10*
    16. Eretrier   *Jahre 15*
    17. Äginäer   *Jahre 10*
    bis zu Alexandros' Übergang auf die andere Seite.

Alexander's name seems to appear here because Macedon, the heading of the next section of the *Chronographia*, caught the translator's or a copyist's eye. The Diabasis of Xerxes, which is the date intended, will have meant for Diodorus (as for all other classical and

5

Hellenistic historians) the sailing and campaigning season beginning in 481/*0* B.C. Consequently, according to the figures of the Diodoran Register, the absolute dates for these historical thalassocracies are:

13. Samos for ⟨ ⟩ years: to 519/*8*
14. Sparta for 2 years: 518/*7* to 517/*6*
15. Naxos for 10 years: 516/*5* to 507/*6*
16. Eretria for 15 years: 506/*5* to 492/*1*
17. Aigina for 10 years: 491/*0* to 482/*1*

The only immediate and certain external evidence for these dates is given by the Diabasis of Xerxes in 481/*0*, and the capture and destruction of Eretria by the Persians in the same campaigning season as Marathon, but earlier—that is, in the Olympic year 491/*0*. This agrees with the dating of the last full year of Eretrian thalassocracy to the Olympic year 492/*1*.

ii. the Eusebian Canons
But the evidence of the extant derivatives of the *Canons* (the second volume of the Eusebian *Chronika*) nowhere agrees with these absolute dates. Thus either (1) the Diodoran evidence is falsely reported (by errors or omissions) through textual corruption; or (2) the evidence of the *Canons* is false through textual corruption; or (3) Eusebius, while reporting the Register in the *texts* of his entries in the *Canons*, in fact placed these entries at *dates* provided by a different historiography.[5]

Moreover, we should note that if Diodorus is accurately reported as covering all the years from the fall of Troy to the Diabasis of Xerxes, Eusebius' Troy was two years later than the orthodox date (no doubt used by Diodorus) of 1184/*3* for Troy. Consequently it is plain that Eusebius must at least have changed the Register so that these two years were lost from it; and he could do this either by shortening the

---

[5] This last is quite possible, as may be shown by another example. At the *annus Abrahae* 1259, Jerome says that the Spartan kings ruled for 350 years: this is quoted from some authority who is not otherwise followed, for the *filum* of royal Spartan years runs only from aA 916 to aA 1240, a total of 325 years. The Armenian *Canons* have moved the quotation back to the 325th year, while the XC edition of Jerome has moved it down to the 350th (aA 1265). Thus what Eusebius did here (though not why), and what his editors made of it, is clear: and we cannot *a priori* exclude such possibilities from the Thalassocracy (or indeed any other) entries.

first, or last, or some intermediate entry by two years, or moving the whole list down two years for every entry.

We cannot exclude the possibility that in re-dating Troy (and therefore the thalassocracies) Eusebius was following a predecessor who was historian enough to know that Eretria was destroyed in 491/0. For such an historian, of course, some of the possible ways of re-dating the list are excluded; and in general it seems unlikely that any changes which were simple mechanical re-datings would be carried out in the historical portion of the Register, either by Eusebius or a predecessor. If there is genuine disagreement between the Register and the Canons for this period, it is most likely to be a historiographic difference.

To decide this question, we must examine the Canonical derivatives in detail.[6]

a. the evidence of the Armenian Canons

The entries of, or relevant to, the historical thalassocracies in the Armenian *Canons* are:

aA 1481 E Samos' Gewalthaber sind Krates und Silos, zu denen
1484 G auch Pandokostos ⟨gehörte⟩, die Brüder, gewesen.

> The date is 536/5 or 533/2, varying between the two manuscripts. The translation is produced by taking the name Συλοσῶν as Συλος ὤν, as in the manuscripts of Jerome. Krates is ⟨Poly⟩krates.

aA 1486 XVI fuhrten die Seeherrschaft die Samier

> According to Karst, the false ordinal XVI is an Armenian textual error: then Myres' suggestion that XVI is taken from the (lost) figure for the duration of the thalassocracy must be abandoned.[7] The date is 531/0.

aA 1503 XIV hatten die Seeherrschaft die Lakedämonier, 2 Jahre.

> The date is 514/3.

---

[6] The following enquiry is anticipated at some points by R. Helm: 'Liste der Thalassocratien in Eusebius' Chronik' in *Hermes* 61 (1926) 241 ff., which does not however use the Syriac evidence. See also Helm's introduction (p. xxix) to his edition of Jerome: *Eusebius Werke VII: Die Chronik des Hieronymus* (*Die griechischen Christlichen Schriftsteller der ersten Jahrhunderte* Vol. 47) Berlin 1956.

[7] So also Mary White 'The Duration of the Samian Tyranny' in JHS 74 (1954) 40 ff.

aA 1514 XVI hatten die Seeherrschaft die Aneretrier, 15 Jahre.
The spelling Aneretrier shows the prefix of A- frequent in the Armenian's proper names. The ordinals of this and the previous entry show that ⟨XV Naxos⟩ has been omitted by a copying error only. The date is 503/2.

aA 1513 XVII hatten die Seeherrschaft die Egypter 10 Jahre, bis zu des Xerxes Hinüberfahrt.
The spelling Egypter (for Aigina) is evidence of transcription from the Syriac. The date is 487/6, but the text of the entry is a quotation from the Diodoran Register.

aA 1534 Xerxes, noch Athen gekommen, äscherte die Stadt ein, unter Kliad dem Fursten.
Kliad is the archon Kalliades of 480/79; but aA 1534 is 483/2 B.C.

aA 1537 Die Kampf bei Thermupolis und die Seeschlacht bei Salamin.
The spelling Thermupolis is again evidence of transcription from the Syriac. The date is 480/79.

The Naxian thalassocracy is omitted entirely, but obviously by a mere copying error; there is no statement of length for the Samian. There is no entry for the Diabasis of Xerxes, and therefore no control for the editors and copyists over the lower terminus of the list. The misdating of the Athenian entry with the name of Kalliades shows that the copyists had no historical knowledge. We are apparently faced only with a mechanical copying, whether from older Armenian texts, or also from the Syriac, is not clear.

The durations obtained by subtraction in this series of dates are: Samos 17 years, Sparta ⟨and Naxos⟩ 11 years, Eretria 16 years. Since Sparta, ⟨Naxos⟩ and Eretria together have 27 years as in the Diodoran Register, there is a presumption that the entry for Eretria is misplaced by one year, and that an earlier Armenian text had:

⟨XIII⟩	Samos, beginning in 531/0 lasting ⟨ ⟩ years		
XIV	Sparta,	514/3	2
⟨XV	Naxos	512/1	10⟩
XVI	Eretria	⟨502/1⟩	15
XVII	Aigina	487/6	(10)

8

Although the periods agree with those of the Register, the absolute dates are either erroneous, or derive from another authority—and it is not easy to think of an authority working on the thalassocracy dates and criticizing the Register, but allowing the Eretrian thalassocracy to survive the city for some three years.

b. the evidence of the Syriac derivatives
Two of the Syriac derivatives of Eusebius contain entries on, or relevant to, the thalassocracies:

The *Epitome* of Eusebius' Chronicle by Dionysius of Tell Mahre:[8]

Anno MCCCCLXXXII filii Sami urbem Poteolos condiderunt

> This is aA 1482=535/4 B.C., a year later than the entry in the E manuscript of the Armenian on the Samian tyranny. Jerome has a slightly longer form of the same entry at 531/0, so it is guaranteed for the Greek original, even though it is omitted by Synkellos and the Armenian *Canons*.

Anno MDXXXVII erat pugna ad Thermopylas et proelium navale Salaminum.

> aA 1537=480/79 B.C. This is presumably the Syriac original of the Armenian's Thermupolis, and is at the same date.

The *Chronicle* of Michael the Syrian:[9]
p.103.20 (after the notice on the tyrannicides): En quatorzième lieu, les Lacédémoniens occupèrent la mer pendant 2 ans; en quinzième lieu, les habitants de Naxos, pendant ⟨ ⟩; en seizième lieu, les Erétriens, pendant 17 ans;
p.107.20 (after the notice on Pompilia): Les Eginètes occupèrent la mer, en dix-septième lieu, pendant 10 ans, jusqu'au passage de Xerxès.

Thus Michael has no entry on Samos, but records the remaining four thalassocracies (without dates). His Sparta follows the tyrannicides, as in the Armenian *Canons*, but unlike those *Canons* adds, in the same entry, Naxos (length lost), and Eretria (length apparently corrupt). His entry on Aigina (presumably the original of the

---

[8] G. Siegfried et H. Gelzer: *Eusebii Canonum Epitome ex Dionysii Telmaharensis Chronico petita* (Leipzig 1884).
[9] J. B. Chabot: *Chronique de Michel le Syrien* I (Paris 1899).

Armenian's Egypt) follows the Pompilia notice instead of preceding it as in the Armenian *Canons*.

The *Canons* from which these Syriac scholars were working were fuller than the Armenian as those survive: the Dikaiarchia-Puteoli entry was present as it is in Jerome, and Naxos still survived though incompletely. There was however one notable difference of form: the Spartan, Naxian and Eretrian entries were placed together in a single compendious entry.

c. the evidence of the Greek derivative

In Synkellos' *Chronographia*,[10] there occur at irregular intervals (and not always in the right order) lists of events which he entitles Σποράδην. These are abstracts of entries in the *Canons* other than dynastic notes or material closely connected with the *fila* of years. Not only are the lists themselves sometimes in the wrong order, but the events within them are sometimes in the order given in our *Canons*, and sometimes not.

For the entries on the historical thalassocracies, two of these Sporaden-lists are concerned, which for the purposes of this enquiry I shall call FIRST and SECOND.

FIRST (451.9 ff.) includes the following entries:

451.10: Σάμου τύραννοι Πολυκράτης καὶ Συλοσῶν καὶ Παντογνόστος ἀδελφοὶ γεγόνασι.

> This entry is out of order, being placed before the fall of Sardis. Perhaps the excerptor omitted it until he came to the entry on Polykrates' destruction, then copied it into his margin, whence it has come to the head of the list (together with another marginalium, on the first Roman consuls, which is part of the preceding section on the Ῥωμαίων βασιλεῖς).

452.4: Πολυκράτης Σαμίων τυραννῶν ἀνεσταυρώθη.

> This entry is missing from all our other representatives of the *Canons*.

452.13: Λακεδαιμόνιοι ιδ΄ ἐθαλασσοκράτησαν ἔτη ιβ΄.

> This entry is also out of place, being after the Roman census dated by Jerome to 504/3 B.C.; but this census

---

[10] *Corpus Scriptorum Historiae Byzantinae: Georgius Syncellus . . .* ed. Dindorf (Bonn 1829).

with its 12 myriads of Roman citizens is probably the source for the 12 years ascribed to the Spartan thalassocracy.

The next Sporaden-list in Synkellos (453.5 ff.) is itself out of place, for its events belong before the fall of Sardis. There follows our SECOND list (469.15 ff.), which begins:

469.15 f.: Νάξιοι ἐθαλασσοκράτησαν ιέ, ἔτη ί, καὶ μετ᾽ αὐτοὺς Ἐρετριεῖς ις᾽, ἔτη ζ᾽.

> Naxos and Eretria (though without Sparta) are here in a single entry, reminiscent of the Syriac.

469.17 Γέλων Συρακούσιος ἐκράτησεν ἔτη ιζ᾽.

> Gelon's entry is at 487/6 in Jerome, and this is the Armenian's date for Aigina.

469.18: Ἐθαλασσοκράτησαν Αἰγινῆται ἔτη ί.

In these three entries, the seven years of Eretria seem to have been stolen from Gelon, who in turn has appropriated the Aiginetan ordinal for the duration of his reign. Synkellos' evidence consequently amply supports Michael's form of a compendious entry, and we may therefore account for Michael's 17 years for the Eretrians by supposing that it was, in his ancestral *Canons*, stolen from the Aiginetan ordinal, as Gelon has stolen the same number in Synkellos' *traditio*. The Greek and Syriac derivatives are therefore connected by the compendious entry and its results, and Jerome and the Armenian are associated in some way with this compendium because one of them places Gelon at 487/6, and the other Aigina at the same date.

d. the evidence of the Latin Canons

Jerome's Latin translation of the *Canons* is in general by far the oldest and best evidence for the original Greek text; but its evidence for the historical thalassocracies is both meagre and disconcerting:

aA 1484: Apud Samum tyrannidem exercent tres fratres Polykrates Sylus et Pantagnostos.

> Syloson's name is already corrupt here, but Jerome's translation preserves ἀδελφοὶ ⟨γ᾽⟩ γεγόνασι lost in Synkellos. The date is 533/2, but the text is poor.

aA 1486: Samii Dicaearchiam condiderunt quam nunc Puteolos uocant.

> The entry is four years earlier in Dionysius' *Epitome*. Jerome's year is 531/0, but the text is not good.

11

aA 1508: XVII mare obtinuerunt Aeginetae an. XX
usque ad transitum Xerxis.

> In this entry, the Aiginetans have retained their ordinal,
> but the duration has become twenty years in all manu-
> scripts but the learned T, in which it is 25. The date
> is 509/8, in a quite good text.

Here, the only direct thalassocracy entry is that for Aigina, at an
eccentric date and with an unparalleled duration. In comparing
Jerome's evidence with that from the eastern scholars, we have to
remember that his hastily dictated translation did not generally alter,
except by inadvertence, the information given in the Greek *Canons*
on any subject but Roman history. We should expect therefore that
he reproduced his original, as he read it, on the Aiginetan thalassocracy, and certainly his last phrase corresponds to the Armenian's
bis zu des Xerxes Hinüberfahrt and to Michael's *jusqu'au passage de
Xerxès*. The phrase therefore seems to be guaranteed for the Greek
Canons, although it is not present in Synkellos.

In this instance, however, the relationship between Jerome and his
Greek original is complicated by the evidence of T, an editor who
collated Greek evidence for his revisions of the Latin text. Jerome
said that Aigina, in 509/8, was twenty years before Xerxes' diabasis,
and since he had no entry on the Diabasis, he had no check on the
figure. Editor T was in the same position, and he retains the date of
509/8; yet he changes the duration of the thalassocracy to 25 years.
This must mean that neither Jerome nor T was exercised by historical
questions: the 20 and 25 years must be textually derived. Helm,
reaching the same conclusion, has suggested that the figure was
appropriated from the Persian *filum* and its notice of Xerxes' 20-year
reign, at a time when the entries on Gelon and Aigina were both
placed at 487/6, but all the stages in this development:

(1) the corruption of a notice about Gelon's victory (at Olympia) in
488/7 to a notice of his conquest in 487/6;

(2) the presumed removal of the Aigina notice from 491/0 to 487/6;

(3) the carrying back of the Aigina notice from 487/6 to 509/8,

can hardly have occurred between the times of Eusebius and Jerome.
We should therefore look instead for an explanation of the numerals
20 and 25 within a Greek text otherwise similar to the Latin, let us
say ιζ' ἐθαλασσοκράτησαν Αἰγινῆται ἔτη⟨δεκ.ἑως τῆς Ξερξου διαβάσεως⟩. With

12

such a text, Jerome and T could have read ἔτη δὲ κ' ἕως and ἔτη δὲ κέ ὡς ...

The Latin *Canons* therefore scarcely add to our information on the Eusebian treatment of the historical Thalassocracies: on the contrary, they pose the questions of why Samos, Sparta, Naxos, and Eretria were omitted, and Aigina treated so eccentrically. Yet the Latin *Canons* are generally to be taken as by far our oldest and best Eusebian evidence. We must therefore work back from the later sources until we make contact of some kind with Jerome's version.

iii. earlier texts of the Canons

The direct evidence from the four derivatives of the Eusebian *Canons* may now be summarized:

Thalassocracy	Armenian	Michael	Synkellos	Jerome
Samos	entry	—	—	—
Sparta	entry	compendium	entry	—
Naxos	(former entry)	which (on the		
		evidence of	compendium	—
		17 years for	which once	
Eretria	entry	Eretria) once	included	—
		included	Gelon and	
Aigina	entry	entry	entry	entry
	(487/6)			(509/8)

Within the eastern sources, the major differences lie between the Armenian with its separate entries on the one hand, and on the other the Greek and Syriac evidence for an earlier and more extensive compendious entry containing the last three or four thalassocrats. The meagerness of Jerome's evidence makes it, without further enquiry, impossible to say whether he was translating from a text of the Armenian, or of the Greco-Syriac, type.

The first attempt at further enquiry should not be addressed to Michael, whose *Chronicle* in general contains much non-Eusebian material, and whose witness might therefore be misleading. But Synkellos' Sporaden-lists are more rewarding.

In FIRST, as already noted, the first two entries are misplaced marginalia, of which only the second (on the Samian tyranny) is part of the Sporaden-list. The first belongs to the previous section, on the Roman kings, and should be printed as part of that section: we shall not count it here, but take the Samian entry as the first.

13

This gives us sixteen entries over the period where there are or should be thalassocracy entries in FIRST, and when we compare this Sporaden-list with the *Canons*, we see immediately:

(1) entries 5–9 in the Sporaden-list are all in the right-hand column of the Armenian *Canons*, p.189 Karst;

(2) contemporary entries in these *Canons*, but in the left-hand column, are NOT in Synkellos;

(3) entries 11 and 14–16 are in the right-hand column of the Armenian *Canons*, pp.190 f. Karst.

It therefore appears, as a first approximation, that the selection certainly, and possibly the sequence also, of entries in FIRST is related to the form of the lay-out in the *Canons* from which the excerpting was done. For this period, two forms of lay-out are known, one in Jerome and one in the Armenian. Jerome had two facing pages, one for Sacred and one for Profane history, on the left and right respectively; each page has columns of royal years of various dynasties on either side, and centrally a *spatium historicum* with entries of events. The Armenian lay-out is more compact, using one page only and placing all the columns of royal years in the centre: on either side are two marginal columns for the entries of events, and there is a marked (but not at all exclusive) preference for placing Sacred events in the left-hand column, and Profane in the right. The correlation of FIRST is, however, with the Armenian and not with Jerome's lay-out: and we must therefore conclude that FIRST was excerpting from a Greek text with the Armenian type of lay-out.

With this hypothesis we proceed as follows:

1st entry, on the Samian tyranny, is a misplaced marginalium which should be in the 530's, that is, between the 9th and 10th entries;

2nd entry, on Thales' death, is in the left-hand column of the Armenian *Canons*, p.189, while

3rd and 4th entries, on Cyrus in Lydia and Harpagos in Ionia, are in the Armenian represented by an entry running across the *fila* (in Jerome they are attached to the Lydian *filum*). It appears therefore that entries 2–4 mark the end of a section dealing with left-hand entries and the end of that epoch. The excerptor then moves to the right-hand column for entries 5–9;

14

10th entry, on the destruction of Polykrates, is not in either of our *Canons*, but since it lies between 5–9 and 11 in the right-hand column, we should probably take it as present in the right-hand column of Synkellos' *Canons*. Herodotus (III 120) dates the destruction of Polykrates to the time of Cambyses' last sickness, so this entry should be in Cambyses' last year 523/2. This would be at the bottom of a page in the original lay-out, and so may have been missed by Jerome.

11th entry has, as an addition, a further (12th) entry on Leaina, not in our *Canons* but perhaps present as a note in Synkellos' copy.

13th entry, on the Roman census, is at 504/3 in Jerome and omitted in the Armenian. Since it is preceded and followed by right-hand entries, we can suppose that it was in the right-hand column also in Synkellos' *Canons*, and that in the course either of excerpting, or of copying the excerpts, it has changed places with the 14th entry, on the Spartan thalassocracy.

15th and 16th entries are in the right-hand column of the Armenian.

This detail therefore seems to mean that, after the fall of Lydia, the entries in FIRST are all taken from the right-hand margin of a Greek edition of the *Canons* with the lay-out known to us from the Armenian. The list has three errors: an omission, marginalization, and false replacement of the entry on the Samian tyranny; an interchange of place between the Roman census and the Spartan thalassocracy; and an interchange of the same kind in entries 15 and 16.

We can therefore produce an approximate picture of the part of the *Canons* from which FIRST excerpted. In this picture, years B.C. stand for the central block of *fila*, and I assume that Jerome's equation of aA 1241 = 776/5 B.C. held also for the Greek edition:

2. Θαλῆς θνήσκει.   549/8
                                       548/7
                                       547/6

3. Κῦρος Σάρδεις εἶλεν.
4. Ἅρπαγος εὐδοκιμῶν παρὰ Κύρῳ κατὰ τῆς Ἰωνίας ἐστράτευσε

15

19. Hibycus carminum
scriptor agnoscitur

20. Anacreon lyricus poeta
cognoscitur

21. Samii Dicaearchiam
condiderunt quam nunc
Puteolos uocant

22. XIII fuhrten die Seeherrschaft
die Samier. 23. Pythagoras
physicus philosophus clarus
habetur. 24. Hipparchus et
Hippias Athenis tyrannidem
exercent

546/5
545/4
544/3
543/2
542/1
541/0
540/39
539/8
538/7
537/6
536/5
535/4
533/3
533/2
532/1
531/0
530/29
529/8
528/7
527/6
526/5
525/4
524/3
523/2
522/1
521/0

520/19

519/8
518/7
517/6
516/5
515/4

514/3
513/2
512/1
511/0
510/09

5. Θέογνις ὁ ποιητὴς
ἐγνωρίζετο.
6. Πεισίστρατος Ἀθηναίων
τὸ δεύτερον ἐβασίλευσε.
7. Φερεκύδης ἱστορικὸς ἐγνωρίζετο. Πυθαγόρου διδάσκαλος.
8. Σιμωνίδης μελοποιὸς ἐγνωρίζετο. 9. Φωκυλίδης καὶ Ξενο-
φάνης φυσικός, τραγῳδοποιὸς
ἐγνωρίζετο.
1. ⟨Σάμου τύραννοι Πολυκράτης
καὶ Συλοσῶν καὶ Πανταγνωσ-
τος ἀδελφοὶ γ΄ γεγόνασι.⟩

10. Πολυκράτης Σαμίων τυραννῶν
'ανεσταυρώθη

17. Note on the building of the Temple

18. Note on the end of the Captivity

11. Ἁρμόδιος καὶ Ἀριστογείτων
ἀνεῖλον Ἵππαρχον τύραννον
καθ' οὓς Λεαίνα ἡ ἑταίρα ὑπ' αὐτῶν ἐταζομένη κατειπεῖν τοὺς
συνωμότας τῆς ἑαυτῆς ἀπέτρισε
γλῶτταν.
14. Λακεδαιμόνιοι ιδ΄ ἐθαλασσοκράτησαν ἔτη β΄.

12. Λεαίναν μόνην ἑταίραν εἰκόνι
Ἀθηναῖοι ἐτίμησαν ἐν ἀκροπόλει.
ἄγλωτταν δὲ Λεαίναν ταύτην
παρεξωγράφησαν ἀντὶ ἐπιγρα-
φῆς τὸ πάθος δηλοῦντες.

16

	509/8	
	508/7	
	507/6	
	505/4	
	504/3	13. Τυμήσεως ἐν 'Ρώμη γενομένης
25. XVI hatten die Seeherr-	503/2	εὑρέθησαν μυριαδες ιβ' τοῦ
schaft die Aneretrier		πλήθους.
15 Jahre	502/1	15. Δημόκριτος 'Αβδηρίτης φυσι-
	501/0	κὸς φιλοσοφος καὶ 'Ηράκλειτος
	500/499	ὁ σκοτεῖνος λεγομενος καὶ
		'Αναξάγορας φυσικοὶ ἐήκμαξον.
	499/8	16. 'Ελλάνικος ἱστορικὸς ἐγνωρίζ-
		ετο.

1. Armenian E dates to 536/5, Armenian G and Jerome 533/2
2. As Armenian. Jerome dates 548/7
3. as Armenian.   ⎧ Jerome dates
4. as Armenian.   ⎨ 548/7 onwards
5. as Armenian. Jerome 544/3
6. as Armenian. Jerome 543/2
7. as Armenian. Jerome 541/0
8. as Armenian. Jerome 539/8
9. as Armenian. Jerome 539/8
10. omitted by both *Canons*
11. as Armenian. Jerome 520/19
12. placed by guesswork to leave room for other entries.
13. at Jerome's date   (omitted in Armenian)
14. at Armenian date (omitted in Jerome)
15. at Armenian date. Jerome 500/499
16. at Armenian date. Jerome 500/499
17. at this date in both *Canons*
18. as Armenian. Jerome part of 17.
19. Jerome only
20. Jerome only
21. Dionysius 535/4, Jerome 531/0
22. Armenian date (omitted in Jerome)
23. Armenian E 533/2, G 532/1 Jerome 530/29
24. at this date in both *Canons*
25. Armenian's date (omitted in Jerome)

The detail in Synkellos' SECOND Sporaden-list presents rather more difficulty. The first entry, on Naxos and Eretria, is paralleled only by the entry on Eretria alone, in the left-hand column of the Armenian *Canons*. The Armenian Aigina is also in the left-hand column, but not associated with Gelon as in SECOND. However, SECOND's entries 4–6 are in the Armenian's left-hand column also, so there is some consistency here.

SECOND's 7th and 8th entries are both in the Armenian's right-hand column; and after this SECOND goes deep into the fifth century before returning in three entries to our period. Of these the first, on the first Roman dictator, appears in the Armenian's right-hand column; the second, on Panyasis, in the left, and the third, on the ostracism of Aristeides, not at all.

In particular it is noteworthy that SECOND has two entries on Aristeides' ostracism. His 9th entry says simply Ἀριστείδης ἐξωστρακίσθη and this corresponds to Jerome's entry at the year 484/3, but is omitted in the Armenian. The second is at the end of the list and is much more informative: Ἀριστείδης ὁ λεγόμενος δικαιός ἐξωστρακίσθη μετὰ πόλλους πόνους ὑπό Ἀθηναίων. From Jerome's evidence, this could be a note either to the ostracism entry of 484/3, or to the entry on Marathon: *Bellum quod in Marathone gestum est et ea quae de Miltiade scribuntur et Aristide qui cognominabatur iustus.* This text almost looks as though it is made out of two entries, one ending at *scribuntur* and one containing the first part of SECOND's longer entry on Aristeides. At least we can say that, in SECOND's *Canons* which are relatively remote from the Armenian version, there seems to be some distant and indirect contact with Jerome, or at least with a Greek text which Jerome would have recognized, and which is not represented, in the Marathon entry, in eastern scholarship.[11]

Returning to the thalassocracy entries of SECOND, and assuming that the *Canons* used were remote from our Armenian text, we may begin by hypothetically placing the beginning of the Naxos-Eretria compendium at the year 512/1, two years after the Armenian's date for Sparta. We then have something like the following:

---

[11] In his Persian dynastic notes, Synkellos 468.6 has a parallel:

Τότε δὴ κακῶς πράττουσιν ἐν Μαραθῶνι Πέρσαι Μιλτιάδου καὶ Ἀριστείδου καὶ Καλλιμάχου καλῶς ἐστρατηγηκότων, ἐν οἷς καὶ ὁ τύραννος Ἱππίας πίπτει μετὰ τῶν βαρβάρων Ἀθηναίοις μαχόμενος.

But this is not the original of Jerome's entry.

18

Νάξιοι 'εθαλασσοκράτησαν	512/1
ιέ, ἔτη ί, καὶ μετ' αὐτοὺς	511/0
'Ερετριεῖς ιϛ', ἔτη ⟨ιέ⟩.	510/09
ιζ' ἐθαλασσοκράτησαν	509/8
Αἰγινῆται ἔτη δεκ ⟨έως	508/7
τῆς Ξέρζον διαβάσεως⟩	507/6

This reconstructed text begins to look like a credible ancestor for (1) Jerome's eccentric date and duration for Aigina, and (2) Michael's 17 years for Eretria. But it does not account for Synkellos' Gelon between Eretria and Aigina, or his seventeen years, or Jerome's placing of Gelon at 487/6, the same year as the Armenian's date for Aigina. However, as we have seen, the Armenian shows no trace of the compendium entry: it followed a *traditio* of separate itemization of each thalassocracy at its own date. We must suppose therefore that SECOND has collated and combined two texts, one ancestral to Jerome and Michael and reconstructed above, and one ancestral to the Armenian, having at the year 487/6 the double entry Γέλων Συρακούσιος ἐκράτησεν ἔτη ζ'. ιζ' εθαλασσοκράτησαν Αἰγινῆται ἔτη ί. The collator would, rightly, consider the compendium version as older and better than the other, but apparently believed that it had omitted Gelon by mistake, and carried that entry back with that of Aigina.

The evidence of Synkellos' Sporaden-list is therefore that FIRST excerpted from a Greek text with the Armenian lay-out, and that we have a record of the entries in the right-hand column of these *Canons*, but not of the entries in the left-hand column; and that SECOND had access to a much older version of the *Canons*, in which the compendious entry ancestral to both Jerome and Michael was present: he combined this evidence with that from a version which, like the Armenian, entered the thalassocracies separately.

iv. the original text

We are now in a position to consider the historical thalassocracy entries in the text of the original Eusebian *Canons*.

For Samos, we have evidence of four entries in the 530s, on the tyranny, the colony, the thalassocracy, and Pythagoras, probably in that order. For the tyranny date, we should accept the evidence of the oldest witness, Jerome, that Eusebius placed it at the year 533/2 B.C. The question for the dates of the colony and thalassocracy is whether Eusebius intended the three entries to make a single paragraph all referring to the year 533/2, or whether these and the Pythagoras entry were placed at successive years. The manuscript evidence is perhaps in favour of the second, but this is by no means conclusive. From the evidence of all the derivatives, we may suppose that the original text, using the wide *spatium historicum* in the centre of the page for its entries, resembled:

533/2 Σάμου τύραννοι Πολυκράτης καὶ Συλοσῶν καὶ Παντάγνωστος ἀδελφοὶ γ' γεγόνασι.

532/1 Samii Dicaearchiam condiderunt quam nunc Puteolos uocant

531/0 XII führten die Seeherrschaft die Samier

530/29 Pythagoras physicus philosophus clarus habetur

> The first entry uses Synkellos' text, but is also present in Jerome and the Armenian; the second entry uses Jerome's text, but is also more briefly present in Dionysius; the third entry comes from the Armenian alone.

*　　*　　*

The last four thalassocracies are all, in one or another source, in or connected with the compendium.

For Sparta, the first question is whether Eusebius intended the Register date of 518/7, or some later year and if so which. For the lay-out at this point we should accept the evidence of Jerome, that the notes on the temple and the captivity were one, and that the tyrannicide entry was placed at 520/19. With the wide *spatium historicum* and that part only of the Leaina entry which is common to Jerome and the Armenian, and the evidence of both Fotheringham and Helm that Jerome in fact has a space of two lines here in his *fila* of years, we may hold that the original text resembled:

520/19 Ἁρμόδιος καὶ Ἀριστογείτων Ἵππαρχον ἀνεῖλον

519/8 τύραννον καθ' οὓς Λεαίνα ἡ ἑταῖρα ὑπ'
αὐτῶν ἐταζομένη κατειπεῖν τοὺς
συνωμότας τὴν ἑαυτῆς ἀπέτρισε γλῶτταν.

518/7 Λακεδαιμόνιοι ιδ' ἐθαλασσοκράτησαν ἔτη β'.

A failure to observe the space of two lines in the *fila*; the narrowing of the *spatium historicum* into a marginal column; or the lengthening of the Leaina entry, would each serve to depress the date of Sparta, and in the Armenian *Canons* it is in fact placed at 514/3. For the

20

Syriac Michael, the Spartan entry has been forced into the first part of his compendium.

If the original text had Sparta at 518/7, its compendium entry for Naxos, Eretria and Aigina should have begun at 516/5. But this is the year of the completion of the Temple, a report which must always have occupied several years, as it does in Jerome; and immediately afterwards the beginning of the Roman republic cannot have had a short entry in Eusebius, even though Jerome may have expanded it. The compendium on the thalassocracies must almost certainly under these conditions have been a marginalium, running from 516/5 to the bottom of the page (188 in Fotheringham, 106 in Helm) at the year 510/09, and at the top of the next page:

	518/7	Λακεδαιμόνιοι ιδ' ἐθαλασσοκράτησαν ἔτη β'.
	517/6	
Νάξιοι ἐθαλ-	516/5	Templum in Hierosolymis
άσσοκράτησαν	515/4	consummatur profetan-
ιέ ἔτη ί	514/3	tibus apud Iudaeos Aggaeo et
καὶ μετ' αὐτοῦς	513/2	Zacharia
'Ερετριεῖς	512/1	Romanorum reges VII a Romulo usque
ις' ἔτη ιέ	511/0	ad Tarquinium Superbum imperauerunt
	510/09	an. CCXL siue ut quibusdam placent CCXLIII

ιζ' ἐθαλασσο	509/8	Ualerius Bruti collega adeo pau-
κράτησαν	508/7	per mortuus ut sumptu publico
'Αιγινῆται	507/6	sepeliretur.
ἔτη δεκ ⟨ἐως	506/5	
τῆς Ξέρξου	505/4	
διαβάσεως⟩	504/3	Censu Romae agitato etc.

With such an original text we can see

(1) how for Michael the Spartan entry was forced out of the *spatium historicum* into the margin above the original marginalium;

(2) how for Synkellos' FIRST in consequence, somewhere in his ancestry, the Spartan thalassocracy followed the Roman census entry at which the whole marginalium ended;

(3) how Jerome overlooked the beginning of the marginalium at the bottom of the page, but noticed and translated the Aiginetan portion at the top of the next page, at 509/8.

21

We conclude therefore that all the historical thalassocracy dates in the representatives of the Eusebian *Canons* derive textually from an original using the absolute dates of the Diodoran Register. The pedigree is:

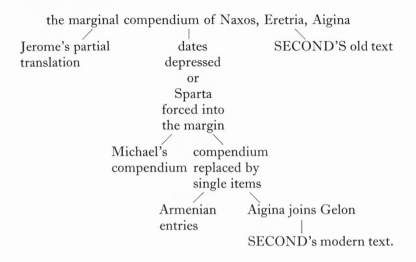

the marginal compendium of Naxos, Eretria, Aigina

Jerome's partial translation   dates depressed or Sparta forced into the margin   SECOND'S old text

Michael's compendium   compendium replaced by single items

Armenian entries   Aigina joins Gelon

SECOND's modern text.

When the compendium was replaced by itemized entries, these were apparently placed and dated by dead reckoning from a Spartan entry already depressed by four years.

B. The Historiography
i. SAMOS

It is fortunate that the first of the historical thalassocracies is also something of a test case for the problems of the concept of thalassocracy. We have, relatively, copious information; Herodotus discusses the meaning of 'thalassocracy' in relation to Samos; and there is sufficient disagreement between the plain implications of his narrative on the one hand, and the dates given by the Register on the other, to illuminate the historiographic questions.

a. Herodotus and the Register

Herodotus explains thalassocracy as Polykrates' use of a fleet 'to rule Ionia and the islands', and in this view the Samian thalassocracy should be dated from Polykrates' usurpation or soon afterwards, to the mutiny of his trireme fleet in the spring of 526/5. In the Diodoran Register, however, the Samian thalassocracy apparently continues until 519/8, or at least is not succeeded (by the Spartan) until 518/7. It is certainly possible that the source of the Diodoran Register assigned the years 525/4 to 519/8 to an interregnum which does not appear in the Register-form in which his conclusions are, for us, represented; but since Herodotus records the survival of the trireme fleet for some years, it is equally possible that the source of the Register regarded the Samian thalassocracy as continuing in being (though now hostile to Polykrates and his successors) while the trireme fleet survived. To understand as fully as possible what Herodotus meant by thalassocracy, and what later historiography may have done to modify or develop his concept, we examine the history of Samos at this period in detail.

b. the history of thalassocratic Samos
1. the policy of Polykrates
When Herodotus says that Polykrates set out, of deliberate policy, to rule Ionia and the islands, and that he was the first man to embark on such a policy since Minos in the Heroic age, he does not relate this statement to the previous history of Samos in any systematic way. Instead, he connects it closely with a centralization of finances—a regular and heavy impost on all merchant vessels using what Polykrates was able to claim as territorial waters.[12]

This appreciation of the financial bases of power was certainly not discovered by Polykrates.[13] The public works which Aristotle[14] calls Polykratean are shown by their archaeology to have been initiated before his time; his early fleet of a hundred pentekonters[15] must at least in part have been inherited from the previous government; and Samian 'piracy' was notoriously successful in the years 548 and 547 B.C.[16] The main architect of Samian power on the financial side was probably Polykrates' father Aiakes, whose grandson and namesake is

---

[12] III 39.4.
[13] M. White, 'The Duration of the Samian Tyranny', JHS 74 (1954) 36 ff.
[14] *Politics* 1313b.
[15] Hdt. III 39.
[16] Hdt III 47 f.; seizure of the Egyptian corselet and of the Spartan wine-bowl.

generally believed to have caused the inscription of the dedication[17] on one of Aiakes' offerings to Hera:

Αεακης ανεθηκεν | ο Βρυσωνος ος τη | Ηρη την συλην ε | πρησεν κατα την | επιστασιν.

'dedicated by Aiakes son of Bryson, who secured the booty for Hera during his *epistasis*'.

Since Aiakes named one of his sons Syloson 'booty-securing', he seems to have been particularly pleased with his organization of the 'booty'; and such indications as we possess suggest that his tenure of the office of *epistasis* was long.[18] Polykrates thus seems to have taken over both the pentekonter fleet, and an established financial machinery for its support: the difference between his father's epistasis and his own tyrannis was presumably that under Aiakes the machinery had a voluntary form, while under Polykrates it was openly obligatory.

One of the Samian local historians[19] seems to have discussed some such difference of administrative form, for he is quoted as reporting, of an unnamed ruler or magistrate, that 'he condemned no-one for not sharing part of the booty'. This is more likely to refer to that would-be just man, Maiandrios, than to Aiakes; but if it refers to the archaic period at all, it implies that some-one, presumably Polykrates, *did* condemn people for not turning in all the booty they secured.

The conditions of our evidence thus seem to be met if we suppose that previously the collection of 'booty' had the form of a co-operative of privateers, while under Polykrates it was enforced by a fleet under orders.

It therefore appears that for Herodotus and for other historians the Polykratean thalassocracy in Samos was (1) definable: rule over Ionia and the islands, shown partly in the enforcement of imposts; (2) a

---

[17] L. H. Jeffery, *The Local Scripts of Archaic Greece* (Oxford 1963) p.414 no.13; pp.330 f.
[18] If the emendation of Suidas' entry on Ibykos is to be trusted, some authority said that Aiakes was already in office (ἦρχεν) in the first year of Croesus (561/0). The statue dedicated to Hera by Aiakes (supposing it to have been rightly identified by his grandson) is dated on stylistic grounds to the last third of the sixth century (M. Richter, *Archaic Greek Art against its historical background*, New York 1949). These witnesses give Aiakes some thirty years in office. See also note 34 below.
[19] Jac 544 F 3: probably Aethlios.

24

matter of deliberate policy, and this for the first time in post-Heroic history; (3) strongly centralized in Polykrates' personal rule.[20]

2. the beginning of the tyranny

The Eusebian evidence places the beginning of the tyranny of the three brothers, Polykrates, Syloson and Pantognostos, in 533/2 B.C. Polyainos[21] provides a longer narrative, in which the name of the third brother has the same spelling as in Eusebius (as against the Pantagnotos of Herodotus[22]), and in which he says that Polykrates summoned and received help from Lygdamis, tyrant of Naxos. This help may have been the fifteen hoplites whom Herodotus[23] mentions as having secured Polykrates' power.

Lygdamis of Naxos, in his turn, was put into power by Peisistratos of Athens after the battle of Pallene.[24]

According to the Common Source on the Athenian tyranny, the battle of Pallene was fought in 533/2 B.C.[25] Thus all our information seems to be consistent with the supposition that Peisistratos established himself in Athens in the summer of 533/2; that Lygdamis, with the Athenian hostages entrusted to him, was settled in Naxos in the autumn, and that he sent help to Polykrates in Samos in the following spring. The date for the beginning of Polykrates' tyranny is therefore 533/2 B.C.

3. Polykrates' Ionian policy

The second entry in the Eusebian account of the Samian tyranny is that on the Samian colony at Dikaiarchia-Puteoli, which is not

---

[20] Previously, the Samian government could disown the activities of the privateers, as in the case of the Spartan wine-bowl: Hdt. I 70.
[21] I 23.
[22] III 39.
[23] III 120.
[24] Hdt. I 64.
[25] *Klio* 37 (1959) 42 ff. It is to be emphasized that there is no evidence in the *ancient* sources for any controversy on the dating of the various episodes in the Athenian tyranny, and it is only the scholiast to Aristophanes *Wasps* 502 who explictly contrasts technical differences of counting the years. We must suppose therefore that for the ancients the tradition was fixed, and that all later historians were aware exactly of how Herodotus had misinterpreted the (oral) Common Source. (Whether the Common Source was historically accurate is a quite separate question.)

mentioned in our other sources except as an ἀποικία ᾿Ιώνων.[26] In Herodotus' narrative,[27] what happens after the establishment of the tyranny is that Polykrates executes Pantagnotos and exiles Syloson. It is tempting to suggest that this 'exile' began as the appointment of Syloson to be the unwilling oecist of Dikaiarchia, and that the colony was planned to relieve Samos rather of Ionian refugees than of Samian citizens. Certainly we can suppose that still in 533/2 there were in the islands numbers of Ionians in flight from the Persian tax-gatherers and without the means to make their own way further to independence: to provide them with transport and a leader would be enlightened policy for a man aiming at 'rule over Ionia and the islands'.

Probably also we should place among Polykrates' earliest activities (if anywhere) an attempt which he is said to have made to secure alliance with Miletos.[28] The attempt, if made, may have been designed to produce failure, and, the failure achieved, to leave Polykrates free to present himself as the leader of the free Ionians.

But the military result of the failure was that the Milesian fleet, with its allied contingents from Lesbos, remained the Persian fleet in the Aegean. As Polykrates embarked on a career of conquest, taking 'a number of islands and many inhabited places on the mainland,'[29] he soon came into collision with Miletos and Lesbos. The episode ended, according to Herodotus,[30] with the defeat of Miletos and the capture of the whole Lesbian fleet; the prisoners were set to dig the moat around the fortress in Samos.

A somewhat romanticized account of this event appears to be quoted from Africanus by Byzantine historians:[31] μετὰ δὲ τὸ ἀπολέσθαι τὴν βασιλείαν τῶν Λυδῶν οἱ Σάμιοι θαλασσοκρατήσοντες ἐβασίλευσαν τῶν μερῶν ἐκείνων, καὶ ἀκούσας μετὰ χρόνους Κῦρος ὁ βασιλεὺς Περσῶν, ἐπεστράτευσε κατ' αὐτῶν, καὶ συμβάλων αὐτοῖς ναυμαχίᾳ πολεμήσας ἡττήθη καὶ ἔφυγε, καὶ

---

[26] Stephanos of Byzantium, s.v. Δικαιαρχία.
[27] III 39.
[28] Schol, Aristophanes *Plut.* 1005: ... ἐν τοῖς παλαιοῖς χρόνοις ἰσχυρότατοι ἦσαν οἱ Μιλήσιοι καὶ ὅπου προστίθεντο πάντως ἐνίκων. Πολυκράτης οὖν ὁ Σάμιος συγκροτῶν πρός τινας πόλεμον ἠθέλησιν λαβεῖν αὐτοὺς εἰς συμμαχίαν, καὶ εἰς τὸ μαντεῖον ἀπῆλθεν ἐρωτήσων περὶ τούτου· ὁ δὲ θεὸς ἔχρησε· πάλαι ποτ' ἦσαν ἄλκιμοι Μιλήσιοι.
Other occasions for this proverbial oracle are given by other sources.
[29] Hdt. III 39.
[30] The same.
[31] Malalas, Migne XCVII 260; Cedrenus 243.

ἐλθὼν εἰς τὴν χώραν αὐτοῦ ἐσφάγη· περὶ οὗ πολέμου Κύρου καὶ τῶν Σαμίων ὁ σοφώτατος †Πυθαγόρας†[32] ὁ Σάμιος συνεγράψατο· ὅστις καὶ εἶπον αὐτὸν Κῦρον τεθνάναι εἰς τὸν πόλεμον.

This great defeat of Cyrus by the Samians is almost certainly the same event as Polykrates' great victory over Miletos and Lesbos. This version of the story contributes the name of Cyrus, and therefore dates the battle to the summer of 530 B.C. or earlier.[33]

With the loss of the works of the local Samian historians, no detail of the 'several islands and many mainland places' conquered (or raided?) by Polykrates survives. But late literary history[34] says that Polykrates' son, Polykrates of Rhodes, persuaded his father to invite Anakreon to Samos. It is natural to suppose that Polykrates placed his son in command of his most important dependency, though it is quite uncertain whether Rhodes came into Polykrates' power by military or diplomatic means.

The culmination of Polykrates' power over Ionia and the islands is marked by his purification of Rheneia and celebration of the Delian festival.[35] This event was later said to be the source of a proverb:

---

[32] The more familiar name has replaced that of the source quoted for the most romantic detail; perhaps the original was Demagoras of Samos, a Hellenistic writer. Africanus apparently did not name his main source, so that we should suppose it was his usual Universal Historian (whoever that may have been).

[33] Cyrus was killed before September 530.

[34] Himerios, *Orat* XXXI 4, presumably from one of Anakreon's poems: C. M. Bowra, 'Polykrates of Rhodes' in *Classical Journal* 29.375 ff. Possibly some similar tradition about the invitation to Ibykos lies behind Suidas' text ὅτε αὐτῆς (in Samos) ἦρχεν ὁ Πολυκράτης ὁ τοῦ τυράννου Πάτηρ, though this is usually emended to ὅτε Αἰάκης ἦρχεν ὁ Πολυκράτους τοῦ τυράννου πάτηρ. See now also J. P. Barron: 'Ibycus: *To Polykrates*' in *Bulletin of the Institute of Classical Studies* 16 (1969) pp.119 ff.

[35] Thucydides I 13.6, speaking of Ionian naval power, says that in the time of Cyrus and his son Cambyses, the navies were employed in fighting ing Cyrus and θαλάσσης - - - ἐκράτησαν for a time; under Cambyses, Polykrates of Samos subjugated, among other islands, Rheneia and dedicated it to Apollo: meantime the Phokaians of Massalia were battling with the Carthaginians. These statements imply (1) that 'thalassocracy' was inter alia leadership of the *free* Ionians; (2) that (as in the Diodoran Register) the Phokaians held this leadership even though after 547/6 their *activities* were all in the far west, until the rise of Samos under Polykrates; (3) that there was fighting against Cyrus in the Aegean (and so presumably by Polykrates) and therefore in or before 530 B.C.; (4) that Rheneia marks the height of Polykrates' power.

27

Polykrates asked an Apolline oracle whether he should name his festival Pythia or Delia, and the god replied ταῦτά σοι καὶ Πύθια καὶ Δήλια,[36] meaning that the name should not concern Polykrates, for he would never hold the festival again. Suidas holds that the prophecy was fulfilled in the death of Polykrates, and on this ground the dedication of Rheneia has been dated to 523 B.C.[37] rather later than is implied by Thucydides.

But after the mutiny of Polykrates' trireme fleet in 525 B.C., and during the continued and (no doubt) hostile existence of that fleet, it is most unlikely that Polykrates found himself in a position to occupy and dedicate Rheneia. For this reason, we should accept the implication of Thucydides' account, and place the dedication not later than 526 B.C. At that date, the occupation of Rheneia is very probably a demonstration in force looking towards the western Aegean, a display of the new trireme fleet.

The progress of Polykrates' policy in Ionia and the islands can therefore to some degree be traced, and that he was by 526 B.C. 'ruling the seas' is clear. But the evidence available does not permit us to interpret with any certainty at all the intended meaning of the four Eusebian entries on the tyranny, the colony of Dikaiarchia, the thalassocracy, and Pythagoras—whether they form one paragraph entered under the year 533/2, or whether they are four separate annals, for the years 533/2, 532/1, 531/0 and 530/29. The colony at Dikaiarchia-Puteoli can hardly have been established without the good will of Rhodian Naples, and we know too little of Polykrates' relations with Rhodes to say whether the colony could have been as early as 532/1. We equally know too little about the sea-battle with Cyrus to say whether this would naturally be regarded by historians as marking the real beginning of the thalassocracy, and whether it was dated to 531/0 B.C. The Byzantine narrative seems to fit a date in the spring of 531/0, but cannot be pressed; and we do not know enough detail to decide whether historians would be more likely to identify the the beginning of the thalassocracy with the initiation of thalassocratic policy (presumably in 533/2), or with its major success in the Cyrus battle.

4. relations with Athens

Peisistratos and Polykrates were connected through Lygdamis of

---

[36] Suidas s.v.
[37] H. W. Parke, 'Polykrates and Delos' CQ 40 (1946) 105 ff.

Naxos in 533/2; both fought Lesbos—one for Sigeion, the other for command of the seas—within a few years if not simultaneously; Peisistratos 'purified Delos' before his death in 528/7, and Polykrates 'purified Rheneia' before 525. Also Athens was, at least traditionally, a candidate for the leadership of Ionia.

Polykrates' decisive defeat of Lesbos must have been most useful to Hegesistratos in Sigeion, but its very completeness may have moved Peisistratos, by way of counter-demonstration, to the Delian purification, as a reminder or assertion of Athenian claims which could not be taken as a direct act of hostility. Similarly, Polykrates' Rheneian purification a short time later could not be regarded, officially, as an act of hostility to Athens, but was certainly an assertion of leadership of the Ionians and islanders.

If this is the correct sequence of events, we have Polykrates' defeat of the Lesbians and Hegesistratos' safe occupation of Sigeion by 531/0; Peisistratos' purification of Delos by 528/7, and Polykrates' purification of Rheneia by 526/5. Lygdamis of Naxos cannot but have been much affected by this development.

5. investment and welfare policies

As we have already seen, Polykrates probably inherited a fleet of a hundred pentekonters, and a good financial administration, from his father's life-work, and it is probable that very early in his reign he added a strong centralization in his own personal power. The funds collected by 'booty' or transit-dues for the use of territorial waters, and from other sources such as (no doubt) the ransoms of his Lesbian prisoners, were invested and spent in various ways of which we are informed:

(1) a new fleet of thirty triremes;

(2) maintenance of the existing pentekonter fleet;

(3) a standing force of a thousand archers, who probably mainly served as marines;

(4) a continuation of the public works programme inherited from the previous government;

(5) transport, and probably some capital, for the colony at Dikaiarchia;

(6) maintenance of the younger Polykrates in Rhodes with his suite or garrison; and no doubt of other Samian representatives in other dependencies;

(7) high wages to immigrant craftsmen;[38] payments to the doctor Demokedes and the poets Anakreon and Ibykos;

(8) special investment imports, probably not confined to breeding sheep from Miletos and Attika, goats from Skyros and Naxos, dogs from Molossia and Sparta,[38] and pigs from Sicily;[39]

(9) such 'welfare' investments as the provision and staffing (presumably by imported slaves) of shore comforts in the notorious λαύρα.[40]

Another welfare action which may be mentioned here, but which probably belongs to the later years, was Polykrates' mode of providing pensions for mothers of the war dead: he assigned them to other families who were made responsible for their maintenance.[41] This may suggest that in the years of thalassocracy and prosperity the Polykratean state paid pensions to the dependents of men killed in war. The 'assigment of mothers' gave rise, like the attempted Milesian alliance and the purification of Rheneia, to a proverb, and since in the story of the mothers Douris is named as the source of the information, he may also be the source for the other proverbs.[42]

6. the Persian alliance

The turning-point of Polykrates' fortunes is marked by his abandonment of the Egyptian alliance. We do not know when this alliance was first concluded: Polykrates may have inherited it from the former government, and renewed it when he took power. Herodotus[43] dates the abandonment sometime before the death of Amasis (which occurred near the end of 526 B.C.); and if the Rheneian purification is rightly dated to the summer of 526, this employment of the new trireme fleet far from the mainland under Persia may show, amongst other things, a desire to avoid clashes with Persian forces as early as the spring of 526 B.C. Herodotus nevertheless represents the Persian negotiations as secret until the spring of 525, when Cambyses' invitation to join in the attack on Egypt was apparently reported by Polykrates to his subjects as a Persian ultimatum.

The new fleet of thirty triremes was despatched, but mutinied. The

---

[38] Alexis 539 F 2.
[39] Klytos of Miletos 490 F 2.
[40] Klearchos, ap. Athen. XII 540.
[41] Douris of Samos 76 F 63; the proverb was Πολυκράτης μητέρα νέμει.
[42] He is known to have been interested in paroemiography: F 84, 85.
[43] III 40 ff.

mutiny of this fleet robbed Polykrates of its services; its attack on, and defeat of, the home fleet (no doubt that part of the pentekonter fleet still in service) robbed him of that also. The mutineers effected a landing on Samos, but were beaten off, and sailed to Sparta.

The result of the loss of both his fleets was that Polykrates, presumably in the following year 524, was unable to prevent the Spartan expeditionary force from landing and besieging the fortress. This expedition has been frequently identified with the Spartan thalassocracy in the Diodoran Register, and it is true that the Polykratean thalassocracy cannot have been held to continue after the mutiny. But the Diodoran Register, whose original source will certainly have known the history of Polykrates, places the Spartan thalassocracy at a later date and assigns it two years, not the forty days of the siege of Samos before the Spartans retired baffled: the author cannot therefore have intended to identify the Spartan thalassocracy with this expedition—and indeed, the Samian trireme fleet continued in existence, though not under Polykrates' command.

By the time the Spartans retired, Polykrates was without a fleet, and without two years' income. Recourse to a token coinage for internal circulation could not help to pay for imports even of such desperate necessities as timber: and this situation—which cannot have much improved over the next twelve-month—explains his anxiety to come to terms with Oroites, the satrap of Ionia. Polykrates was killed 'during Cambyses' last sickness', in the summer of 522. In Samos his secretary Maiandrios, after some hesitation and executions, continued the government until the arrival of Syloson with a Persian force to claim his inheritance, probably in the summer of 521 B.C.[44]

7. the mutineers' thalassocracy

After the Spartans retired from Samos, the mutineers' fleet exacted a hundred talents of silver from Siphnos: they obviously shared with

---

[44] Herodotus III 139 says that Samos was the first city, Greek or barbarian, that Darius conquered: he thus places Syloson's arrival earlier than the revolt of Babylon (III 149) by which he means the second revolt in September 521. Samos was important to Darius as a part of the suppression of the Median revolt, in which Oroites was implicated (III : 126) the revolt broke out towards the end of 522 and was crushed in a battle of 8th May 521. The securing of Samos is thus a part of the mopping-up operations against Oroites after the end of the revolt. See also *Klio* 37 (1959) 29 ff., where the Spartan attack on Samos is placed at the other possible date, 523.

Polykrates and his predecessors a strong appreciation of the importance of finance. With this money they bought the island of Hydrea, but left it to the care of the Troizenians while they went to expel the Zakynthians from Cretan Kydonia.[45] Presumably some enemies of these Zakynthians, either in Crete or the Peloponnese, had hired the mutineers' formidable services.

The mutineers, however, remained in Kydonia for five years, where they 'flourished greatly' and continued the Samian tradition of public works by building temples. In the sixth year they were destroyed by the Aiginetans in alliance with the Cretans: the triremes also were destroyed and the figure-heads dedicated to Athena in Aigina.

If the Spartan expedition against Polykrates is datable to the sailing season of 524, the attack on Siphnos and purchase of Hydrea will have occupied the rest of that summer. The five years in Kydonia will then cover the sailing-seasons of 523–519, and the destruction will have occurred in the summer of 518. In Olympic years, therefore, this mutineers' control of the trireme fleet lasts from 525/4 to 519/8. There can be little doubt that the Diodoran thalassocracy of Samos, which also ends in 519/8, includes both Polykrates and the mutineers.

8. Sparta and the mutineers' thalassocracy

The mutineers' attack on Siphnos must have alarmed all the island and coastal states of the Aegean. Herodotus does not state who found this dangerous fleet employment in Kydonia: we have to consider whether it may have been Sparta.

It was probably in 547 B.C. or a year or two earlier that the Spartans, after their victory over Argos at Thyrea, annexed Kythera. The island was made the property of the kings, and was the traditional stopping-place for vessels bound out of the Aegean westwards—that is, a principal haven of international trade. No doubt while it was Argive, before 547, the administration (the collection of anchorage and port dues and so forth) had been in Aiginetan hands: Sparta had no reason to change this, so long as the revenues now went to her treasury and not to that of Argos.

Other havens for ships bound westward were in Crete. Apparently in 524 Kydonia in western Crete was occupied by a settlement from Zakynthos (an island further on the western route). The directing of the mutineers' fleet against this settlement would be explained if the

---

45 Hdt. III 59.

Zakynthians had been imposing transit dues in their 'territorial waters' without coming to some agreement with the Spartans and Aiginetans in Kythera.

The suggestion is therefore that after the attack on Siphnos, the Spartans and Aiginetans negotiated anew with the leaders of the Samian mutineers; that the sale of Hydrea was to some degree a device or reserve fund; and that the planting of the Samians in Kydonia was agreed upon by the Spartans and Aiginetans, to support their interests in the western trade.

The 'great flourishing' of the Samians in Kydonia, and the Aiginetan destruction of their fleet and settlement (with Cretan assistance) after only a few years, suggests however that the arrangement—at least from the Aiginetan point of view—was a failure: that the Samians were as piratical (and probably more efficient at piracy) as the Zakynthians had been. But such a destruction must have at least seemed to have Spartan consent: and we have some evidence on this point in the story of the mission of Maiandrios.

When Maiandrios abdicated the tyranny of Samos in favour of Syloson, he went to Sparta, where he found Kleomenes already the senior king.[46] If he left Samos in 521, and arrived in Sparta in the same year, this would mean that Kleomenes was already ruling two years before any other activity of his is reported. We are bound to ask whether Maiandrios did not spend some time first elsewhere, and whether his mission was not in fact on behalf of the Samians in Kydonia, hoping to re-animate Spartan interest on their behalf at the beginning of a new and energetic reign.

In our other sources, the first datable action of Kleomenes is his sponsoring of the Plataian alliance with Athens in 519/8 B.C.[47] Herodotus[48] gives a brief narrative: the Plataians, having had already long struggle with Thebes, applied for aid and alliance to Kleomenes (who happened to be nearby). He sent them to Athens, wishing to weaken that city by embroiling it with Thebes. The Athenians accepted the alliance; the Thebans marched; the Athenians moved to support Plataia. The Corinthians (who happened to be nearby) intervened and arbitrated: if any of the Boiotians wished to leave the Theban federation, they were to do so. The Corinthians then de-

---

[46] Hdt. III 148.
[47] Thk. III 68.
[48] Hdt. VI 108.

33

parted, the Athenians were withdrawing when the Thebans attacked them, were defeated, and lost their territory south of the river Asopos.

This artless tale has caused much debate. Why was Kleomenes nearby? Why did he wish to weaken Athens? Why were the Corinthians nearby? Why did they wish so radically to weaken Thebes?

It has been suggested that Kleomenes was in the northern Peloponnese on League business, perhaps enrolling Megara among his allies. Though there is no direct evidence, this is probable.

But if so, we must surely ask what the Athenians had to say about their ancient enemies securing such powerful protection: there must have been some complicated negotiations between Kleomenes and Hippias leading to a fairly full convention and agreement on spheres of influence. If Hippias now gave up all claims on Megara, such a result of the negotiations would be sufficient to explain the belief of Herodotus' informants that Kleomenes' actions were directed against Athens (though it is clear from the sequel that the League was rather thinking of Thebes). Plataia then was surely part of the price which Kleomenes paid for Megara; and on this view of a convention of 519/8, we should probably place also at this date the Spartan arbitration of Salamis, finally yielded to Athens as another instalment of the price of Megara.

There is another implication of this view: Megara could find no protectors against this 'alliance' with Corinth and Sparta—an 'alliance' which led to the presence of a Corinthian army nearby to Plataia, or some kind of (political and temporary?) Corinthian occupation. This means that we must look once more at Pausanias' mention[49] of a war between Kleomenes and Argos at the beginning of his reign. Pausanias identifies this war with that of 493: he may well have been wrong on this point without also being wrong that there was an Argive war in the first year of Kleomenes' reign.[50] A Spartan demonstration in force in Argive territory and some visible evidence of Argive inability to meet it seems a probable and perhaps almost a

---

[49] III 4.

[50] This suggestion was first put forward by Curtius, and though dismissed as 'a compromise which will satisfy no-one' requires re-examination. The dismissal implies that, in one source or another, we have an exhaustive and total record of all wars between Sparta and Argos—an implication which only has to be stated to be seen untenable.

necessary part of the enrolment of Megara in the Peloponnesian League.[50a]

We thus seem to have for 519/8 a Spartan defeat of Argos, the enrolment of Megara in the Peloponnesian League, and a convention with Hippias from which Athens gained Salamis and the alliance with Plataia and, a few weeks later, Boiotia south of the Asopos.

But a new Spartan reign beginning with such vigour and success could have inspired the Samians in Kydonia with new hope: the mission of Maiandrios as a mission on their behalf directed especially to Kleomenes makes sense in this context. Kleomenes' rebuff to Maiandrios was however, according to Herodotus,[51] exceedingly brusque. If the Aiginetans (who must already have been uneasy about some of the details of Kleomenes' convention with Hippias) were already annoyed with the Samians in Kydonia, they may have seized upon this disagreement between the Samians and Sparta as an opportunity to concert with the Cretans for the destruction of the Samians during the sailing season of 518 B.C.

It may be useful to tabulate the dates assigned in the preceding discussion:

533/*2*: Polykrates and his brothers usurp power in Samos.

? Attempted alliance with Miletos?

530 or earlier: Victory over Cyrus, Miletos and Lesbos.

? Rhodes becomes a dependency of Samos?

? Colony of Dikaiarchia near Rhodian Naples.

526 (or earlier): Purification of Rheneia: display of the new trireme fleet.

525: Mutiny of the trireme fleet; destruction of the pentekonter fleet.

524: Spartan and Corinthian attack on Samos.

523: the mutineers settle in Kydonia.

522: murder of Polykrates: Maiandrios maintains the tyranny.

521: Syloson and the Persians arrive in Samos; Maiandrios abdicates (and goes to Kydonia?).

519/8: Convention of Kleomenes and Hippias (Megara, Salamis, Plataia). Mission of Maiandrios to Sparta.

518: destruction of the Samians in Kydonia by Aigina and the Cretans.

[50a] The Megarian Treasury at Olympia implies some such event: L. H. Jeffery, *Local Scripts of Archaic Greece* (Oxford 1963) p. 135.
[51] III 148.

c. the historiography of the Samian thalassocracies

The drama of Polykrates' career is meteoric, splendid, and sudden; the learned tradition seems to have been fixed by Herodotus, and all later sources seem to be consistent, in general, with his account. There is a long list of local historians of Samos,[52] and no doubt they added detail and precision, but we do not seem to be able to trace any historiographic development.[53]

The great problem is the question of who first extended the predication of thalassocracy to the mutineers. The reasons for the extension seem to be that when Polykrates turned to Persia, he ceased to be the leader of the free Ionians, and when the trireme fleet mutinied, it was against the new alliance that they revolted; also that the effect of Polykrates' thalassocracy on other Greeks was that he was capable of exacting imposts on traffic in his 'territorial waters' and so were the Samians in Kydonia. The reasons do not seem to be very well worked out, for the actions of the mutineers show no enterprises against Persia, unless the Spartan expedition of 524 and the mission of Maiandrios are to be so interpreted.

For the development of the Herodotean notion of the Polykratean thalassocracy therefore we should look in two directions:

(1) supposing that an anti-Persian policy was ascribed to the mutineers, and they were represented as consistently attempting and failing to find support, we might look to the Samian historians anxious to glorify their past, and in particular to Douris, whose use of proverbs shows him adding detail (and precision?) to accepted accounts; or

---

[52] The earliest poetic sources (Asios and Semonides) are earlier than Polykrates. The primary source and contemporary witness was Anakreon. The earliest prose source was Euagon (Jac 535), followed by Aethlios (Jac 536), Douris (Jac 76, also a Universal Historian), Olympichos (Jac 537), Ouliades (Jac 538), Alexis (Jac 539), Potamon of Mitylene (Jac 147, also a Universal Historian), Leon (Jac 540), and in Roman times Xenophon (Jac 540a) and Menodotos (Jac 541). Prose mythographers or romancers include Demagoras (Jac 840 F 22) and Aineias (Jac 543). Among these authors the horographers or annalists were Aethlios, Douris, Alexis and Potamon.

[53] Our named sources may be divided into (1) the universal historians, Herodotus and Thucydides; (2) the local historians: Aethlios (?), Douris, Alexis (Klytos, Klearchos); (3) specialist historians: of literature: biographers of Ibykos and Anakreon; of war: Polyainos; of geography: Steph. Byz.; of constitutional matters: Aristotle (on the public works); and (4) romancers: †Pythagoras†

(2) supposing that no such policy was attributed to the mutineers, but that the Herodotean tradition of their interest only in other Greeks was sustained, then the *evidence* upon which thalassocracy could be ascribed to them might have been found in the local historians of Aigina especially; or of Sparta and Crete. In this case, we should suppose that the ascription of thalassocracy was not earlier than the original author from whom Diodorus abstracted his Register.

ii. SPARTA

So far as can be seen from the meagre information at our disposal, a Spartan 'thalassocracy' in 517 and 516 means in the first place that the Spartan state took over the direct administration of the havens at Kythera and elsewhere. This would imply, it seems, that any Aiginetan administration there was ended; and if so, the cause must have been that the Aiginetan destruction of Samos-in-Kydonia displeased Sparta. In that case, Kleomenes' rebuff to Maiandrios was a diplomatic blunder, offering the Aiginetans an unforseen opportunity, and depriving the Spartan treasury of that portion of the exactions which the Samians had passed on to her.

This hypothesis finds no direct supporting evidence, but is consistent with some other information about Sparta at this time.

The years of the thalassocracy of the Samian mutineers seem, on the archaeological evidence, to have been critical for the relations between Sparta and the international market. After the end of the Aristomenian war,[54] Sparta began an export—apparently politically organized and controlled—of fine pottery, especially to her ally Samos (whence it was sold in Naukratis and Kyrene) and her colony Taras in Italy (whence a little was sold to other western cities). About 525 this export ceases, at the same time as Polykrates becomes the object of Spartan hostility and the Persian conquest of Egypt closes the Naukratite market. There remained the possibility of direct communication with Kyrene and the west: if Sparta could pay, she could buy leather from Kyrene and metal from the west, both important to her army. But it is during the last quarter of the sixth century that the Carthaginians succeed in excluding the Greeks from Tartessos, and political changes in the Gallic hinterland depress or extinguish Massaliote trade, which had included fine bronze-work from the Spartan

---

[54] See *Sicilian Colony Dates* Part VIII.

smiths. Thus, as Lakonian pottery exports declined towards their extinction, we have to suppose that the Spartan smiths imported metal and paid for it by exporting finished metal goods—a trade of small bulk but high value, easily organized politically, but in a diminishing market.

The shifting pattern of Spartan trade, or relations with the international market, at this time cannot have been easily managed overall; and the loss of the revenues from Samos-in-Kydonia must have been irritating. The expulsion of an Aiginetan administration from Kythera would be petty, but natural.

Within Sparta itself we have some historical evidence which seems relevant. Kleomenes' father Anaxandrides had married twice and simultaneously: Kleomenes was the eldest son but by the second wife. This queen was the daughter of Prinetadas son of Demarmenes,[55] who seems (as we should expect) to have been of a notable family: Kleomenes' colleague Demaretos was married to Perkalos daughter of Chilon son of Demarmenes,[56] apparently a cousin. The name of Chilon is the same as that of the great ephor, son of Demagetos: we are probably to infer either blood-relationship or close political affiliation. The ephor's displeasure at the annexation of Kythera,[57] Kleomenes' expansion of the Peloponnesian League, the rebuff of Maiandrios, are consistent with one another and suggest attachment to the army as the traditional mainstay of Spartan power.

On the other hand Dorieus and the younger sons of Anaxandrides were the children of Anaxandrides' first wife, his sister's daughter. We are not told who was the father of this queen, but there are some indications: when Dorieus was planning his second emigration, the principal oracles he consulted were those of Laios,[58] whose descendants, the Aigeidai, were not only prominent at Sparta but provided the kings of Thera and had kinsmen in Rhodes and Akragas in Sicily. When Dorieus first emigrated, he was assisted by men of Thera, and when he departed for Sicily, one of his synoecists was named Euryleon—and this name appears as that of an Aigeid in earlier Spartan history.[59] Consequently, it seems fair to infer that Dorieus had a body of kinsmen and supporters led by the Aigeidai, and that

---

[55] Hdt. V 41.
[56] Hdt. VI 65.
[57] Hdt. VII 235.
[58] Hdt. V 43.
[59] Paus. IV 7.8.

the Aigeidai treasured and maintained their overseas connections.

Thus, behind Herodotus' brief account of dissension between Kleomenes and his half-brother Dorieus, it appears that there was a division among the Spartiates themselves, each party organized around the kinsmen of Anaxandrides' queens and pursuing divergent policies: Kleomenes' policy is fairly clearly based on the army, Dorieus' is directed to the sea and overseas connections. Any consistent handling of the relationships between Sparta and the international market is not, in these circumstances, to be expected.

Consequently, we are probably to take the Spartan 'thalassocracy' as an episode in the quarrel between the Chilonian and Aigeid parties in Kleomenes' Sparta.[60] Apparently Kleomenes' Chilonian rebuff to Maiandrios resulted in a loss of revenues and power, and gave Dorieus' Aigeid party an opportunity to establish their own policy, first in the 'thalassocracy', then in Dorieus' settlement in Kinyps (threatening Carthage and Carthaginian shipping), then in his Sicilian venture. The ending of the 'thalassocracy' in this context is not to be ascribed to any external defeat, but to a shift in the party struggle in Sparta, an increase in the power of Kleomenes which led to Dorieus' decision to emigrate and turn his energies against the constriction of the Greek metal trade by the Carthaginians.

But if this hypothesis is anything like the true explanation of the appearance of a Spartan thalassocracy in the Diodoran Register, we have to consider what can have been its historiographic ancestry. Herodotus' Spartan source, so extremely hostile to Kleomenes, is likely to have been Aigeid; and in general Aigeid influence on accounts of Spartan history is marked. But not all Aigeid influence need have been Spartan: the Aigeids of the Aegean and the west may have contributed information to other local histories, especially in Rhodes, Kyrene, and Sicily—and indeed it is likely that the beginnings of the construction of a 'thalassocracy' out of Dorieus' career took place outside Sparta. Since this 'thalassocracy' can hardly have been associated with rule over 'Ionia and the islands', or with leadership of the free Ionians, it was possibly based on the capacity to exact transit and haven dues from shipping bound westwards from the Aegean: so the ascription may have arisen first on the basis of Theraian or Rhodian Aigeid information.

---

[60] The struggle probably existed at least from the time of the Lydian treaty negotiations in 548; and (since no kings are mentioned) the Samian expedition of 524 may have been led by Aigeids.

iii. NAXOS

The connection between Peisistratid Athens and Lygdamis of Naxos may have politically weakened in 528/7, if Hippias (as seems probable) declared an amnesty on his succession and allowed the hostages to come home. Lygdamis also can hardly have regarded with complacence the activities of his erstwhile protégé, Polykrates, at Rheneia. No direct information however survives about the politics of his tyranny; there is an anecdote[61] about his finances. The exiled or fugitive oligarchs were invited to buy back their confiscated lands and their unfinished dedicatory statues. Apparently the second of these offers was not accepted, for the unfinished statues are still in Naxos; we are told nothing about the first. It seems, however, clear that the offer amounts to some kind of amnesty, perhaps after Hippias' example.

A tradition of unknown origin[62] says that Lygdamis' tyranny was ended by the Spartans. The context is that of a long list of tyrants said to have been so suppressed, beginning with the Kypselids of Corinth with whom the Spartans certainly had nothing to do. The list-form itself suggests that the tradition does not come from history but from apologetics: certainly the whole contention was unknown to Herodotus, otherwise his speech of the Corinthian Sosikles,[63] warning the Spartans not to restore Hippias, would have quite a different content and force. We cannot therefore take the statement about Lygdamis as historical without supporting evidence, and the financial anecdote suggests rather that the restoration of the Naxian oligarchy occurred as the result of Naxian developments. It is also the only indication of date, and points to sometime after 528/7.

The next appearance of Naxos in our surviving sources is just before the Ionian Revolt,[64] and therefore after the thalassocracy. At this time, Naxos is said to have an army of 8000 men and many boats, and to rule over Paros, Andros, and the Cyclades. Paros and Andros were the metropoleis of colonies in Chalkidike, Thasos, and Thrace, which in the second half of the sixth century had flourishing exports of wine and, more especially, of silver. The Naxian rule over Paros

---

[61] Aristotle *Oeconomica* II 2.
[62] Plutarch *de Mal. Her.* 21, schol. Aisch. II 77. Lygdamis' name does not appear in what survives of a shorter list in Rylands Papyrus 18=Jac 105 F 1.
[63] Hdt. V 92.
[64] Hdt. V 30 f.

and Andros implies some control, in the Naxian interest, of the links of these cities with their colonies, so that we should probably see in the 'Naxian thalassocracy' an attempt to impose some centralizing organization on the Ionian wine and metal trades, at the time when the the Carthaginian constriction of the western metal trade was becoming severe.

The archaeological evidence[65] from Egypt and the near east shows that in the latter part of the sixth century the coinages of the cities in Thrace were largely used for export, more or less as bullion, and remained in demand in Egypt even when ordinary Naukratite trade had almost ceased to exist under the Persians. The historical evidence is that Peisistratos spent his second exile in Thrace, and came back to Athens with considerable funds and accompanied by Lygdamis of Naxos; while Herodotus[66] reports that Aryandes, satrap of Egypt (until winter 519–8 B.C.), refined silver with the intention of coining. Both the archaeological and the historical evidence therefore agree that the extensive exploitation of the Thracian mines and copious minting from their metals coincided, in the last third of the sixth century, with a strong demand for silver and coins in the near east.

When we add to this the claim of a Naxian local historian[67] that the Naxians invented coinage, it becomes possible to suggest that the 'Naxian thalassocracy' represents an organization of this sector of the international market.

In that case, the Naxian claim to thalassocracy was probably made by local historians, and accepted by the original source of Diodorus' Register. If, however, it was Lygdamis who laid the foundations of this organization of the Cycladic metal trade, which was sustained, and perhaps expanded, by the succeeding oligarchy, it is likely that the local historians claimed a longer period of thalassocracy than the author of the Register allowed. It is also likely that at the lower terminus the local historians carried the thalassocracy down to the expulsion of the oligarchs about 500 B.C., which began the train of events leading to the Ionian Revolt and the Persian Wars.

iv. ERETRIA

The Diodoran Register, however, places the beginning of the Eretrian

---

[65] C. M. Kraay, 'Hoards, small change, and the origin of coinage' in JHS 84 (1964) pp. 76 ff.; J. Boardman, *The Greeks Overseas* pp.79, 146 f.
[66] IV 166.
[67] Aglosthenes 499 F 7.

thalassocracy in 506/5. This date probably refers not to any conflict between Eretria and Naxos, but to the Athenian capture and occupation of Chalkis in the early years of the democracy,[68] and the release thereby effected of Eretria from Chalkidian rivalry. If this is the case, the fall of Chalkis is to be dated to the campaigning season of 506, leaving Eretria to take command of the sea in the sailing season of 505 B.C. No doubt Eretria was allied to Athens, against Chalkis and Boiotia at this time; and she had a trireme fleet by 498/7.[69]

The most famous action of Eretria during her thalassocracy was her assistance to the Ionian cities in their revolt against Persia in 498/7. In Herodotus' account, Eretria is represented as decidedly subordinate to Athens, but Plutarch reports as Herodotus' chief critic on this subject Lysanias of Mallos,[70] who apparently gave the Eretrians credit for intervention in Cyprus as well as in Ionia. The date of Lysanias is unknown, and so also is any reason why a citizen of Mallos in Kilikia should write a book Περὶ 'Ερετρίας.

The thalassocracy necessarily came to an end in 492/1, for in 491/0 Eretria was captured by the Persians and the population transported to Arderikka near Susa.

The original author from whom Diodorus abstracted his register may have drawn his information on the Eretrian thalassocracy from Lysanias of Mallos, but if so Lysanias himself may only have been working within a tradition which spoke of Euboians and thalassocrats together, though only mythographic allusions seem to survive. Archemachos[71] speaks of Aigaion as the inventor of the pentekonter, and Arrianos[72] enlarges: Aigaion-Briareus was ruler of Euboia, thalassocrat, and eponym of the Aegean Sea. The eponymy of a thalassocrat is rare in Greek mythography, for the names of seas and gulfs are usually accounted for by stories of drowning.[73] But a thalassocrat eponym is as old as the fourth century in at least one case: Theopompos of Chios[74] held that the Ionian Sea was named from an Illyrian called Ioneus, a native of those parts who ἐκράτησε

---

[68] Hdt. V 77.
[69] Hdt. V 99.
[70] Jac 426 F 1.
[71] Jac 424 F5.
[72] Jac 156 F 92.
[73] As Archemachos himself (424 F 8) ascribes the name of the Ionian Sea to τῶν ἀπολομένων ἐν αὐτῷ 'Ιώνων.
[74] Jac 115 F 128=424 F 8.

τῆς θαλάσσης. Theopompos was not a local historian, even of Chiote history; but his notion of thalassocracy may not be wholly unconnected with the fact that Chios herself claimed to have exercised thalassocracy at one time.[75] The original source of the Diodoran Register did not include this Chiote thalassocracy in his list: nevertheless it may be that the traditions of Euboia and her daughter Chios, especially (in the former case) as represented for us by Lysanias of Mallos, were a main contributor to the historiographic concept of thalassocracy.

v. *AIGINA*

Although the Naxian and Eretrian thalassocracies are represented as successive in the Register, they represent different kinds of 'leadership of the Ionians' and these leaderships probably overlapped in time to a considerable extent. The visits of Persian fleets to the Aegean from 493 onwards however ended both: Thasos twice submitted to Persia and this would affect her relations with Paros and Naxos; Eretria was destroyed. The Aiginetan 'thalassocracy' is of a new kind.

Aiginetan prosperity in general was probably deeply affected by the Persian conquest of Egypt and the decline of the western metal trade; also she had probably suffered from the thalassocracy of the Samian mutineers and that of Sparta. When she next appears in the records, after 506, it is as the new ally of Thebes and new enemy of Athens.[76] By 493/2 however she was enrolled in the Peloponnesian League.[77] We must suppose that these various twists of policy were due to a relative reduction of Aiginetan wealth and power from about 525 onwards, also shown in the claim of Naxos to thalassocracy in what were almost Aiginetan home waters.

When the Persian heralds reached Greece in the spring or summer of 491, the Aiginetans decided to medise, and the Register dates their thalassocracy from the following sailing season 491/0: as Persian subjects, they would have access to ports and markets in the east on preferential terms. Our detailed information on the following years is from Herodotus, who is concerned entirely with Aigina's political and

---

[75] Strabo XIV 1.35.

[76] Hdt. V 80. Both the alliance and the enmity are furnished with legendary aitia: the sisterhood of Aigina and Thebe daughters of Asopos; and the 'ancient feud'.

[77] and provided ships for Kleomenes' attack on Argos: Hdt. VI 92.

43

military relations with Athens and Sparta. For Aigina certainly, and probably for Athens also, the commercial aspect would be more important: Aiginetan raids on the Attic coast and shipping must have reduced Athenian trading profits both by direct losses, and by the use of alternative export channels involving some land transport (either to Megara or to the eastern and safer coast of Attika).

By early 481/0 Xerxes was in winter quarters in Sardis, and the Aiginetans decided to revolt and join the Greek alliance being prepared. Something must of course be allowed to the Aiginetans of the general exciting feeling of defiance, but the deciding factor in this change of policy would certainly be the new Athenian fleet.

The Aiginetan thalassocracy thus seems to appear in the Register, not as a leadership of the Ionians, but on the same grounds as that of the Samian mutineers (and of the Spartans); a capacity to exact imposts, to harass trade, to control in a negative sense. Both aspects were present in the Polykratean thalassocracy: the author from whom Diodorus abstracted his Register seems to have given them equal weight in deciding on the later entries in his list.

vi. the concept of thalassocracy

The comparison of the entries in the Register with the surviving knowledge about these states has shown that Herodotus had a very clear and definite meaning for the word 'thalassocracy'; that Thucydides enlarged the concept to include also the Phokaians of Massalia; that for Theopompos the notion was already current in mythography; and that probably statements of Euboian and Chiote tradition and history were familiar with the notion.

We have also seen that from the beginning, in Herodotus' description of the Polykratean thalassocracy, the notion had positive and negative aspects: rule or leadership on the one hand, systematic exactions on the other. In the Register, Polykrates, Naxos and Eretria are entries which emphasize the positive; the Samian mutineers, probably Sparta, and Aigina emphasize the negative.

The difference between Herodotus and the Register lies preeminently in the fact that the Register predicates the *continuity* of thalassocracy. We have seen reason to believe that this continuity involved the rejection of the Chiote claim to thalassocracy, the limitation of the Naxian, and admission of the Aigeid-Spartan claim—in other words a detailed knowledge of the local historians, critically used.

The problem is to find and state the criteria by which the evidence of the local histories was judged. Certainly more than politics was involved: the piratical thalassocracy of the Samian mutineers was scarcely a political entity at all. But like other fleets, theirs meant investment (at least in its upkeep), and the collection of funds for this purpose: so we return to the two aspects already explicit in the Herodotean notion of thalassocracy. In the Polykratean example, the fleet is backed by 'tyranny' and centralized administration, and directed to the aim of ruling Ionia and the islands; in the cases of the mutineers and Aigina, the piracy both collects funds and is aimed at control of trade and communications: in the Spartan case, the control of Kythera achieves the same objects; Naxos apparently aimed at the organization of trade rather more positively; Eretria used her fleet politically.

Thus there is a recurrent theme: thalassocracy is not merely an objective fact—the most prosperous maritime state at the time: thalassocracy means the possession of a fleet and an aim, a concentration of force and purpose.

And there is a continuous succession of such concentrations—necessarily through changing and developing historical circumstances. The identification of these concentrations consequently *organizes* the writing of history, and determines periodization. The Register, that is to say, is not only an historical model; it is also a theory of historiography. Such historiography is neither institutional in the ordinary ancient sense, nor is it concerned with processes and trends in the ordinary modern sense: it is however analytical in an historiographical technical sense. It is concerned to identify the greatest concentration of forces and purposes at any given time, and to see the permeation of their effects throughout contemporary events. This approach is nearer to modern economic than to modern historiographic thinking —which may account for the relevance of the archaeological economic evidence to the interpretation of the entries as (for example) is especially clear in the case of Naxos.

It is of course involved in this continuous succession of concentrations that the *degree* of concentration varies as between one thalassocracy and another, or between different periods in one thalassocracy. Polykrates' concentration was intense; that of Sparta was probably small and due to one of two conflicting parties in the state—nevertheless, the author of the Register judged that for two years the Spartan concentration exceeded others: and his judgement tells us

45

something of the nature of the evidence, available to him, though lost to us. Similarly, his placing of the beginning of the Eretrian thalassocracy in 506/5, eight years before the outbreak of the Ionian Revolt, tells us that he judged Eretria in these eight years to have had a concentrated purpose, though we do not know what that was.[78]

Thus when we move from the historical to the ante-historiographic thalassocracies we have some information to guide us in examining the entries.

---

[78] We may perhaps guess that Eretrian policy was concerned with the cities of Chalkidike and Thrace, and their metals.

PART 2

THE ANTE-HISTORIOGRAPHIC THALASSOCRACIES

IT IS THE FIRST twelve of the thalassocracies in the Diodoran Register which present great and numerous difficulties: Who was the original author of the list? Why did he choose these twelve communities? Over which seas did they (supposedly) exercise power? What were the dates in the Register? Did the dates in the *Canons* originally agree, either with each other, or with the Register, or both? Why was the continuity of thalassocracy so important, to the original author that he composed the list, or to Eusebius that his thalassocracy entries were often specially written, in coloured ink or in emphatic placing on the page? It is by no means certain that satisfactory answers can be found to all these questions, but a beginning on some of them can be made.

A. The Texts
i. the Diodoran Register
The fourth part or chapter of the Armenian version of Eusebius' *Chronographia* is devoted to Greek Dates. At the beginning of the chapter the sub-headings are given:[1] kings of Athens, kings of Argos, kings of Sikyon; kings of Sparta, kings of Corinth; Thalassocrats and their periods; Olympiads; early kings of Macedon; kings of Macedon, Thessaly, Syria and Asia after Alexander.

In general, this is a rational succession of subjects. The heroic dynasties in Sikyon and Argos, and the Heroic and Dark Age dynasties in Athens are followed by the Dark Age dynasties of Corinth and Sparta; the Thalassocracies cover the whole period from the fall of Troy (the beginning of the Dark Age) to the fully historical Persian wars; the Olympiads begin at the end of the Dark Age and cover the whole Macedonian period and its derivatives. Each set of dates thus provides a set of reference-points overlapping with the next, and the

---

[1] Karst p.80.

47

whole would form a connected chronological argument. The only exceptionable detail is that the Sikyonian dynasty is misplaced in the list: as the earliest it should come first.

But the order of treatment actually followed in the chapter is not the same as that of this list of contents. Sikyon is given first, as it should be, then Argos and Athens. All three dynasties are said to be taken from Kastor's *Epitome*, and this first section thus forms a unity in itself.

The second section begins with a quotation from Pophyrius (260 F 4) of Apollodoros (244 F 21) on the numbers of years separating Troy, the Return, the Ionian Migration, Lykourgos, and the First Olympiad. This list of epochal dates is not mentioned in the Table of Contents, and may have been inserted in the first place to give the commencing dates for the dynasties of Sparta and Corinth, even though these could have been adequately given by the ends of Argos and Sikyon, and a note on the change of dynasty in Athens.

The order of the Contents Table is however definitely broken with the following of this epochal list by the Olympic Register: only after this is there a section on Corinth, Sparta, and the Thalassocracies, all quoted from Diodorus. Finally, there is an anonymous list of the early Macedonian kings, then Porphyrius' lists of the dynasties of the Diadochoi. Thus a block of matter from Diodorus, instead of following on directly from the Kastor quotations, is inserted into the information cited from Porphyrius.

The first question is whether this irrational sequence is due to Eusebius himself. There is some equivocal evidence from a fifteenth-century Greek manuscript[2] which contains quotations from this part of the *Chronographia*, with considerable difference of arrangement. The Porphyrian histories of the Diadochoi are placed after the Achaemenids of Persia in the preceding chapter; and consequently the Greek Dates are reduced to: Sikyon, Argos and Athens from Kastor, the Porphyrian epochs, and the Olympic register 'from Eusebius': all the Diodoran material is absent. The moving of the Diadochoi from the Greek to the Asiatic chapter is sufficient to show that in eastern scholarship the sequence of subject-matter was not sacrosanct, and that at the latest by the fifteenth century the succession of institutions (in this case, empires) was preferred to the more abstract chronological argument. We cannot therefore be by any

---

[2] Cramer, *Anecdota Graeca* II 118 ff.

48

means sure that the Armenian version of the *Chronographia* (in our thirteenth century manuscripts) follows the sequence of subjects in the original Eusebian text.

What does seem to be clear is that Eusebius was using at least three books from which to compile his Greek Dates: Kastor's *Epitome*, Porphyrius, and Diodorus. The problem, consequently, is why he used all three.

There seems to be, at least *prima facie*, no reason to doubt that Kastor accepted the Apollodoran epochal dates; Eusebius may however have found Porphyrius a better authority on the Diadochoi, and having him to hand for that subject, may have quoted him, either as a sort of footnote, or as a more explicit authority on the epochal dates—which Kastor may have accepted without giving a special account of them. The nub of the problem is therefore why Eusebius used Diodorus for Sparta, Corinth, and the Thalassocracies —for we must assume that Kastor's *Epitome* listed the Spartan and Corinthian kings. In the *Canons*, Eusebius follows his Diodoran lists of the Spartan and Corinthian kings only with considerable modifications, of unknown source. The possibility seems to be that Eusebius is quoting Diodorus on all three lists at second-hand, and that in the *Canons* he accepts the criticisms of the Diodoran lists given by his main authority.

Thus, so far as the Diodoran Register of Thalassocracies is concerned, we may have to reckon with (1) the original from whom Diodorus abstracted; (2) Diodorus' Register, which itself may not have corresponded exactly to his original; (3) a reporter and critic who was Eusebius' own main source; (4) Eusebius himself in the *Canons*; and (5) successive editors in the Eusebian tradition, both in the *Chronographia* and the *Canons*. Under (5) we may possibly have to allow for considerable excisions from Eusebius' text, for example a statement why Kastor's *Epitome* was disregarded for Sparta, Corinth, and the Thalassocracies.

In spite of all these possibilities however we shall continue for convenience sake to call the Register of Thalassocracies in the Eusebian *Chronographia* the 'Diodoran Register'. It consists of no more than the following:

Aus denselben Diodor-schriften auszugweise von den Zeiten der Meeresbeherrscher, die die Seeherrschaft hatten.

Nach dem Troischen Kriege hielten die Seeherrschaft

1. Lyder und Mäoner   Jahre 92

2. Pelasger	Jahre	85
3. Thraker	Jahre	79
4. Rhodier	Jahre	23
5. Phrygier	Jahre	25
6. Kyprier	Jahre	33
7. Phynikier	Jahre	45
8. Ägypter	Jahre	
9. Melesier	Jahre	
10.	Jahre	
11. Lesbier	Jahre	
12. Phokier	Jahre	44
13. Samier	Jahre	
14. Lakedmonier	Jahre	2
15. Naxier	Jahre	10
16. Eretrier	Jahre	15
17. Äginäer	Jahre	10

Bis zu des †Alexandros† Ubergang auf die andere Seite.

This notice tells us only that, in the time of Eusebius or that of his main authority, there existed in the universal history of Diodorus a list of thalassocracies covering the whole period from the fall of Troy to the diabasis of Xerxes. It does not tell us where Diodorus obtained his list, whether he used it himself as a means of organizing universal history in its period, whether he copied it unchanged from his source, or whether it fitted his dates for contemporary epochs—there is no note, for example, stating which Thalassocrat year is contemporary with the First Olympiad. This silence is matched by almost all our other sources: the two exceptions are dubious.

a. Pliny and the power of 'free Mitylene'
Myres was the first[3] to connect with the Lesbian thalassocracy the remark by Pliny[4] that free Mitylene was powerful for MD years, and to suggest that MD was a false transliteration of MΔ, 44 years. The suggestion is that Diodorus gave to Phokaia the 44 years which his source gave to Lesbos—and presumably gave to Lesbos whatever figure his source gave to Phokaia. Helm[5] added that Pliny is just the sort of man who may have read Diodorus' source for himself.

---

[3] See Part I note 3 above.
[4] NH VI 31.39.
[5] See Part I note 6 above.

Myres' suggestion was that Pliny had miscopied the figure, his eye falling to the next line on the list. But if Pliny was reading the original work, he was surely not reading a list but a history. The same will of course be true for Diodorus himself, so at this stage we have to choose between supposing either (a) that a 44-year thalassocracy for Lesbos does not belong to the Diodorus-Eusebius tradition at all, but (for example) to the same source as spoke of a Chiote thalassocracy; or (b) that Diodorus deliberately changed the date of the transfer of sea-power from Lesbos to Phokaia by interchanging the durations of the two thalassocracies; or (c) that the interchange occurred by a copying error either in the manuscripts of Diodorus or those of Eusebius' primary authority.[6] The first and third of these possibilities cannot be either excluded or confirmed; the second is however a distinct possibility.

We have seen that when Thucydides speaks of Phokaian sea-power, he seems to have in mind solely the Phokaians of the west, based on Massalia. The foundation of Massalia is dated to 600/599 by Timaios and to 598/7 by Eusebius:[7] a Phokian thalassocracy beginning in the early 570's (44 years before 532/1 or 531/0) presumably allows time for the colony to establish itself, to be followed by Alalia in Corsica in the 560's.

On the other hand, the Lesbian thalassocracy in its naval aspect must have been conceived as primarily concerned with the Euxine and, more especially, its approaches—the fight with Athens over Sigeion is an obvious illustration. Jerome has the Lesbian thalassocracy in being when the Megarians found Byzantium: the notion of the thalassocracy therefore probably included an understanding with Megara and her Propontine colonies. But (according to Jerome) in 601/0 Samos planted the colony of Perinthos in the Propontis (in the teeth of extreme Megarian opposition:[8] Lesbos is not mentioned, so she was either no longer thalassocrat or her understanding with Megara had come to an end). If the original of the Register shared this historiography and ended the Lesbian thalassocracy by 601/0, then his Phokaian thalassocracy was nearly 70 years in duration, up to Polykrates in the later 530's. Jerome's report on the length of the

---

[6] A copying error within the Eusebian tradition is for the most part excluded by the mention of the 44 Phokaian years by Synkellos and the Armenian *Canons*.

[7] *Sicilian Colony Dates* (Index of Years).

[8] Plut. QG 57.

51

Lesbian thalassocracy gives it 68 or 69 years, so that the interchange of figures for Lesbos and Phokaia is possible, either deliberately by Diodorus, or erroneously by his copyists or critic.

If Diodorus changed the dates deliberately he transferred the fall of Lesbos and rise of Phokaia from the last decade of the seventh century to the early 570's. This thirty years is the period in Apollodoros of the career of Pittakos, aisymnetes of Mitylene, who bore two characters: according to Alkaios he was a tyrant, according to our prose sources he was one of the Seven Sages and champion of freedom. Thus the possibility that Diodorus changed the date and duration of the Lesbian thalassocracy involves the supposition that he took the kinder view of Pittakos,[9] as against his and Pliny's source, whose 'free Mitylene' will then be the oligarchic city before Pittakos' appointment. This appears to be possible.

But it would follow that the Diodoran Register is at best that and nothing more—for we cannot exclude the possibility that Diodorus altered other figures too. So far as the historical thalassocracies, from Samos onward, are concerned, this is unlikely both on general grounds and because examination of the Eusebian texts has shown a single tradition. But for the thalassocracies before Samos, where the Eusebian derivatives show wide variations in dates, it is clearly possible that there was current more than one version of thalassocratic historiography, even if there was a single succession of powers.

b. 'Suidas' on Kastor of Rhodes

In a muddled notice, Suidas states that Kastor of Rhodes published a two-volume work entitled *Register of Babylon and of Thalassocrats of the Past*.[10] There is the double question whether the alleged work existed, and whether it was Diodorus' source, at least for the notion of thalassocracy as a concept in Universal History.

Kastor is also said by Suidas to have been the author of *Chronological Unknowns*, and by Eusebius to have written the six-volume *Chronological Epitome* which he quotes directly for Assyria, Sikyon, Argos, Athens, and Rome. So far as subject-matter in general is concerned therefore, a *Register* of Babylonian and Thalassocrat dates

---

[9] Though in that case the Perinthos problem remains: but the foundation may have had other dates in other sources.
[10] Jac 250 T 1. Jacoby, following Berhardy and von Gutschmid, distrusts the text, and regards the title as 'sicher korrupt' (p.818).

would be quite possible for Kastor, and there is one small piece of evidence[11] which suggests that he knew of the Babylonian Venus-cycle: if this is right, then Suidas' title is to that extent confirmed at least for Babylon.

The main difficulty is of course to conceive why a single work should treat both of Babylon and of thalassocracy, subjects which at first sight seem to have nothing in common. A similar juxtaposition is however found in Kastor's *Epitome*, where kings of Assyria and kings of Sikyon succeed in parallel series over many centuries: the idea of contemporary and parallel series of dates in Greece and the East was therefore one which appealed to *Kastor*.

It is more illuminating to contrast a *Register of Babylon and Thalassocrats* with the structure of Herodotus' history, where the parallel series are those of the Herakleid genealogies for Greece and Lydia on the one hand, and on the other the 'empire of upper Asia' for Assyria, Media and Persia.[12] Herodotus, that is to say, has a register of Herakleid generations for Greece and Lydia, and an abstract empire which descends on successive peoples for Asia; Kastor's Register, on the other hand, is of Babylon, and his abstract thalassocracy descends on successive communities in Greek waters. The contrast suggests that Suidas' report of this book is true, and that the title proclaimed Kastor's intention to put universal history on a new footing, reducing to second place for Greece the reliance on Herakleid genealogies which had been constant (in various ways) since Herodotus' time. 'Thalassocracy' in that case is not only a new concept for universal history, but involves a new conception of Greek history especially.

If we accept Suidas' report that Kastor wrote such a book, it follows that Diodorus included in his Dark Age discussions a reference to, and summary of, the latest development in Greek and universal historiography. It seems improbable on the other hand that it greatly affected his disposition of his data, so that his version of the Register may in the main be Kastor's without alteration, even if it was Diodorus who gave the Phokaians the 44 years which Kastor perhaps gave to Lesbos.

It also follows, since he quotes the thalassocracies from Diodorus, that Eusebius did not know Kastor's *Register of Babylon and Thalas-*

---

11 250 F 9.
12 *Klio* 46 (1966) 118 ff.

socrats. This should mean that Kastor himself wrote the *Epitome* before the *Register*, and that, therefore, the *Epitome* did not contain any reference to the thalassocrats. Indeed, the Eusebian quotations from the *Epitome* show Kastor working (so far as we can see) purely as a constructionist, making elegant chronographic patterns out of material already well-worn: there is no trace of the innovations suggested by the title of the *Register of Babylon and Thalassocrats*.

So far as can be made out from such general arguments therefore the pedigree of the thalassocratic tradition is:

(1) Kastor's *Register of Babylon and Thalassocrats of the Past*, published perhaps about 60 B.C., and later than the *Epitome*.

(2) Diodorus' abstract from Kastor, possibly with some figures changed;

(3) a reporter and critic of Diodorus' abstract, used as a primary source by Eusebius;

(4) Eusebius;

(5) his successive copyists, translators and editors.

ii. the derivatives of the Eusebian Canons

The texts of the surviving entries on the ante-historiographic thalassocracies, as found in the four derivatives[13] of the Eusebian *Canons*, are set out in Table I. Out of the fifteen entries, Jerome has fourteen, and two are found only in him. The Armenian version has two considerable lacunae in this period, which accounts for the absence of five entries, but the surviving text also omits another four. Synkellos' abstracts also fail for a considerable time; otherwise the only entry missing in the Greek is one of the two duplicates 5 and 6, found in Jerome's earlier manuscripts (OM/SA/F/B/L) but not in some later ones (TXC/D/Q). One of these duplicates is presumably an unerased error, but there is little textual evidence which this is: the learned T, and Q, retain the second while the other single-entry manuscripts prefer the first.

---

[13] Jerome (Fotheringham); the Armenian (Karst); Synkellos: *Georgius Syncellus et Nicephorus Cp. ex recensione Guilielmi Dindorfii* Vol. I (*Corpus Scriptorum Historiae Byzantinae* 10) Bonn 1829; the Syriac entries from J. B. Chabot, *Chronique de Michel le Syrien* Tome I fasc. I (Paris 1889).

I have added to the Syriac column in the Table references (according to Karst) to evidence in the Armenian of transcription from the Syriac, though no such entries survive in Michael. Michael however is the only witness we possess for the number of years in the Egyptian thalassocracy.

TABLE I
TEXTS OF THE *CANONICAL* ENTRIES

Synkellos	Jerome	Entry	Michael	Armenian
324.16 Λυδοὶ οἱ καὶ Μαίονες ἐθαλασσο κράτησαν ἔτη ϙβ΄.	101.16 Lydi mare optinuerunt	1		172.15 Zuerst führten die Lyder die See-herrschaft 92 Jahre.
339.18 Πελασγοὶ β΄ ἐθαλασσοκράτησαν ἔτη πέ.	113.25 Pelasgi mare obtinuerunt.	2	⟨Pelesger in *Arm. Can.*⟩	175.10 Zweitens herrschten die Pelesger zur See 85 Jahre.
340.17 Τρίτοι ἐθαλασσοκράτησαν Θραῖκες ἔτη οθ΄.	119.18 Tertio mare optinuerunt Thraces an. XVIIII.	3		
340.18 Θραῖκες ἀπὸ Στρυμόνος διαβάντες κατέσχον τὴν νῦν Βιθυνίαν, τότε δε Βεβρυκίαν καλουμένην.	123.14 Thraces Bebryciam, quae nunc Bithynia uo-catur, transeuntes a Strymone occu-pauerunt.	4	66.24 Les Thraces traversèrent le Strymon et occu-pèrent la Bébry-cie qui est appelée Bithynie.	lacuna
340.20 Θραῖκες ἐθαλασσοκρατοῦν.	125.4 Thraces mare obtinuerunt.	5		lacuna
	125.10 Thraces mare obtinuerunt.	6		lacuna
341.1 Τέταρτοι ἐθαλασσοκράτησαν Ῥόδιοι, κατὰ δέ τινας πέμπτοι, ἔτη κγ΄.	130.9 Quarto mare obtinuerunt Rho-dii an. XXIII.	7	69.17 Les Rhodi-ens occupèrent la mer en quatrième lieu.	lacuna
341.4 Φρύγες πέμπτοι εθαλ-ασ-σοκράτησαν ἔτη κέ. κατὰ δέ τινας ζ΄.	135.3 Quinti mare obtinuerunt Fryges an. XXV.	8		178.26 Die See-herrschaft be-sassen die Phry-ger 25 Jahre.
lacuna	137.15 Sexti mare obtinuerunt Cyprii an. XXIII	9	73.30 En sixième lieu les Cypriotes occupèrent le mer pendant 24 ans.	

55

TABLE I (*Continued*)
TEXTS OF THE *CANONICAL* ENTRIES

Synkellos	Jerome	Entry	Michael	Armenian
lacuna	141.10 vii Foenices mare obtinuerunt an. xlv.	10		lacuna
lacuna	147.15 Aegyptii post Phoenices mare optinuerunt.	11	78.26 en huitième lieu les Egyptiens occupèrent la mer pendant 50 ans.	
lacuna	153.16 mare optinuerunt Milesii an. xviii construxeruntque urbem in Aegypto Naucratin.	12	85.19 Les Milésiens occupèrent la mer, en neuvième lieu, pendant 18 ans; ils fondèrent une ville en Egypte: Naucratès.	
lacuna	157.20 mare optinuerunt Cares.	13	86.22 en dixième lieu, les Cariens obtinrent ⟨ ⟩ pendant 69 ans.	182 *ad fin:* Zehntens führten die Seeherrschaft die Karier 61 Jahre.
lacuna	165.5 post Caras mare optinuerunt Lesbii an. lxviii.	14	⟨Libyer in *Arm. Can.* (but also *libii* in Jerome N)⟩	184.44 nach dem Karern beherrschten das Meer die Libyer.
454.4 ιβ' φωκαεῖς ἐθαλασσοκράτησαν ἔτη μδ '		15	100.18 Les Phocéens occupèrent la mer, au douzième lieu, pendant 34 ans.	187 *ad fin.* xii führten die Seeherrschaft die Phokier, Jahre 44.

8. κατὰ δέ τινας ἔτη ζ' Dindorf: ἔτη secl. Casaubon	8. uiginti APN 9. xxiii APN/T/D/B xxxiii M/XC xxiiii L xxxii F xii Q 10. an. xlv F only 12. xviii M/APN/T/FD/BQ xvii O xv L xviiii XC 14. lxviii OM/T/FD/BQ/L lxviiii APN/XC	15. 34 cod., 44 Chabot	

Statistics (1) out of the 15 entries, the following are found in:

Synkellos	Jerome	Michael	Armenian
8	14	7	6

(2) no entry is found in all four sources;
  7 entries are found in three sources: nos. 1, 2, 4, 7, 8, 13, 15
  6 entries are found in two sources: nos. 3, 5, 9, 11, 12,14
  2 entries are found in Jerome only: nos. 6 and 10.

In the four derviatives of the *Canons*, the surviving entries sometimes translate one another, and sometimes not: leaving any figures
on one side, translation is found in entries 3, 4, 9, 12 and 15, while
entries which do not translate are found in items 1, 2, 5, 7, 8, 11 and
13. Thus in seven cases against six, something more than simple
translation has occurred: in 1 and 2 Jerome shortens and simplifies
the entry; in 5 the Greek and Latin verbs do not translate one
another; in 7 and 8 Synkellos collates from more than one source; in
11 and 13 Jerome is again the simpler. Thus, on the usual assumption
that Jerome's hasty translation did not normally—except by inadvertence which applies perhaps to the verb in 5—alter the text of
his original, the more elaborate entries in the other derivatives are
due to expansion and editing. The principle serves also as a guide in
considering differences of dating in the various derivatives.

a. the dated sources
The dates given to the thalassocracies in the two surviving versions
of the *Canons* never exactly agree: the differences range from 2 years
in the case of Lesbos to 32 years in the case of the Pelasgoi. In Table
II, I set out the two series of dates, and also for comparison two
further columns showing the dates which would hold if, in the first
case, Troy fell at the orthodox year 1184/3, and in the second case at
the Eusebian year *anno Abrahae* 835. It is clear from this confrontation
that *the Armenian entries appear to oscillate between the two calculations,
while Jerome's entries are generally quite independent.*

Thus if we take the evidence from the texts of the entries, and from
their dates, together it appears that Eusebius-Jerome did not generally follow the Register in the placing of these entries, though quoting
it in some of his texts. The Armenian's ancestral editors on the other
hand not only expanded the texts upon occasion in conformity with
the *Register*, but also changed the *canonical* placings.

The Armenian date for Lydia, as Helm pointed out, is probably a
merely textual variant from Jerome's date, being driven down from
aA 842 by a Sacred History entry. This and Lesbos seem to be the
only survivors in the Armenian of the datings of Eusebius-Jerome,
and these may be common therefore to the *Register* and the source of
Jerome's dates.

b. undated sources
The Greek and Syriac derivatives of the *Canons* give no dates for the

thalassocracies, but probabilities can be established by examining the sequence of their entries and comparing it with, in each case, the sequence in the dated sources.

TABLE II
THALASSOCRACY DATES IN THE LATIN AND ARMENIAN CANONS

Jerome	Armenian			if Troy = 1184/3	= 835 aA
842	848	1.	Lydia 92 years	(834 = 1183/2)	836
960	928	2.	Pelasgoi 85 years	926 = 1091/0	928
1011	om.	3.	Thrace 79 years	1011 = 1006/5	1013
1044			Strymon		
1050			Thrace		
1054			Thrace		
1101	om.	4.	Rhodes 23 years	1090 = 927/6	1092
1125	1113	5.	Phrygia 25 years	1113 = 904/3	1115
1152	om.	6.	Cyprus 33 years	1138 = 879/8	1140
1180		7.	Phoenicia 45 years	1171/= 846/5	1173
1234		8.	Egypt ⟨50 years⟩	1216 = 801/0	1218
1268	om.	9.	Miletos ⟨18 years⟩	1266 = 751/0	1268
1296	1286	10.	Caria ⟨61 years⟩	1284 = 733/2	1286
1347	1345	11.	Lesbos	1345 = 672/1	1347
om.	1441	12.	Phokaia 44 years	1440 = 577/6	1442

1. Synkellos
LYDIA

The Lydian thalassocracy is the last entry in a Sporaden-list, and immediately follows the notice on the fall of Troy. This might imply that Synkellos' copy of the *Canons* had Lydia at an earlier date than aA 842, but in the left-hand column of the Armenian *Canons* the Lydian thalassocracy is the first Profane entry after Troy. Also Synkellos' previous Sporaden-list ends with a comparison of Samson and Herakles which is expanded from Jerome's Sacred entry at aA 842, so that both Sporaden-lists seem to end at the same time. The balance of the indications (they can hardly be called evidence) is therefore in favour of aA 842 as the date for the beginning of Lydia in the Greek as well as in the Latin and ancestral Armenian texts.

PELASGOI

The Pelasgian thalassocracy is the first entry in a Sporaden-list, and is

58

immediately followed by an entry not in our *Canons*, on Neleus and the Ionian Migration, with which is placed the long note on the Homeric question found in our *Canons* at aA 913 (Jerome) or 915 (Armenian). There is thus no immediate evidence whether Synkellos' *Canons* placed the Pelasgoi at aA 960 with Jerome or at aA 928 with the Armenian: certainly the context of the entry has been much edited.

The Neleus entry is Νειλεὺς Πελοποννησίων καὶ Ἀθηναίων ἡγούμενος εἰς Ἀσιάν ἐλθὼν τὰς Ἰωνίας ᾤκισε πόλεις ἐκβάλων τοὺς Κᾶρας. This is the orthodox and systematic tradition of the Ionian Migration, present already in Herodotus[14] and applying especially to Miletos: it is a question whether the editor of the *Canons* to whom this is due was also connecting the Ionians with the Pelasgians, and the Lydians with the Carians, in the Herodotean manner.[15]

The Eusebian Ionian Migration is placed at aA 980=B.C. 1037/6 with a reticent text:[16] *Ionica emigratio, in qua quidam Homerum fuisse scribunt.* This is the foundation of the entry which Synkellos has at the name of Akastos of Athens:[17] ἐπὶ Ἀκάστου Ἰώνων ἀποικία. καὶ Ὅμηροι ἱστορεῖται γεγονὼς παρ' Ἕλλησιν ὡς τινές, οἱ δὲ ὀλίγῳ πρότερον καὶ ἄλλοι ὕστερον. In Synkellos' *Canons* therefore the original Eusebian entry, slightly elaborated, has been demoted to a note on Akastos, and replaced by the Neleus entry as the principal notice on Ionia.

A note to the name of Akastos would normally in the *Canons* be written at the beginning of his reign, at aA 968. This seems to be confirmed by Michael,[18] who has the foundations of Ephesos and Samos at this year; by Dionysius[19] who has Ephesos at this year; and by the manuscripts F and X of Jerome, probably copying from a Greek source. There was thus a marked tendency in eastern scholarship to correct and amplify Eusebius on the Ionian Migration.

The derivatives of the *Canons* therefore show two traditions on the Ionian Migration. One is the Eusebian, represented by Jerome, in which Ionia has a short entry 20 years after the beginning of the Pelasgian thalassocracy. The other places Ionia (Ephesos and Samos

---

[14] I 147; IX 97.
[15] I 56; I 171.
[16] So dated both in Jerome O and the Armenian: see for the chronography *Sicilian Colony Dates*, Part V.
[17] 336. 3 f.
[18] p.61 f.
[19] See Part I note 8 above.

in the Syriac) at the first year of Akastos. This is eight years after the beginning of Jerome's Pelasgian thalassocracy: it is therefore possible that the Pelasgians and Ionians were connected in the Herodotean manner in this tradition, and a faint echo of this may account for the dating of the Pelasgoi to aA 968 in one of Jerome's worse manuscripts, L.

This indirect evidence of a Pelasgian thalassocracy eight or twenty years before the Ionian migration is therefore probably in favour of the conclusion that Synkellos' *Canons* had the Pelasgoi at Jerome's date, aA 960.

THRACE

Synkellos' entries on Thrace follow immediately upon an entry on Carthage which represents the notice in our *Canons* at aA 974 (Jerome) 978 (Armenian), but which was probably identified or confused with a similar entry at aA 1003(J) 1005(A)—Dionysius has the *text* of the later entry at the earlier *date* (which he renders as aA 971). If this is right, Synkellos' Thrace began after aA 1003; that is, probably about Jerome's date, aA 1011. This is consistent with the fact that Synkellos like Jerome has a multiple Thracian entry (items 3, 4, and either 5 or 6).

The differences between Synkellos and Jerome are that Synkellos omits one of the two duplicate entries (5 and 6) and that in his single third entry on Thrace the verb is in the imperfect. By using this tense, Synkellos' *Canons* presumably meant to convey that the Thracian thalassocracy continued after the migration to Asia: this agrees with the counting of the next two thalassocracies as the fourth and fifth. But Synkellos also reports that 'some' counted them as the fifth and sixth, which probably means that the same authority counted two Thracian thalassocracies, one in Europe and one in Asia. It is possible therefore that Jerome correctly translated the Greek verb before him (and that Eusebius counted two Thracian thalassocracies), and that Synkellos' imperfect tense comes from the alternative tradition.

Synkellos' first entry reports or quotes the 79 years of Thrace given in the Register; Jerome, without any textual variant, reports 19 years. It has been universally supposed that Jerome's figure is a misreading of ΟΘ as ΙΘ, but in that case we should expect some of his editors (especially T and F) to show variation or correction.

So far as we know, Jerome and the eastern scholars alike had only two sources on the thalassocracies: the Register in the *Chronographia* and the entries in the *Canons*. With the Thracian evidence before us we are bound to ask whether the Register is even more damaged textually than appears at first sight. For example, the entries in the *Canons* either assert, or are textually compatible with the assertion, that the first thalassocracy began in aA 842=B.C. 1175/4, while the orthodox date for the fall of Troy (no doubt used by the Diodoran Register) was 1184/3, nine years earlier; and the Eusebian date is aA 835=B.C. 1182/1. These nine years (reduced to six by Eusebius) could readily have been assigned to the Nostoi in general, or more especially to the fleet of Aeneas, up to his settlement at Alba which Jerome places in the eighth year after Troy. We have therefore to consider the possibility that the Register in the *Chronographia* is even more lacunose than it appears, and that its early entries once had this form:

1184/*3*   Fall of Troy
1183/*2*   ⟨Nostoi, or Aeneas⟩ 8 years
1175/*4*   Lydia, 92 years
1083/*2*   Pelasgoi, 85 years
998/7   Thrace in Europe ⟨19 years⟩
979/*8*   ⟨continued as Thrace in Asia⟩ 79 years
900/*899* Rhodes

If this was the original form of the early entries in the *Register*, used side by side with the different historiography shown in Jerome's entries, then:

(1) both historiographies recognized the ⟨Nostoi or Aeneas⟩ period; Eusebius shortened it by two years to suit his date for Troy, but he gave no entry in the *Canons* and it was lost from the *Register*. The continuation of the date aA 842=1175/4 for Lydia was therefore mechanical; and the Armenian's placing of the Pelasgoi at aA 928 shows an attempt to reckon 92 years from aA 836= 1183/2.

(2) in one historiography Thrace counted as one thalassocracy, in the other as two; Jerome's figure of 19 years, as well as the figure of 79 years given by the *Register* and Synkellos both come from the original *Register*. Jerome, who recognized two Thracian thalassocracies (if his verbs are to be trusted) quoted the '19 years' as he quoted other durations which his entries do not observe, and all

these will be simple translations from Eusebius' *Canons*. Synkellos *Canons* on the other hand have been influenced by the *Register* and regard the two Thraces as one, but remember the older Canonical tradition in the statement that 'some' counted Rhodes as the fifth thalassocrat.

RHODES and PHRYGIA
These entries follow on from Thrace in Synkellos' Sporaden-list, and are separated from one another only by a brief note on Homer κατά τινας. If this represents the rather longer note in Jerome at aA 1104, then Synkellos' dates for Rhodes and Phrygia were probably the same as Jerome's.

PHOKAIA
Synkellos' entry comes after a note on the Seven Sages which is not in our *Canons*, and before the entry on the Nemean Games, at aA 1444 in both versions. It is likely both that Jerome's original placed the beginning of Phokaia at or near its place in the Armenian, aA 1441, and that Synkellos' *Canons* agreed.

*　　*　　*

So far as can be seen therefore Synkellos' main source had a very similar text to Jerome for the thalassocracies. Synkellos however (or an ancestor) had also another source which—so far as we know— must have been the *Register* in the *Chronographia*, in a better text than ours.

2. Michael of Syria
Michael's entries on the thalassocracies, in so far as their dates can be inferred, seem to be farther from Jerome's than those of Synkellos. The surviving notices are such that in Michael's case it is most convenient to begin with Phokaia, and work backwards.

PHOKAIA
The entry on Phokaia, with a stated length of 34 years, is between the deaths of Aesop (aA 1453 J, 1452 A) and of Stesichoros (aA 1457 J, 1458 A): that is, within the years aA 1455 ±3. But as we have seen, Samos as thalassocrat in the *Canons* began either in 533/2 (aA 1484) or 531/0 (aA 1486). Michael therefore, on the evidence of his

Phokaian entry, understood for Samos the same date as the Armenian *Canons*, aA 1486, and his Phokaian entry was placed in aA 1452=B.C. 565/4. His text should not be altered,[20] as the 34 years agrees with the placing, and is not a quotation of the 44 years given in our other sources.

This innovation may be another piece of quasi-Herodotean scholarship in the tradition, for 565/4 is approximately the date of the Phokaian colony at Alalia.[21] Michael's source may have regarded the Phokaians as primarily thalassocrats of the western seas.

CARIA

The entry on the Carians succeeds a number of items on Sacred History, and precedes the notices of the battle of Thyrea (aA 1297 in both *Canons*), Midas' coinage (not in our *Canons*), and Numa's calendar (attached to his accession aA 1303 J). The abstracting here seems to have followed events in the reign of Hezekiah down to the foundation of Chersonesos in aA 1300, then from aA 1300 to the end of Hezekiah in 1304 to have given first the Sacred, then the Profane, items. Michael's Caria will then have fallen in aA $1302+2$=B.C. $715/4\pm2$ (which is later than in either of our *Canons*, aA 1296 J, 1286 A). It is possible that the 69 years stated may be a variant of the 61 years reported by the Armenian, but in view of the soundness of Michael's figure for Phokaia we should more probably trust the 69 years here, which would place the beginning of Lesbos at B.C. 646/5 ±2.

MILETOS

Miletos follows the Erythraian Sibyl (aA 1273 J, 1275 A) and precedes Midas (aA 1275 J, 1278 A): although the stated length is 18 years (as in Jerome), the actual placing thus gives 28 years (before $1302+2$ for Caria) as also in Jerome; and Michael's date will be aA 1274 ± 2=B.C. $743/2\pm2$. In this case the '18 years' will be a quotation from the *Register*, as in Jerome's text.

EGYPT

Egypt, with a stated length of 50 years, follows the accession of Menahem of Israel (aA 1222), and precedes the attack of Phul on

---

[20] Chabot prints 44 years in his text.
[21] Hdt. I 165 f.

Menahem, dated by Dionysius to aA 1224. The date is therefore aA $1223\pm1=$B.C. $794/3\pm1$, which is 50 years before Miletos in $743/2\pm2$.

*　　*　　*

Thus for the later ante-historiographic thalassocracies in Michael we seem to have the dates:

$793/2\pm1$: Egypt for 50 years (783/2 Jerome)

$743/2\pm1$: Miletos 'for 18 years' (749/8 J)

$715/4\pm1$: Caria for 69 years (721/0 J)

$\langle646/5\pm1$: Lesbos$\rangle$

$565/4$: Phokaia for 34 years ($576/5\pm1$ Arm).

CYPRUS
The earlier thalassocracy entries in Michael are perhaps not so informative. Cyprus is said to have been thalassocrat for 24 years as in Jerome L, and as against the *Register*'s 33 years. The entry follows the notice of Hazael's attack on Israel (aA 1144 in Dionysius) and precedes the death of Aremulus of Alba (aA 1160 J): this would be consistent with Michael's acceptance of Jerome's absolute date in aA 1152=B.C. 865/4.

RHODES
Michael's entry on Rhodes is in a context where quotations from pseudo-Epiphanes on various prophets have been interpolated. The notice to which these form an appendix appears in Jerome extended over the years aA 1086–1090; Michael places next a notice of Homer which may represent Jerome's longer item at aA 1104; then, after interpolations, the Rhodians. Jerome's Rhodes is at aA 1101, but if Michael used the *Register* years, 23+25 for Rhodes and Phrygia, and his Cyprus began in aA 1152, his Rhodes will have begun in aA 1104.

THRACE
The earliest of Michael's entries is that of the Thracian crossing from the Strymon into Asia. Here again the context is confused: a list of true and false prophets (which in Jerome occupies the years aA 1041–44) is followed by the Egyptian war attributed to the tenth year of Asa: in Jerome this is the year aA 1050, but Dionysius gives the date

aA 1047. Then comes the Strymon entry, followed by the first appearance of Baasa of Israel, whose accession is at aA 1045 in Jerome. It seems therefore that Michael probably intended Jerome's date, aA 1044, for the Strymon entry.

*   *   *

The derivatives of the Eusebian *Canons* therefore seem to show a fairly consistent development, away from the original Canonical entries and on the whole towards a rendering of the *Register*. Jerome, we may suppose, does not alter Eusebius' own entries unless by inadvertence; Synkellos is probably very near to Jerome throughout the thalassocracies but innovates on the Herodotean model on the Ionian Migration and knows another source besides his *Canons*: this may have been a better text of the *Register* in the Greek *Chronographia*. Michael appears to show this quasi-Herodotean scholarship affecting the thalassocracy entries at Phokaia; and the *Register* durations appear to be preferred to Jerome's at Rhodes and Phrygia. Finally, the Armenian *Canons* bring the thalassocracy entries into conformity with the lacunose text of the *Register* as known.

iii. the original text of Eusebius-Jerome

Comparison of the derivatives of the *Canons* has shown that one of the characteristics of Jerome's entries is that the text often shows a quotation from the *Register* but that the placings follow some different authority. This conclusion is confirmed when we examine the manuscript evidence for the placing of the entries: there is not often any substantial doubt of the year intended:

Lydia: aA 842 in OM/S/T/F/BQ, and? in A/L; ±2 years in the remainder; XC/D. (In the conditions of a *Canons* text, variation within ±2 years may be taken as confirming the standard text.) This is a good text.

Pelasgoi: aA 960 in O/S/BQ; ±1 in M/XC/D. Erased in A and no entries in T and F, perhaps because the Greek texts they consulted had the 'Armenian' date of aA 928. L has the entry at aA 968, the first year of Akastos, and a year for the Ionian Migration in the later eastern tradition.

Thrace: aA 1011 in PN/T/FD/Q; ±2 in M/A/XC/B/L; 1016 in O, the oldest manuscript.

Strymon: aA 1044 in OM/SA; 1045 in TXC/D/B/L; 1036 in F.

Thrace: aA 1050 in OM/SA/XC/D/L; 1051 in B; 1047 in F.

Thrace: aA 1054 in OM/SA/Q; ±2 in N/F/BL(Helm); 1057 in T.

Rhodes: aA 1101 in OM/APN/TX/F/BQ; omitted in C/D; 1098 in L. A very good text.

Phrygia: aA 1125 in O/APN/TC/FD/Q; ±2 in M/X/B; 1117 in L.

Cyprus: aA 1152 in M/APN/TXC; ±2 in FD/BQ/L; omitted by O.

Phoenicia: aA 1180 in O/APN/T/D/BQ; ±2 in M/C/F/L; 1191 in X after the fall of Assyria.

Egypt: aA 1234 in OM/T/Q; ±2 in APN/F/B; 1230 in C, 1231 in X/D; Fotheringham reports 1230 for L, Helm gives 1231.

Miletos: aA 1268 in O/APN/B/L; ±2 in M/T/F; 1252 in D; 1254 in XC; 1265 in Q. Several of D's entries are very early in this period.

Caria: aA 1296 in OM/P/T/F/B/L; ±2 in AN/Q; 1284 in XC; 1289 in D. XC here approach the Armenian date.

Lesbos: aA 1347 in OM/PN/T/Q/L; ±2 in A/D; 1341 X; 1342 C; 1343 F. B is reported for 1344 by Fotheringham, 1345 by Helm.

On this evidence, it seems certain that Jerome gave the dates mentioned as standard for Lydia, Thrace in aA 1050, Rhodes, Phrygia, Cyprus, Phoenicia, Caria and Lesbos; the others are probable though not so well-evidenced.

Consequently the thalassocracy-list of Eusebius-Jerome is:
B.C.

1181/0	⟨Nostoi or Aeneas: 6 years⟩	
1175/4	Lydia lasts	118 years
1057/6	Pelasgoi lasts	51
1006/5	Thrace quotes '19 years' but lasts	33
973/2	Strymon crossing placed	6 years before next
967/6	Thrace, placed	4 years before next
963/2	Thrace lasts	47
916/5	Rhodes quotes '23 years' but lasts	24
892/1	Phrygia quotes '25 years' but lasts	27
865/4	Cyprus quotes †23 years† but lasts	28
837/6	Phoenicia quotes '45 years' but lasts	54
783/2	Egypt lasts	34
749/8	Miletos quotes '18 years' but lasts	28
721/0	Caria lasts	51

670/69 Lesbos quotes '68 years' but lasts ⟨　⟩
　　⟨Phokaia⟩
⟨533/2 or 531/0 the historical thalassocracies⟩
⟨481/0　the diabasis of Xerxes.⟩

This gives a total of 700 years with Troy at the Eusebian date of 1182/1 B.C., but we should almost certainly suppose that the source of this version accepted the orthodox Eratosthenic date for Troy in 1184/3 B.C. The original list would then be 702 years long, and Eusebius will have changed it only by reducing the 8 years of the ⟨Nostoi or Aeneas⟩ entry to six.

This means that Eusebius in the *Chronographia* quoted the Diodoran *Register*, item (2) in our pedigree of thalassocratic historiography; in the *Canons*, he placed these quotations at dates determined by another authority, item (3) in the pedigree. Jerome simply translated these entries at the places given by Eusebius. This is most clearly seen when we tabulate Jerome and his nearer relatives, Synkellos and Michael:

Jerome		Synkellos[22]		Michael	
⟨1181/0	Nostoi, Aeneas⟩				
1175/4	Lydia	⟨1175/4⟩	Lydo-Maionians '92 years'		
1057/6	Pelasgoi	?⟨1057/6⟩	Pelasgoi '85 years'		
1006/5	Thrace I '19 years'	⟨1006/5⟩	Thrace '79 years'		
973/2	Strymon	⟨ 973/2⟩	Strymon	⟨973/2⟩	Strymon
967/6	Thrace II	?	Thrace II		
963/2	Thrace III				
916/5	Rhodes '23 years'	⟨916/5⟩	Rhodes '23 years'	⟨916/5⟩	Rhodes
892/1	Phrygia '25 years'	⟨892/1⟩	Phrygia '25 years'		
865/4	Cyprus †23 years†			⟨865/4⟩	Cyprus †24 years†
837/6	Phoenicia '45 years'				
783/2	Egypt			793/2±1	Egypt 50 years[23]
749/8	Miletos '18 years'			743/2±1	Miletos '18 years'
721/0	Caria			715/4±1	Caria 69 years[23]

---

[22] The inferred dates are not of course intended to be exact reconstructions, only to summarize the arguments given above for supposing that Synkellos and Michael more or less agreed with Jerome on the placing of these thalassocracies.
[23] Because of lacunae in the *Register*, it is uncertain whether these are quotations: see further below.

Jerome	Synkellos[22]	Michael
670/69 Lesbos 68 years[23]		⟨646/5 ±1⟩ Lesbos
⟨Phokaia⟩	⟨576/5⟩ Phokaia '44 years'	⟨565/4⟩ Phokaia
		34 years[24]
⟨Samos⟩		⟨531/0 Samos⟩
⟨Sparta⟩	Sparta †12 years†	Sparta '2 years'
⟨Naxos⟩	Naxos '10 years'	Naxos '⟨ ⟩ years'
⟨Eretria⟩	Eretria †7 years†	Eretria †17 years†
†509/8 Aigina †20 years	Aigina '10 years'	Aigina '10 years'

It seems likely that in perhaps the majority of the entries Eusebius quoted durations from the *Register*. The Greek and Syriac scholars found this erudition perplexing, and gradually altered the items, either by innovation, or into greater conformity with the *Register*.

iv. the original text of the Register
The evidence for the original *Register* now consists of:

(1) the lacunose text in the *Chronographia*

(2) the quotations and possible quotations in the texts of the *Canons* entries

(3) the inference that Lydia (beginning in 1175/4) was originally preceded by a ⟨Nostoi or Aeneas⟩ entry of 8 years

(4) the dates established in Part One for the historical thalassocracies, beginning with Samos in 533/2 or 531/0, and ending with 482/1, the year before the Aegean was occupied by the Persian fleets in 481/0.

The various statements of durations in years are collected together in Table III. The first column shows the figures surviving in the *Register*; the second the figures of the quotations or quasi-quotations in Jerome, Synkellos, Michael, and the Armenian *Canons* respectively. I have added a third column, of those figures which, on the textual evidence, were certainly to be found in the original—the 44 years of Phokaia (or Lesbos) are included in these because, as we have seen, the 34 years of Michael are due to innovation.

The total period covered by the thalassocratic list is determined by the dates of 1184/*3* for the fall of Troy and 481/*0* for the diabasis of Xerxes. But these facts alone do not settle the technical dating question. If Diodorus was quoting from Kastor, we have to bear in

---

[24] This is not a quotation from the *Register*.

mind that Kastor was probably dating the thalassocracies in parallel with Babylon, which used the March-April year. In dating thalassocracies moreover it is natural to have sailing seasons particularly in mind, and these might be more easily calculated in March–April than in Olympic years, even if the calculations were later translated into the Olympic notation.

TABLE III
EVIDENCE FOR THE FIGURES OF THE ORIGINAL DIODORAN REGISTER

Thalassocrat	*Chronographia* Text	Quotations J.	S.	M.	A.	Original ⟨Nostoi/Aeneas 8 years⟩
Lydia	92		92		92	92
Pelasgoi	85		85		85	85
Thrace		19				
	79		79			79
Rhodes	23	23	23			23
Phrygia	25	25	25		25	25
Cyprus	33	23		24		
Phoenicia	45	45				45
Egypt				50		
Miletos		18		18		18
Caria				69	61	
Lesbos		68				
Phokaia	44		44	34	44	44

Thus if Kastor agreed with Eratosthenes that Troy fell at the end of the Olympic year 1184/*3*, he would almost certainly have allowed the rest of that sailing season, 118*3*/2, for the dispersal and partial destruction of the Greek fleet. The first entry in his thalassocrat list can therefore not have begun before the next sailing season, 1183/*2*. Similarly at the lower terminus: the Aegean was commanded by the Persian fleet in the year of the diabasis, 481/*0*, which must therefore have been excluded from the thalassocrat years. Consequently we must conclude that for *Kastor* the first thalassocrat year was 1183/*2*, and the last 482/*1*, a total of 702 years.

Table III shows that the total of textually certain years in the evidence for the ante-historiographic thalassocracies of the *Register* is

419, which leaves 283 out of the total of 702 to be accounted for. Of these, either 50 or 52 (depending on the initial date for Samos) belong to the historical thalassocracies, leaving either 231 or 233 for the textually uncertain places. We need therefore those figures from the uncertain entries which amount to one or another of these totals, and 231 years is the sum of 19 years for Thrace in Europe (Jerome), 33 years for Cyprus (*Register*), 50 years for Egypt (Michael), 61 years for Caria (Armenian), and 68 years for Lesbos (Jerome).

From the hypothesis that these figures are the originals of the Diodoran Register, it follows that the initial date of Samos in that list was 533/2 B.C.

The original text of the Diodoran Register may therefore be reconstituted with absolute dates as shown in Table IV.

TABLE IV
THE ORIGINAL REGISTER

1184/*3*	Fall of Troy
118*3*/2	the Nostoi occupy the rest of the sailing season
1183/*2*	⟨Aeneas' fleet commands the seas for 8 years⟩
1175/*4*	Lydo-Maionians, 92 years
1083/*2*	Pelasgoi, 85 years
998/*7*	Thrace ⟨in Europe, 19 years⟩
979/*8*	⟨Thrace continues, in Asia⟩ 79 years
900/*899*	Rhodes, 23 years
877/*6*	Phrygia, 25 years
852/*1*	Cyprus, 33 years
819/*8*	Phoenicia, 45 years
774/*3*	Egypt, ⟨50 years⟩
724/*3*	Miletos, ⟨18 years⟩
706/*5*	⟨Caria, 61 years⟩
645/*4*	Lesbos, ⟨68 years⟩
577/*6*	Phokaia, 44 years[25]
533/*2* to 482/*1*	the historical thalassocracies

v. the chronographic structure of the Diodoran Register
The 702 years of the thalassocracies represent the chronographic equation $39 \times 18 = 27 \times 26$ years, and an examination of the series of figures in our reconstituted *Register* shows that they are grouped in chronographic periods, both on a 27-year and on a 39-year reckoning.

---

[25] So in the *Chronographia*, but perhaps in Kastor: 645/4 Lesbos 44 years (Pliny), 601/0 Phokaia 68 years: *see* further below.

These groupings are set out in Table V. It is perhaps unfortunate that they are such that they throw no light on the possible interchange of the numbers of Lesbos and Phokaia since the grouping of the numbers would suit either sequence. We are therefore forced to leave this problem aside until we come to more detailed enquiries.

Chronographic groupings offer a historian a good opportunity to express his view of periodization, and if we look at the *Register*'s 39-year grouping with periodization in mind, we see immediately that the third group comprises the $52 = 39 \times \frac{1}{3}$ years of the historical thalassocracies. We should therefore assume that the *Register*'s originator—probably the experienced constructionist Kastor—took full advantage of the opportunity.

There are three 39-year periods. The first and longest begins with ⟨Aeneas⟩ and ends with Cyprus, and for none of the communities mentioned (so far as we know) did the Greeks have access to any archives of this period. The second period extends from Phoenicia to the Phokaians, and in Kastor's time translations of the archives of Phoenicia and Egypt were available. We shall see, moreover, that they were used; in Greece the poets were comparable contemporary witnesses for this period. The three 39-year periods are therefore those of traditional, of archival and other contemporary, and of historical, source-material.

There are also three periods in the 27-year groupings. The first extends from ⟨Aeneas⟩ to Rhodes: it consists of Aegean powers, all barbarian except the last, which is on the eastern margin of the Aegean. The second begins with Phrygia and follows with Cyprus, Phoenicia and Egypt, ending with Miletos the founder of Naukratis: the period is concerned therefore with the Levant—it is Kastor's counterpart to 'the eastern adventure' of the modern archaeologist. The third period returns to the Aegean, and comprises all the thalassocracies from Caria to Aigina. The three 27-year periods are therefore those of the old Aegean, the eastern adventure, and the new Aegean

We shall be discussing later the details of the historiography for the traditional and the archival periods. Here we should note that the chronographic structure is, in a certain important sense, dominant whether the source-material is traditional, archival or historical. For example, if the Samian thalassocracy had been defined as beginning with the 'Cyrus battle' or other event in 531/0, the 50 years of historical thalassocracies would not have formed a chronographic period; similarly we shall see that the archival material has been used in something of the same way; if the sailing seasons had not been carefully kept in mind, the total from the fall of Troy to the diabasis would have been the non-chronographic period of 703 years. Thus the chronographic structure is dominant in the sense that, when the point of fixing on a date was reached in the work on the source-material, the precise year was finally decided on chronographic grounds.

TABLE V
THE DIODORAN REGISTER

	B.C.		years	
	1183/2	⟨Aeneas⟩	8	
	1175/4	Lydo-Maionians	92	
$364 = 39 \times 9\frac{1}{3}$ years	1083/2	Pelasgoi	85	$306 = 27 \times 11\frac{1}{3}$ years
	998/7	Thrace in Europe	19	
	979/8	Thrace in Asia	79	The Old Aegean
Traditional Sources	900/899	Rhodes	23	
	877/6	Phrygia	25	
	852/1	Cyprus	33	$171 = 27 \times 6\frac{1}{3}$ years
	819/8	Phoenicia	45	
$286 = 39 \times 7\frac{1}{3}$ years	774/3	Egypt	50	Eastern Adventure
	724/3	Miletos	18	
	706/5	Caria	61	
Archival etc. Sources	645/4	Lesbos	68	
	577/6	Phokaians	44	$225 = 27 \times 8\frac{1}{3}$ years
	533/2	Samos	15	
$52 = 39 \times 1\frac{1}{3}$ years	518/7	Sparta	2	
	516/5	Naxos	10	The New Aegean
Historical Sources	506/5	Eretria	15	
	491/0	Aigina	10	

$702 = 39 \times 18$ years $702 = 27 \times 26$ years

vi. the chronographic structure of the list of Eusebius-Jerome
The assembling of the full list of thalassocracies as known to Eusebius-Jerome still has some textual difficulties unresolved. We are, on the evidence available, to ascribe to this list the recognition of two separate Thracian thalassocracies, of which the first begins in 1006/5 B.C. This lasted, it would seem, until the Thracian crossing from the Strymon into Asia, dated to 973/2; and it is in conformity with the ascription of two separate Thracian thalassocracies to this list that the second is not entered until some years after this crossing. This can only mean that from 973/2 until Thrace II there were some years of interregnum. If therefore we examine the early figures of this list for chronographic grouping, it is useful, and not surprising, that we find they fall into periods of $(39 \times 5\frac{1}{3})+2$ years and $(39 \times 2\frac{2}{3})-2$

years around a six-year interregnum. This means that it is the second of the two duplicate entries for Thrace II in Jerome that is the un-erased error, and it is so shown in Table VI.

TABLE VI
THALASSOCRACIES OF EUSEBIUS-JEROME

Traditional Period	B.C.		years	
$210 = 39 \times 5\frac{1}{3}+2$	1183/2	⟨Aeneas⟩	8	The Old Aegean
	1175/4	Lydia	118	
	1057/6	Pelasgoi	51	$216 = 27 \times 8$
	1006/5	Thrace in Europe	33	
6 years' interregnum	973/2	Strymon crossing	6	
	967/6	Thrace in Asia	51	The Eastern
$102 = 39 \times 2\frac{2}{3}-2$	[[963/2	Thrace]]		Adventure
	916/5	Rhodes	24	
	892/1	Phrygia	27	$297 = 27 \times 11$
Archival-Historical	865/4	Cyprus	28	
Period	837/6	Phoenicia	54	
$195 = 39 \times 5$	783/2	Egypt	34	
	749/8	Miletos	28	
	721/0	Caria	51	
	670/69	Lesbos	?93	The New Aegean
	577/6	Phokaia	44	
	533/2	Samos	15	
$189 = 39 \times 5-6$	518/7	Sparta	2	$189 = 27 \times 7$
	516/5	Naxos	10	
	506/5	Eretria	15	
	491/0	Aigina	10	
$702 = 39 \times 18$ years			$702 = 27 \times 26$ years	

In the case of the Thraces therefore the chronographic structure is helpful with a textual problem. The other unresolved difficulty in the list is the date for Phokaia. Here a preliminary chronographic grouping does not help, since in the 27-year reckoning from Lesbos in 670/69 to the end of the list is $189=27 \times 7$ years, and this total throws no light on the disposition of the years within the period. The same group also gives $189=(39 \times 5)-6$ years, where the residue balances the six interregnal years in the early part of the list.

The periodization shown in the 27-year grouping in this list uses the same principles as Kastor, but applies them differently. The Old Aegean is much shorter; the Eastern Adventure is greatly lengthened, going back to Thrace in Asia at the beginning, and including Caria at the end; the New Aegean is consequently also shorter than Kastor's. The 39-year reckonings (whether our reconstruction is correct or not)

73

do not accept Kastor's principles governing his three periods: they seem to show two main divisions, the boundary falling between Phrygia and Cyprus. Probably the earlier of these two periods was regarded as traditional, and the later as archival and historical, thus treating barbarian archives and Greek history as of equal value. This is a profound change from Kastor's viewpoint, and dates our author to well within the Roman period, and even perhaps nearer to Eusebius than to Kastor.

vii. the residue patterns in the lists
One of the technical numerical (and therefore stylistic) aspects of a chronographic document may be seen in its residue patterns within the periodization groupings. Most of the individual figures within a group are not exact multiples of the generation-length or its fractions, there is an excess or deficiency of years which we may call the *residue*. If we examine Kastor's list from this point of view, his figures show:

TABLE VII
KASTOR'S RESIDUE PATTERN

Thalassocracy and Duration in Years	Residue of 27-Year Calculation	Residue of 39-Year Calculation
⟨Aeneas 8⟩	−1	−5
Lydia 92	+2	+1
Pelasgoi 85	+4	+7
Thrace 19	+1	+6
Thrace (continued) 79	−2	+1
Rhodes 23	−4	−3
Phrygia 25	−2	−1
Cyprus 33	−3	−6
Phoenicia 45	0	+6
Egypt 50	+5	−2
Miletos 18	0	+5
Caria 61	−2	−4
Lesbos 68	−4	+3
Phokia 44	−1	−8
Samos 15	−3	+2
Sparta 2	+2	+2
Naxos 10	+1	−3
Eretria 15	−3	+2
Aigina 10	+1	−3

74

It is clear from these residue patterns that *Kastor* operated with numerical as well as historical considerations when constructing his thalassocracy series; and the residue patterns seem to be used to demonstrate sub-periods within the main periodizations, which can be used to interrelate these periodizations—notice, for example, that a period in the 39-year calculations ends with Cyprus, and so does a sub-period in the 27-year column; while a 27-year period ends with Miletos, and so does a sub-period in the 39-year column.

In Jerome's list the residue pattern is very different (Table VIII).

TABLE VIII
JEROME'S RESIDUE PATTERN

Thalassocracy and Duration in Years	Residues of 27-Year Calculation	Residues of 39-Year Calculation
⟨Aeneas 8⟩	−1 ⎫0	−5 ⎫
Lydia 118	+1 ⎭ ⎫0	+1 ⎬
Pelasgoi 51	−3 ⎫ ⎬	−1 ⎬ +2⎤
Thrace I 33	−3 ⎬0 ⎭	+7 ⎭
interregnum 6	+6 ⎭	+6 +6⎤
Thrace II 51	−3 ⎫	−1 ⎫
Rhodes 24	+6 ⎬+3	−2 ⎬ −2⎦
Phrygia 27	0 ⎫	+1 ⎭
	⎬+1	
Cyprus 28	+1 ⎭	+2 ⎫
Phoenicia 54	0 0 0	+2 ⎬
Egypt 34	−2 ⎫	−5 ⎬ 0⎤
Miletos 28	+1 ⎭−1	+2 ⎭
Caria 51	−3 −3	−1 ⎭
Lesbos 93	+3 ⎫	+2 ⎫
Phokaia 44	−1 ⎭+2	−8 ⎭−6⎦
Samos 15	⎫	
Sparta 2	⎬0	+1 ⎫
Naxos 10	⎪ 0	⎬ 0⎦
Eretria 15	⎬	⎪
Aigina 10	⎭ −2	−1 ⎭

Whereas Kastor shows a preference for +x −x patterns in his sub-period residues, this authority clearly likes to arrange the residues in patterns of three: +*x* (*y*) −*x*, and variations of this: Kastor uses this three-member pattern only where *y*=0 as at Phoenicia.

75

It is clear from these examples that chronography tended to include an element of number-play, in which different authors show different preferences. What is not so clear as yet is how freely or how seriously this was used, with or without a close connection with sub-periodization; probably this also varied with style and author. It seems likely too that as an aspect of periodization this number-play was sometimes used by Kastor to express a sense of the movement of time—musically rather than arithmetically. This kind of musical use of residue figures seems on the other hand to be completely missing from the chronography of Jerome's list, and may be a useful indicator of style and authorship.

B. The Historiography
i. the author of the list of Eusebius-Jerome
The textual and chronographic enquiries have led us towards recognition of certain characteristics of the second author of thalassocratic history: he accepted Kastor's list of powers; he altered all Kastor's dates for the ante-historiographic thalassocracies except those of ⟨Aeneas⟩, Lydia and Phokaia; he combined Kastor's archival and historical periods into one, and this last marks him as of considerably later date than Kastor. To make any further progress towards his identification however—and indeed to advance further towards understanding either thalassocracy list—we have to consider the problem of how any of the dates were arrived at.

a. the general problem of identifying the calculations
The first component of the problem is our immense ignorance, due to the loss of all the books of the local historians of the communities mentioned in the list of thalassocracies, and of the works of universal history in the period when we might look for the author of the second list. On the other hand, Eusebius appears to have taken his list from one of his main authorities, so that other Eusebian dates very probably come from the same source; and since the thalassocracies are as much of universal as of local history, it is likely that the base-dates of local calculations (in addition to that of the diabasis) in some cases come also from universal history.

A second component of the problem is the absence of any narrative accompanying the lists, with two fragmentary exceptions: the thalassocracies of the Thraces are connected by the crossing from the Strymon valley into Bebrykia, and the Milesian thalassocracy is

76

connected with the foundation of Naukratis. We may be sure therefore that the author gave a narrative: but since (as it happens) no
other ancient dates survive for either of these events[1] we cannot from
these fragments judge its quality.

Indeed, for a source so late as this author seems to be, no quality
can *a priori* be excluded: it may have been very bad, at least upon
occasion. If however the author relied upon good sources, his continuous differences with Kastor may be due either to a genuinely
superior erudition; or to a different view of the nature of, for example, archives and history; or to pretentiousness. None of these
possibilities can be ruled out *a priori*, but a genuinely and consistently
superior erudition is perhaps the least likely.

In these circumstances, the best approach to the question of the
characteristics and identity of this author is probably to attempt to
discover parallel calculations which show him as a critic of Kastor.

b. the author as critic of Kastor

The simplest form of criticism undertaken by this author appears in
those cases where he seems to accept the historiography of Kastor but
to change the arithmetic:

(1) PELASGOI: 1083/2 Kastor: $585 = 39 \times 15$ years before the
Ionian Revolt in 498/7[2]

        1057/6 critic: $559 = 39 \times 14\frac{1}{3}$ years before the
Ionian Revolt in 498/7.

By this change, the critic is able to create
chronographic connections for the Pelasgian
thalassocracy with that of ⟨Aeneas⟩ (who
crossed from Asia into Europe) in 1183/2, 126
$= 27 \times 4\frac{2}{3}$ years earlier; and with that of the
Thracians in Asia (who had crossed from
Europe) in 967/6, $90 = 27 \times 3\frac{1}{3}$ years later.
Presumably therefore he wished to emphasize

---

[1] Hdt. II 178 implies that Naukratis was founded in the time of Amasis
(570–526), but perhaps the implication is not necessary, and certainly it
was not accepted: Polycharmos of Naukratis (Jac 640 F 1) had Naukratis
already in being by 688/7–685/4; Strabo XVII.1.18 places Milesion
Teichos earlier than Naukratis but in the time of Psammetichos I (from
about 660 onwards). The archaeological date is about 620: Boardman
p.138.
[2] For this precise year see *Klio* 37 (1959) p.40.

an intercontinental aspect of Pelasgian history, but from these connections there is no evidence that he used any information refused by, or unknown to, Kastor.

(2) THRACE in Asia: 979/8 Kastor: 324 = 36×9 years before Lampsakos in 655/4.

STRYMON crossing: 973/2 critic 312 = 39×8 years before Lampsakos founded in 655/4.

Here Kastor's critic has the count of nine generations back to Thrace in Europe: 1006/5 is 351 = 39×9 years before 655/4.

(3) PHRYGIA: 877/6 Kastor: 135 = 27×5 years before Midas accedes in 742/1 (Jerome)

892/1 critic: 216 = 36×6 years before Midas dies in 676/5 (Africanus[3])

The change here is mainly arithmetical, though slightly disguised by altering the base-date. The notable feature of both base-dates is that they seem to be archival: in 743 the Assyrians decisively defeated Urartu at the battle of Musasir, thus leaving power in the north-west to Phrygia, so that Midas' 'accession' means the (re-)establishment of the Phrygian empire. Jerome dates the 'death of Midas' to 696/5, when Assyria reconquered Kilikia and defeated Mita of Muski; Africanus' date presumably refers to the Kimmerian disaster, independently of Assyrian complications.

(4) CYPRUS: 852/1 Kastor: 156 = 36×4⅓ years before Tarsos became Assyrian in 696/5[4]

865/4 critic: 169 = 39×4⅓ years before Tarsos became Assyrian in 696/5.

---

[3] J. A. Cramer, *Anecdota Graeca e codd. manuscriptis Bibliothecae Regiae Parisiensis* (Oxford 1839) II 264.6.
[4] See Boardman, *The Greeks Overseas* p. 70, and 'Tarsus, Al Mina, and Greek Chronology' in JHS 85 (1965) pp.5 ff.

The change here, so far as we can see, is wholly arithmetical. Greek knowledge of the Assyrian building of Tarsos is guaranteed by Hellanikos (4 F 63); knowledge of the date is guaranteed by Jerome's entry on 'the death of Midas' at that year as well as, of course, by the references in Berossos and Abydenos: see below, CYPRUS.

(5) PHOENICIA: 819/8 Kastor: $333 = 27 \times 12\frac{1}{3}$ years before the Persian reconquest of Egypt 486/5[5]

837/6 critic: $351 = 27 \times 13$ years before the same date.

Although these calculations were probably made, they were perhaps subordinate to a synchronism with the beginning of Media: see below PHOENICIA. In this case there is a difference (though not immediate) of historiography between *Kastor* and his critic.

(6) EGYPT: 774/3 Kastor: $288 = 27 \times 10\frac{2}{3}$ years before the Persian reconquest of Egypt 486/5.

783/2 critic: $297 = 27 \times 11$ years before the same date.

These were probably the calculations actually made, on the basis of Egyptian archives: see below, EGYPT.

In these six cases the criticism of Kastor is simple: only in the instance of Phoenicia (and that indirectly, through Media) does there seem to be a historiographic difference between the two lists, while in some cases (pre-eminently Cyprus), the criticism seems, so far as we can tell, to be wanton. There are however also examples of differences of greater substance:

(7) The Ionian Migration: 1044/3 Kastor: $546 = 39 \times 14$ years before the Ionian Revolt, 498/7

---

[5] Dated to the Persian year beginning 6th April 485 by Herodotus: the Olympic translation into 486/5 was necessary to keep the 'four full years' of preparation for the diabasis thereafter: see *Klio* 37 (1959) p.40.

$$1037/6 \text{ critic}: \quad 594 \quad = \quad 36 \times 16\tfrac{1}{2} \quad \text{years}$$

before the expulsion of
the Neleids from Miletos
in 443/2[6]

Here the assumption that Kastor would follow Eratosthenes and Apollodoros for an epochal date is confirmed by: 1083/2 PELASGOI, 39×1 years before 1044/3; 979/8 THRACE in Asia, $65 = 39 \times 1\tfrac{2}{3}$ years after 1044/3; 706/5 CARIA, $273 = 39 \times 7$ years after 1044/3; and 628/7 Byzantium founded,[7] $130 = 39 \times 3\tfrac{1}{3}$ years before the Ionian Revolt 498/7. This series and the associated dates (see below) mark the 39-year construction from 1044/3 to 498/7 as one of Kastor's main stemmata. The critic on the other hand seems to go back to Hellanikos for the date of the Ionian Migration, and 1037/6 is $288 = 36 \times 8$ years before his Milesian thalassocracy in 749/8.

(8) The Lydian king-list: the Hellanikan date for Ionia carries with it the date of 623/2 for the beginning of the Lydian war with Miletos, and this is the Olympic-year equivalent of the 'summer' 623 given by the Herodotean king-list for Lydia:[8] the critic's Milesian thalassocracy in 749/8 is $126 = 36 \times 3\tfrac{1}{2}$ years before the Lydian war so dated. Kastor's Milesian thalassocracy in 724/3 on the other hand is $108 = 36 \times 3$ years before 616/5, which is the date yielded by the Lydian king-list of the Eusebian Common Source for the Milesian war. This Common Source seems to have been Kastor himself.

---

[6] *Sicilian Colony Dates* Part V.
[7] Kastor 250 F 2(a) quoted by John of Lydia.
[8] *Klio* 41 (1963) p.65. In addition to the reasons given there for ascribing the Eusebian Common Source on Lydia to Kastor, we may note the residue pattern:

King and Duration		*Residues of 27-Year calculation*		
Ardys I	36 years	0		
Alyattes I	14	−4 ⎤		
Meles	12	+3 ⎟ −2 ⎤		
Candaules	17	−1 ⎦		
Gyges	36	0	0 ⎬ 0	
Ardys	37	+1 ⎤		
Sadyattes	15	−3 ⎬ +2 ⎦		
Alyattes	49	+4 ⎦		
Croesus historical				

Very pretty; more artificial than the patterns of the thalassocracy list, but of the same general style, particularly in the characteristic that the middle member of a three-member pattern=0.

We should note that where Kastor and his critic agree on an absolute date, 1175/4 for the Lydian thalassocracy, their calculations were different if they were using different king-lists: 1175/4 is 459 = 27×17 years before 716/5, the translation of the Herodotean 'summer' of 716 for the accession of Gyges; but it is 477 = $27 \times 17\frac{2}{3}$ years before 698/7, the date for the accession of Gyges in the Eusebian Common Source. We infer that Kastor gave his Lydian king-list in his *Epitome* (whence it passed to Eusebius), and used it when he came to date his thalassocracies. His critic did not quarrel with Kastor's Lydian thalassocracy date (apparently accepting Troy in 1184/3 and ⟨Aeneas'⟩ eight years beginning in 1183/2), but preferred Hellanikos-Herodotus for the dating of the Mermnad kings.

(9) LESBOS: 645/4 Kastor: 17 years before his date for the foundation of Byzantium in 628/7: this presumably means that he accepted Herodotus' dating[9] of Kalchedon 17 years before Byzantium, and synchronized with it the beginning of the Lesbian thalassocracy. There is also a synchronism with the career of Terpandros of Lesbos, as dated by Phainias: see below, LESBOS.

670/69 critic: there is no synchronism with the Eusebian Kalchedon of 685/4, but there is with the career of Terpandros as dated by Hellanikos and Sosibios: see below, LESBOS.

Thus it seems that in three cases at least, Kastor's critic preferred to base his calculations on those of Hellanikos and Herodotus instead of those of later historians. One of his characteristics is therefore that he archaizes; the other is that, for whatever reason, he always changes Kastor's calculations even when (as in the Lydian case) he agrees on the absolute date, or (as in the cases of Cyprus and others) when he agrees on the historiography.

c. the author as constructionist
We may also examine the thalassocracy-list of Eusebius-Jerome in its own right as a construction, to elicit its characteristics in this respect.

---

[9] IV 144.

In looking at the pure chronographic system, we have already seen, for example, that the author does not value a distinction between barbarian archives and Greek history, and this is an important characteristic. Other matters of construction are:

(1) Jerome dates the beginning of Minos' thalassocracy (notoriously based on his Carian seamen[10]) to 1250/49, which is $529 = 23 \times 23$ years before the Carian thalassocracy in 721/0. Jerome also reports the death of Minos in 1204/3, which may[11] be attributed to Antiochos of Syracuse, but in this context gives Minos a thalassocracy of $46 = 23 \times 2$ years. Eusebius here[12] therefore is probably reporting from his main source on the thalassocracies, and the author had no hesitation about carrying his thalassocratic record back into the Heroic Age.

(2) in the Heroic Age, Eusebius-Jerome naturally shows considerable interest in the Trojan ancestors of Rome, and their Tantalid adversaries. Tantalos himself, as king of 'Phrygia or Maionia' is dated to 1360/59, which is $690 = 23 \times 30$ years before the thalassocracy in 670/69 of Lesbos, where the ruling Penthilidai claimed descent from Agamemnon and Tantalos. (It is also $387 = 27 \times 14\frac{1}{3} = 36 \times 10\frac{3}{4}$ years before the Strymon crossing in 973/2; and this is $81 = 27 \times 3 = 36 \times 2\frac{1}{4}$ years before Phrygia as thalassocrat in 892/1.). Here also therefore, the author of the second thalassocracy list carried his construction well back into the Heroic Age.

This case is also important in that it seems to involve the thalassocracy lists in an ethnographic controversy. Kastor's Lydian thalassocracy is a thalassocracy of the Λύδοι οἱ καὶ Μαίονες: on the other hand, Jerome's is of the Lydi alone (the Maiones are not mentioned), and Tantalos is king of Φρυγία ἤτοι Μαιονία. There was an ancient disagreement about the Phrygians, whom some (following Homer) brought to Asia before Troy, while others followed Xanthos of

[10] Hdt. I 171.

[11] *Sicilian Colony Dates* (Index of Years).

[12] At another date, 1406/5, Minos bears no relationship (it seems) either to Kastor's or to the Eusebian source's thalassocracies: if Kastor reached back into the Heroic Age, this alternative Minos does not seem to be evidence for it. The very early date is reminiscent of Philistos' very early date for Carthage, and in fact is $650 = 39 + 16\frac{2}{3}$ years before Philistos' era-date of 756/5: whether this arithmetical fact is historiographically relevant is another matter. (The event attributed to this date does not survive: it was possibly the foundation of Zankle or of the 'first' Gela.)

Lydia[13] in making their migration from Europe and arrival in Asia occur after the War. Undoubtedly the Phrygian empire was of heterogeneous origins, and this is reflected in the various Greek forms of the name of the Phrygians alone[14]—apart from the names of the Mygdones and others; there is no reason to doubt that at various times it varied in composition and extent, and that its Midas came from various ruling groups. Kastor's Λύδοι οἱ καὶ Μαίονες presumably means that these Lydians (if not also the Hesioneis of Sardis) were very closely connected with the people called Maiones by Homer; his critic's Phrygia-Maionia presumably means that his Tantalos ruled that part of the Phrygian empire which was the province or territory of Maionia.

It seems therefore to be clear that the author of the second list of thalassocracies did not confine his interests either to the list or to its period; and that he wrote in narrative form, of which there are occasional traces in the *Canons*.

A longer fragment may be the narrative with sources which appears in Jerome immediately following Tantalos in 1360/59, and of which Synkellos[15] gives a longer version: Γανυμήδην ὁ Τάνταλος ἁρπάσας υἱὸν τοῦ Τρωός, ὑπ᾽ αὐτοῦ κατεπολεμεῖτο Τρωός, ὡς ἱστορεῖ Δίδυμος ἐν Ἱστορίᾳ Ξένῃ (F 2 Schmidt) καὶ Φανοκλῆς (in the Ἔρωτες F 4). μάτην ἄρα τοῦ Διὸς ὡς ἀετοῦ τοῦτον ὁ μῦθος καταψεύσεται. If this fragment belongs to our author, then to his other known characteristics we must add a kind of erudition and parade of authorities, and a politico-military interpretation of mythodic history. If we add that the source should, in view of his importance to Eusebius, preferably be sought amongst those listed in the bibliography of the *Chronographia*, the candidates are few,[16] and seem to be confined to Kephalion, the pseudonym of a Hadrianic author who wrote a history of the period from Ninos to

---

[13] Jac 765 F 14, 15, 26: he explained that the Homeric Phrygians came from a *far* Askania, i.e. in Europe.

[14] Phryges; Briges (in Europe); Bebrykes, Berekyntes; Phorkys and Phrixos as eponyms.

[15] 305. 11 ff.

[16] The list consists (Karst p.125) of Alexander Polyhistor and Abydenos for oriental history, Manetho for Egypt; Kephalion and Diodorus for Greek universal history; Cassius Longinus and Phlegon for *Olympiades* annals; Kastor's *Epitome* (the authoritative handbook); Thallos' summary history; Porphyrius. Diodorus is impossible, since he is the source for Kastor's list; the annalists and handbook probably lacked narrative: this leaves Kephalion.

Alexander in a work, imitative of Herodotus, which he called *The Nine Muses*.

d. Kephalion (Jac 93)

There are not many named fragments of Kephalion, but they agree with the characteristics we have elicited for our author: he called Priam a Phrygian,[17] no doubt in the same extended sense as the Maiones were; he paraded his authorities;[18] his sources are very various; he regarded mythodic history as μάτην;[19] he reinterpreted the myths politically—fragment 4, for example, (on Pentheus) begins: 'So the senate and people of Thebes did not admit the claim of Dionysus to the throne . . .'

His work survived to be read by Photius, who says that he was childishly prolix and erudite; he wrote (after the manner of his idol Herodotus) in literary Ionian; and he certainly had access to a considerable library.[20] His main theme appears to have been excision of the supernatural (as of Zeus and the eagle in the tale of Ganymede), and therefore a reduction of all genres and periods of history to the politico-military, salted[21] with biography and anecdote.

It is of course a problem why Eusebius took such an author as one of his main sources in preference—in the case of the thalassocracies—to Kastor. The first reason may be that Kephalion covered a long period and was consistent in his treatment of it throughout, at however low a level, and gave his references. But perhaps the decisive point was that Kephalion excised the (pagan) supernatural, and in this way did half the Christian chronicler's work for him. Photius, living in a Christian world, would have no appreciation of this point, and therefore could see Kephalion's deficiencies more clearly.

A full justification of the identification of the author of the second thalassocracy list with Kephalion would of course require a collection of all the Eusebian entries of this style, and their comparison, in analytical detail, with Kephalion's named fragments. Until this work is done we may for convenience's sake use Kephalion's name for the author of the second list, as we use Kastor's name for the author of

---

17 93 F 1.
18 Hellanikos, Herodotus, Ktesias and ⟨Deinon⟩ F 1; Sophokles F 3; Deinarchos, Philochoros F 4; Euripides F 5 and 6.
19 F 6.
20 Jac 93 T 2.
21 Suidas calls his work παντοδάπαι ἱστορίαι.

the first while awaiting a detailed stylistic comparison of the chronography of Kastor's named fragments. To mark the unfinished state of
these identifications however, both names are from this point onwards italicized.

ii. the separate items from Egypt to Phokaia
a. Kastor's *EGYPT 774/3–725/4*

An Egyptian thalassocracy covering the middle fifty years of the
eighth century is unexpected and astonishing, and cannot (so far as
we know) be derived from Aegean tradition, either of the mainland or
East Greece. This implies that *Kastor* was unable to find a Greek
state of the middle eighth century whose activities fulfilled his
definition of a thalassocracy; and since this is the time when Euboian
activity reached from Cumae to Al Mina, our suspicions that there
was a lacuna where there should have been Euboian tradition[1] is to
that extent confirmed.

If *Kastor* was unable to admit a Greek state to thalassocracy at this
period, we must suppose that he believed he had found the appropriate
evidence for a thalassocracy in the Egyptian archive. This archive, as
accessible to him, was in the main available from Manetho's *Egyptian
History*, a three-volume translation of one version of that history. The
Greeks, and after them the Christians, both found this archive in part
incredible; at the same time, they explored it for confirmation of the
biographies of Danaos and Menelaos on the one hand, and of Moses
on the other. It is therefore doubtful whether any of the surviving
quotations are wholly unedited and unrevised transcripts of what
Manetho wrote, but we can divide the versions into two groups:
Manetho as quoted by Africanus and known to us through Synkellos
(609 F 2), and a heavily revised version used by Eusebius in his
Chronographia (609 F 3a) and his *Canons* (609 F 3c), and excerpted by
Synkellos (609 F 3b).

The part relevant to our problem of finding *Kastor*'s reasons
for an Egyptian thalassocracy consists of the period beginning with
the Twenty-third Dynasty. This dynasty is presented:

Manetho (F 2)	*Revision (F 3)*
1. Petoubates 40 years contemporary with Ol.1	1. Petoubastis 25 years

---

[1] SCD Part VI.

2. Osorcho 8 years whom
    whom the Egyptians
    call Herakles
	2. Osorthon 9 years
	    'whom the Egyptians
	    called Herakles'

3. Psammous 10 years	3. Psammous 10 years
4. Zet 31 years altogether 89 years	altogether 44 years

The difference between the 40 and 25 years attributed to the first Pharaoh of this dynasty is apparently due to the division of the 40 years of Manetho into 15 pre-Olympic and 25 Olympic years.[2] Since however Eusebius does not observe this absolute dating, the division of the years probably belongs to Manetho himself, and the omission of the first part of the reign to the revisor. We may conclude that this revisor did not have access to, or did not use, Manetho's original source.

The total of 44 Olympic years correctly (if mechanically) reported in the Revision, has become 31 (ΛΑ for ΜΔ) years at some stage in the copying of Manetho; and then at a second stage been queried: ΖΗΤ (εῖται).[3] At a third stage, the query has been taken as the name Zet, and the figure of 31 years taken as the length of a reign: this new reign has then been added to the rest to produce the total of 89 years for the dynasty. At one of these stages also the figure for Osorcho (which must be 9 years to give the total of 44) has been miscopied as 8 years: Θ has been misread as H.

It thus appears that Manetho's Twenty-third Dynasty was:

1. Petoubatis of Tanis: 15 pre-Olympic years: 791/0–777/6
                       25 Olympic years: 776/5–752/1

2. Osorcho, 9 years: 751/0–743/2

3. Psammous, 10 years: 742/1–733/2

But the Twenty-third Dynasty, according to Egyptian sources now known, was not Tanite but Theban, and its second Pharaoh, Pedubaste, reigned in the ninth century. 'Petoubatis of Tanis' was Pedubastit of Tanis recorded by the Assyrians in 671/0, and in later demotic romance a hero who fought Thirteen Asiatics for the Sacred Boat of Amon, and duelled with the Syrian warrior Mentu-Baal for

---

[2] So Pessl, probante Jac III C 1, p.76 note 39.
[3] Flinders Petrie ap. Jac ad loc.

the armour of Inaros.[4] It seems clear that Manetho has made a false identification of the Theban and the Tanite, on the basis of another false identification of Assyrians with Phoenicians already made in demotic romance. So, when *Kastor* read his Manetho, he found, about the time of the first Olympiad, an Egyptian dynasty which began or established its rule by a most successful fight with the Phoenicians involving the Boat of Amon. It was natural that *Kastor* should see in this archive an explanation of the end of the Phoenician thalassocracy, in the sense at least that the Phoenicians were now unable to work their will in Egyptian waters.

Kastor's choice of the exact year 774/3 for the establishment of the Egyptian thalassocracy in this sense is perhaps more probably his own than Manetho's. It allows the Phoenicans to have a thalassocracy of respectable length; and it places Egyptian independence of Phoenician domination $288 = 36 \times 8$ years before the Persian re-conquest of Egypt under Xerxes[5] in 486/5. But it is possible that *Kastor* was anticipated in the choice of the year, as we shall see.

Nothing further is known of Manetho's Dynasty XXIII which throws light on *Kastor*'s thalassocracy, but the following dynasties are:

Manetho	*Revision*

Dynasty XXIV

(732/1)	Bocchoris of Sais, 6 years in whose time a lamb spoke 990 years	Bocchoris of Sais, 44 years 'in whose time a lamb spoke' altogether 44 years

Dynasty XXV

(726/5)	1. Sabakon the Ethiopian who captured Bocchoris and burnt him alive, and who reigned 8 years	1. Sabakon 'who captured Bocchoris and burnt him alive' and who reigned 12 years
(718/7)	2. Sabichos his son, 14 yrs	2. Sebichos his son, 12 years

---

[4] H. R. Hall, CAH III[1], 290.

[5] Egyptian historiography succeeded in forgetting the Assyrian occupation, and in regarding the early Persians as legitimate Pharaohs. Xerxes however refused any concessions to Egyptian feeling: yet his reconquest was too recent to be denied. It is therefore very possible that for Manetho's version of the archive, Xerxes' reconquest of Egypt marked an epoch.

(704/3)	3. Tarkos, 18 years	3. Tarachos 20 years
	altogether 40 years	altogether 44 years

Dynasty XXVI

(686/5)	1. Stephinates 7 years	1. Ammeris the Ethiopian 12 yrs
(679/8)	2. Nechepsos 6 years	2. Stephinathis 7 years
(673/2)	3. Nechao I 8 years	3. Nechepsos 6 years
(665/4)	4. Psammetichos 54 years	4. Nechao 8 years
(611/0)	5. Nechao II ⟨1⟩6 years	5. Psammetichos 44 years
(595/4)	6. Psammouthis 6 years	6. Nechao II 6 years
(589/8)	7. Ouaphis 19 years	7. Psammouthis 17 years
(570/69)	8. Amosis 44 years	8. Ouaphris 25 years
(526/5)	9. Psammecherites $\frac{1}{2}$ year	9. Amosis 42 years
	altogether 150 years 6 months	altogether 167 years.

Bocchoris of Sais appears in Diodorus[6] as a considerable person-ality, famous particularly for his reform of the law of contract. Diodorus may be drawing on Manetho direct, but in any case we may suspect that *Kastor*'s Egyptian thalassocracy, established by defeating the Phoenicians, developed into the avaricious and crafty policies attributed to Bocchoris.

The absolute dates calculated for Manetho in the above list are confirmed at the second year of Ouaphris by Clement of Alexandria,[7] who equates this regnal year with the Olympic year 588/7. The num-ber of 990 years noted at the end of Dynasty XXIV is clearly not a dynastic total and may be neglected here;[8] the date given for the Ethiopian conquest is 726/5, which is unhistorical but $240 = 36 \times 6\frac{2}{3}$ years before Xerxes' reconquest of Egypt in 486/5.[9] The Assyrian

---

[6] I 79: the tradition continued to develop: an elegy, the *Bokchoreis*, was written by a Pankrates in Hadrian's time (625 F 1), and the years attributed to this king much increased; pseudo-Manetho 609 F 28.

[7] *Str.* I.127.1.

[8] It may be, for example, a total of years for native Egyptian Pharaohs before the Ethiopian conquest from some earlier foreign domination; if correct (within Manethonian terms), $990 = 36 \times 27\frac{1}{2}$ years: and the figure may show the influence of Greek chronography.

[9] It is this arithmetical fact, and the possibility of chronography in Manetho, which make it conceivable that Manetho himself dated the 'war with Phoenicia' to 774/3 B.C.

conquest of 686 B.C. is expunged from the record, and this agrees with the identification of Petoubatis of Tanis with the Pharoah of Dynasty XXIII.

It appears therefore that after the military activities of Petoubatis and the economic and legal activities of Bocchoris, *Kastor* will have brought his Egyptian thalassocracy to an end with the Ethiopian conquest and allowed an interregnum of two years before the rise of Miletos to thalassocracy in 724/3.

In relation to his archival source, *Kastor*'s construction of an Egyptian thalassocracy is solid and persuasive: it was accepted in principle by *Kephalion*. That it is entirely unhistorical is due to the nature of the archive as represented by Manetho, whose chief errors here are (1) the identification of Petoubatis of Tanis with the Theban Pharaoh; (2) the misdating of Bocchoris; and (3) the omission of the Assyrian conquest. It is possible also that Manetho was to some degree influenced by Greek chronography, which would make his work more acceptable to *Kastor* though less so to us: an examination of his text from this point of view might be fruitful.

b. Kastor's *MILETOS 724/3–707/6*

The commencing date for *Kastor*'s Miletos is $108 = 36 \times 3$ years before the Lydo-Milesian war dated to 616/5 (–605/4) according to the dynastic years in the Eusebian common source for Lydia, *Kastor* himself. We are to infer that *Kastor* published his Lydian dates in the *Epitome* (whence they came to Eusebius), and used them for this further construction when he came to write *Babylon and the Thalassocrats*. The 36-year generation interpretation of the 108 years is to be preferred to a 27-year generation because the 36-year generation was traditional for Miletos under the Neleids since Hellanikos' time:[10] the 18 years of the thalassocracy then represent half a generation.

In the *Canons*, Eusebius has a single entry for the Milesian thalassocracy and the foundation of Naukratis: at the date of 749/8 this comes from *Kephalion*. The first question about *Kastor*'s Miletos is therefore whether he preceded *Kephalion* in ascribing Naukratis to the time of the eighth-century thalassocracy.

The archaeological date for Naukratis is *c.*620, and this date seems

---

[10] SCD part V.

89

to have been known to the literary tradition, for Strabo[11] reports the arrival of thirty shiploads of Milesians who settled first at Milesion Teichos, then at Naukratis, in the time of Psammetichos of Egypt and Kyaxares the Mede. The last year of Psammetichos in Manetho is 612/1; the first year of Kyaxares is usually placed by the Greek historiographers in the 620's:[12] Strabo's date therefore is within the period 620 ± 10, which agrees with the archaeology.

Consequently we can reconstruct the argument which put Naukratis back to the eighth century somewhat as follows:

(1) the Lydo-Milesian war began in the generation of the Neleid X son of Y;

(2) Naukratis, at Strabo's date, was founded in the generation of Y;

(3) BUT the name of Naukratis shows thalassocracy consciously pursued;

(4) and thalassocracy in this sense is otherwise fixed to the generation of Y's grandfather, Y 1;

(5) so Naukratis was founded in the time of Y 1.

Therefore the question about *Kastor*'s Naukratis is the question of whether this kind of verbal argument about names and nomenclature cycles is one which he could have used. It seems likely that he did, for Athenaios quotes Polycharmos of Naukratis[13] for contact between Naukratis and Cyprus in 688/7 (36×1 years after 724/3). Polycharmos' date is unknown, but he is clearly more likely to have drawn on *Kastor* (or a predecessor) than on *Kephalion*: and we can therefore provisionally assume that *Kastor* dated Naukratis to the time of his Milesian thalassocracy, and made it the event which marked the appearance of Miletos as successor to Egypt in the rule of the sea.

It also follows from this assumption that *Kastor* fixed the date of the Milesian thalassocracy on other evidence than that of Naukratis, and this evidence seems to be traceable, beginning with one of *Kastor*'s main series of dates.[14] This series is:

1083/2 Pelasgian thalassocracy begins
          39×1

---

[11] XVII.1.18.
[12] For the detail see below: Phoenicia.
[13] Jac 640 F 1.
[14] Noted (i)b(7) above.

1044/3 Neleus of Miletos leads the Ionian Migration

$$65 = 39 \times 1\tfrac{2}{3}$$

979/8 thalassocracy of THRACE in Asia

$$247 = 39 \times 6\tfrac{1}{3}$$

732/1 Maroneia in Thrace founded from Chios

$$26 = 39 \times \tfrac{2}{3}$$

706/5 CARIAN thalassocracy begins

$$13 = 39 \times \tfrac{1}{3}$$

693/2 Glaukos of Chios, ironmaster

$$65 = 39 \times 1\tfrac{2}{3}$$

628/7 Byzantium founded (named fragment of *Kastor* 250 F 2 a)

$$130 = 39 \times 3\tfrac{1}{3}$$

498/7 Ionian Revolt begins

The Chiote dates of 732/1 and 693/2 in this series seem to represent *Kastor*'s version of what Strabo[15] calls Chiote thalassocracy and ἐλευθερία. Strabo no doubt represents the local historian more faithfully than does *Kastor*, who refuses to admit Chios to thalassocracy in his full sense: but *Kastor*'s selection of Chiote subjects for dating is significant: the wine of Maroneia prefigures the Chiote wine trade,[16] and Glaukos is a representative of the metal trade.[17]

The Chiote dates overlap the Milesian thalassocracy, and show, first, that when *Kastor* refused to admit Chios to thalassocracy he did not thereby deny her importance; and, second, that he found in Miletos a quality which distinguished her activities beyond the purely economic at this time. Miletos and Chios were often closely associated,[18] and it seems probable that the 'Milesian thalassocracy', as conceived by *Kastor*, represents Miletos as in some sense the leader and planner of activities wider than her own, as in fact the typical Neleid Miletos, the leader of Ionia.

Consequently we may note another series of dates as either due to *Kastor*, or showing this influence in the Eusebian sources. :

741/0 Foundation of Naxos in Sicily

$$9 = 27 \times \tfrac{1}{3} = 36 \times \tfrac{1}{4}$$

732/1 Foundations of Maroneia, and of Leontinoi in Sicily

$$36 = 27 \times 1\tfrac{1}{3} = 36 \times 1$$

---

[15] XIV.1.35.

[16] Boardman, *op. cit.* p.32 and almost *passim* (sixth century).

[17] Boardman, *op. cit.* p.106 f.: from the eighth century onwards, connected with Phrygian originals in some cases.

[18] e.g. Thales' wine-presses are in both places: Ar. *Pol* I *ad fin.*

696/5 Tarsos becomes Assyrian (historical date)
$$135 = 27 \times 5 = 36 \times 3\tfrac{3}{4}$$
561/0 accession of Croesus in Lydia
$$45 = 27 \times 1\tfrac{2}{3} = 36 \times 1\tfrac{1}{4}$$
516/5 thalassocracy of NAXOS
$$18 = 27 \times \tfrac{2}{3} = 36 \times \tfrac{1}{2}$$
498/7 Ionian Revolt begins.

This series adds Naxos to the Ionians of Miletos and Chios, and relates their histories to that of the Assyrians at Tarsos.

Tarsos in 696 B.C. is known to us chiefly as the culmination of the Assyrian hostility to the Greeks of Al Mina and Kilikia, which had a substantial history of which we plainly have only fragments. In 709/8 Cyprus submitted to Assyria after 'the Ionians were drawn like fish from the sea', presumably in a series of naval engagements. In 696/5, Berossos and Abydenos report Greek fleets in action off Kilikia. For all this period *Kastor*, who had the full texts of Berossos and of Menandros' *Acts of the Kings of Tyre*, must have been much better informed than we are: and it must have been this information which led him to identify and date the Milesian thalassocracy.

It seems therefore that *Kastor* attributed to Neleid Miletos at this time a concentration of force and purpose sufficient to meet the requirements of thalassocracy; and that he did not find this quality in other important Ionian states of the time, Chios and Naxos. It would also appear that, in the local histories of the Ionian states, Chios had the most claim to be the rival of Miletos for thalassocracy: and Chios was settled from Euboia. We are therefore bound to suspect that the 'Milesian' thalassocracy as envisaged by *Kastor* is a construction which in part fills the Euboian lacuna in tradition of the eighth century. Apparently what has happened is that Egypt has taken the place of Euboia, and Miletos represents the beginning of the development of East Greece, as a result of Euboian influence through Chios.

Kastor's Milesian thalassocracy ends in 707/6 (ten years before Assyrian Tarsos), and finds no Greek successor. The fall of the thalassocracy therefore probably was not ascribed to external eastern enemies; and the cause of Miletos' fall probably was also the reason why no other Greek thalassocracy succeeded. These indications, taken together with the somewhat Euboian flavour (through Chios) of the 'Milesian thalassocracy', suggest that *Kastor* ascribed the end of this rule of the seas to Miletos' entry into the Lelantine War as ally of

Eretria. We should therefore connect this dating, both with the ascription of the foundations of Spartan Taras and Corinthian Corcyra to 706/5 in the *Canons* (which points to a historiography of joint action by Corinth and Sparta on the western trade-route 195 = 39×5 years before Dorieus in 511/0 and 216 = $36 \times 6 = 27 \times 8$ years before the destruction of Eritria in 491/0), and with Plutarch's story that the Eretrians were the original settlers of Corcyra.[19] The *date* seems to be derived from Timaios;[20] but he knew nothing of the Eretrians: perhaps their story was first published from the traditions of their refugee settlement in Macedonian Methone after his time.

There seems to have been no ancient specialist history of the Lelantine War. But it must have been mentioned in the local histories of Euboia, Thessaly, Chalkidike, Miletos and Samos; and it must have been mentioned in any thalassocrat history. It was probably also referred to in a number of biographies of Hesiod, but no direct and explicit statement of date survives. The suggestion that *Kastor* dated its outbreak or general spread in 706/5 cannot therefore be checked against other traditions, but seems probable.

Kastor's Milesian thalassocracy therefore seems to have begun with the establishment of Naukratis in Egypt; continued under Neleid leadership with campaigns in Cyprus and Kilikia; and come to an end with Milesian involvement in the Lelantine War. It is (quite apart from Naukratis) probably unhistorical in the sense that the Ionian enemies of Assyria were not under the leadership of the Neleids of Miletos.

c. Kastor's *CARIA 706/5– 646/5*

This is the last of the barbarian thalassocracies, and has been much discussed. Myres[21] wished to take the 'Milesians and Carians' as a single entry to be dated to the time of the Dodekarchy or Psamme-tichos I; Burn[22] has suggested the reading 'Megarians'. It is import-ant therefore that there is other evidence for a historiography which gave the Carians some importance at this time: Plutarch[23] reports a story that the Carian Arselis, dynast of Mylasa, killed Candaules of Lydia and put Gyges on the throne, removing the 'Amazon' double-

---

[19] QG 11.
[20] Who placed the event two years earlier: SCD Part IV.
[21] *op. cit.*
[22] *op. cit.* and *Lyric Age of Greece* (1960) p.217 f.
[23] QG 45=Jac 742 F 5.

axe (which Candaules had inherited and dishonoured) to the sanctuary of Zeus Labrandeus in Caria. It seems a most probable inference that *Kastor* knew and used this story to account for at least the beginning of his Carian thalassocracy: his Gyges accedes in 698/7, and Arselis must be supposed to have himself acceded some time before he grew to power over Lydia, so that the Carian thalassocracy probably began in 706/5 with Arselis' reign, or some notable event near its beginning.[24]

But it seems certain that the Carian thalassocracy must have been, for *Kastor*, considerably shorter than 61 years, and that this period must include an interregnum. We have to bear in mind on the one hand the evidence from the Egyptian, Milesian, and historical thalassocracies that *Kastor* required some concentration of force and purpose from the powers he admitted to thalassocracy; and on the other that, given this, he was prepared to concede complex situations, as in the appearance of Chios and Naxos alongside Miletos. The period of the Carian thalassocracy was certainly complex: in addition to the Lelantine war, there was the Greek defeat at Tarsos in 696/5; the Kimmerian destruction of Phrygia in 696/5 or 676/5; Gyges' first Kimmerian war, his policy to the Greek cities on his west and their colonies on his north; and the second Kimmerian war in which, according to Ashurbanipal, Gyges was killed in 648 or later. According to Herodotus, Greek knowledge of Gyges did not include the first Kimmerian war, and ascribed the second to Ardys his son; although Ashurbanipal believed that Gyges was killed,[25] it is possible that with communications disrupted by the barbarians he was misinformed and the Greek tradition is right, and that Gyges had died on the eve of the Kimmerian invasion.

Kastor's Gyges accedes in 698/7, and his Ardys in 662/1: but these dates do not give us his placing of the Kimmerian invasion. It is of course tempting to suppose that after Herodotus, and especially in Pergamene scholarship, the true date (in 648 or later) of the Kimmerian devastation of Lydia and Ionia had become known, and is represented in *Kastor*'s dating of the end of the Carian thalassocracy (and interregnum) in 646/5. We can show the probability that it was known; and the possibility that *Kastor* used it:

---

[24] Arselis' name seems to be theophoric, for a Solymian divinity named Arsalos is reported: Plutarch *de defect. orac.* 21.

[25] See now Campbell Thomson and Mallowan, 'A New Inscription of Ashurbanipal' in *Liverpool Annals* XX pp.96 f.

(1) there is the probability that the true date (i.e. in the 640's) was known to the Lydian source of the Marmor Parium, for there Alyattes' reign is dated as beginning in (or about) 605/4. For the Parian therefore Alyattes had a reign of 44 years, less than Herodotus' 57 or *Kastor*'s 49 years. It is consequently probable that the reigns of Ardys and Sadyattes (who together have 69 years in Herodotus and 64 years in *Kastor*) were shorter than the other figures we possess, and that the second Kimmerian war dated in Ardys' time, was placed at, approximately, its true date;

(2) the possibility that *Kastor* knew and used the true date is shown by the appearance in Eusebius at 1078/7 the entry Ἀμαζόνες τῇ Ἀσίᾳ ἐπῆλθον ἅμα Κιμμερίοις: this is $416 = 39 \times 10\frac{2}{3}$ years before *Kastor*'s Ardys accedes in 662/1. There is clearly the possibility that *Kastor*'s actual reckoning was the tidier 39×11 years from 1078/7 to ⟨649/8⟩ taken as the year of the Kimmerian devastation in Ardys' time.

There is therefore the possibility that *Kastor* ended his Carian period with the Kimmerian devastations.

But this period, as we have seen, almost certainly included a thalassocracy and an interregnum: and here the questions are of what the Carians did during their thalassocracy, and when and how it ended.

If *Kastor* placed the outbreak of the Lelantine War in 706/5, and saw in this absorption of Greek energies the opportunity of the Carians, it may be that he ascribed the Ionian defeats of 696/5 as in part due to Carian interference with reinforcements. The Carian thalassocracy in this sense was therefore probably imagined as a pirate regime which preyed on Greek shipping at a time of internecine Greek war: in particular, perhaps, affecting communications between Miletos and Rhodes, and derived therefore by *Kastor* from his native Rhodian tradition.

The Ionian and Carian mercenaries of Psammetichos I are generally connected with Ashurbanipal's report of Gyges' alliance with Psammetichos around 660; and both with Greek reports of his wars with Miletos and Kolophon, and his promotion of Greek colonies at Abydos, Priapos and Prokonnesos, and the archaeological evidence from Daskyleion, in the southern Propontis. If, as is often supposed, Gyges sent these mercenaries to Psammetichos, and if *Kastor* supposed that Gyges' policy towards Mylasa was similar to that towards Miletos, then for him by 670–660 Lydia was overlord of Caria: the 'thalassocracy' therefore probably ended within Gyges' reign, even for *Kastor*. If he agreed with Africanus that Phrygia fell to the Kimmerioi in 676/5, he may have placed the expansion of Gyges' power after that date, so that the Carian thalassocracy would come to an end somewhere around 670, and be succeded by an interreggnum. When *Kephalion* dated the end of Caria to 671/0, he may have been following *Kastor* closely for the end of the thalassocracy, though he omitted the interregnum.

The historicity of the Carian thalassocracy is a question. If the tradition came to *Kastor* from Rhodian history, it may have been well-based in the context of the Lelantine war: we should expect piracy to flourish at that time. The length of the thalassocracy is however too great, and the commencing date too early, being connected with Gyges' accession dated to 698/7. The fall of the old Lydian dynasty is most reasonably seen as resulting from difficulties consequent upon the Kimmerian devastation of Phrygia; and if this is dated to 676/5, the Lydian changes may have come to a head, and produced Gyges as king, about 670. Arselis of Mylasa should then be seen as ruling already by 676/5, and taking advantage of the disorganization to invade Lydia. The Carian thalassocracy, in the sense of a pirate regime organized from Mylasa, should therefore perhaps be assigned to the decade 680–670.

The historicity of the thalassocratic interregnum, if rightly dated 670/69—646/5, seems assured. In general Greek history, this is the time of the rise of Lydia under Gyges and his westward restriction and northward expansion of the Ionians, ended by the Kimmerian devastation; of the wealth of Bacchiad Corinth before the collapse of the market; of the flourishing of the Hyameian kingdom before its conquest by Sparta.[26] No single power commands the seas at this period: on the contrary, these are the years when the international market is, to the Greeks for the first time, far enough advanced in its own organization for unwary governments, like that of the Bacchiads, to become dependent upon it.

d. Kastor's *LESBOS 645/4–(?)602/1*

Lesbos begins in 645/4, seventeen years before *Kastor*'s date[27] for Byzantium in 628/7. Consequently it seems fair to infer that *Kastor*

---

[26] SCD parts VII and VIII.
[27] Preserved for us by John of Lydia, who names Kastor and his book, the *Epitome* (250 F 2a).

followed Herodotus[28] in placing the foundation of Kalchedon seventeen years before Byzantium. His thalassocracy of Lesbos in its early years was therefore probably closely connected with the Megarian colonies in the Propontis.[29]

The dates of these colonies had undoubtedly been fixed by *Kastor* in the *Epitome*, so that when he came to the *Thalassocrats* he would have to explain the power of Lesbos. But most of our surviving information is about the Megarian colonies.

Byzantium in 628/7 is chronographically connected with the cluster of foundations on the Thracian coasts (Akanthos, Stageira, Kardia, Lampsakos, and the failure at Abdera) 27×1 years earlier in 655/4, and with the Samian foundation at Perinthos 27×1 years later in 601/0. This 27-year series of dates is in turn closely connected with the Eusebian colony dates for Sicily, so that *Kastor* emerges as a major contributor to the Eusebian main source for Sicily—as we have already seen reason to suspect for Naxos in 741/0 and Leontinoi and Maroneia in 732/1. Eusebius however does not use *Kastor* for his Megarian colonies (711/0 Astakos, 685/4 Kalchedon, 659/8 Byzantium: the authorship of Megarian Trotilon is dubious, for 758/7 is both $99 = 27 \times 3\frac{2}{3}$ years before 659/8 and $130 = 39 \times 3\frac{1}{3}$ years before 628/7).

Kastor was very interested in the *character* of the Megarian colonies in the Propontis: he asserted that the Megarians at Byzantium commemorated king Zeuxippos of Sikyon, and that some Megarians at (Milesian) Kyzikos commemorated the last pre-Dorian eponym of Sikyon, Charidemos the priest of Apollo Karneios.[30]

In his Sikyonian king-list,[31] *Kastor* listed reigns totalling 962

---

[28] Hdt. IV 144.

[29] There is no evidence for *Kastor*'s dates for Selymbria ('a few years before Byzantium' [Skymnos] 715), or for Astakos, which was either founded from Kalchedon (Charon of Lampsakos 262 F 6) or in 711/0 (Memnon 434 F 1.12; Eusebius).

[30] Jac 250 F 2a. Also Jerome preserves the note to the accession of Zeuxippos (aA 857): Quidam ad huius memoriam conseruanam balneas Byzantiorum multo post tempore appellatas putant. Other references to these baths are found in the *Chronicon Paschale* 265b (494.15), Malalas V 124d (291.17), Hesychius Illustris *Orig. Const.* 37 (=390 F 1.37, with a different Zeuxippos), Cedrenus 252b (442.15). The Megarian colonies worshipped some obscure heroes, and it was a hobby of the learned to identify them: see Promathidas 430 F 1 and 3.

[31] Jac 250 F 2.

years, [32] which end in the Eusebian *Canons* 352 years before the First Olympiad. In the *Chronographia*, Eusebius reports that the priests who followed the kings ended at that date, but this is probably an error, for such a dating throws out the synchronisms (with other Greek events[33]) which Eusebius reports and which were probably from *Kastor*. If therefore we take *Kastor*'s Sikyonian *kings* as ending $351 = 27 \times 13 = 39 \times 9$ years before the Eratosthenic era-year 777/6, the latter part of his eponymous list for Sikyon is:

1210/09 Polypheides reigned 31 years
and was contemporary with the fall of Troy 1184/3
1179/8 Pelasgos reigned 20 years
1159/8 Zeuxippos (Βασιλεὺς Ἑλλήνων,[34] presumably to distinguish him from Pelasgos his predecessor): reigned 31 years. According to Pausanias,[35] Zeuxippos was the son of Apollo and the nymph Syllis. The year 1159/8 is $531 = 36 \times 14\frac{3}{4} = 27 \times 19\frac{2}{3}$ years before Byzantium in 628/7.
1128/7 beginning of the priests of Karneian Apollo: Archelaos, 1 year
1127/6 Automedon, 1 year
1126/5 Theoklytos, 4 years
1122/1 Euneos, 6 years
1116/5 Theonomos, 9 years
1107/6 Amphigyes, 12 years
1095/4 Charidemos, who fled. His accession is $338 = 39 \times 8\frac{2}{3}$ years before the Eusebian date for Kyzikos I in 757/6, which is $78 = 39 \times 2$ years earlier than the Eusebian date for Kyzikos II in 679/8: these therefore may be *Kastor*'s dates.

We should probably connect Charidemos' flight from Sikyon with the general flight of the Ionians of the Aigialos to Attika, which Jerome enters as *Iones profugi Athenas se contulerunt* at 1085/4, 48 years before his Ionian Migration in 1037/6. But *Kastor* will have

---

[32] So the best witness (Jerome, probante Jac), and confirmed by the chronography: $962 = 39 \times 24$.
[33] The biblical synchronisms will of course not be *Kastor*'s; nor in fact are the Assyrian, for he gave no years to the god Belos: 250 F 1.
[34] 250 F 2a.
[35] II 6.7.

used the orthodox date of 1044/3 for the Ionian Migration, so that the Ionian flight from the Aigialos, and probably that of Charidemos from Sikyon, will for him have been 48 years earlier in 1092/1. This agrees with the relevant portion of his Athenian king-list:[36]

1183/2   Demophon reigned 33 years
1150/49 Oxyntes   12
1138/7   Apheidas   1
1137/6   Thymoites   8
1129/8   Melanthos   37
1092/1   Kodros   21
⟨1092/1 Ionians arrive in Attika⟩
1072/1   death of Kodros and foundation of Dorian Megara,
         $444 = 36 \times 12\frac{1}{3}$ years before Byzantium founded in 628/7.

The attribution of a sort of Heroic ancestry to the Megarians of the Propontis illuminates one part of *Kastor*'s historiography. Kalchedon in ⟨645/4⟩ and Byzantium in 628/7 are probably both seen as events in, or associated with, the tyranny of Theagenes, which[37] was in existence at the anciently uncriticisable date of 636/5. With their Heroic background, the colonists must have been taken as Megarian notables, opponents of Theagenes; and the Heroic connections with Athens glance at Theagenes' son-in-law Kylon of Athens, and his enemies among the Athenian nobility. There are two implications: first that the thalassocracy of 'free Mitylene' was exercised in connection with the 'free Megarian' opponents of tyranny, at least in its early years; and second, that *Kastor* probably thought of the *foundations* of Sigeion and Elaeus as made by an Athens friendly to Lesbos and her Megarian allies.

It is likely also that *Kastor* thought of Lesbos as friendly to Miletos, even if the Eusebian dates of 631/0 for Sinope and 627/6 for Kios come from another source. Since however he dated the Milesian war with Lydia to the years 616/5–605/4, it is probable that he thought of this friendship as more beneficial to Miletos than to Lesbos during these years, even if he did not date the rapprochement of Thrasyboulos of Miletos with Periandros of Corinth before the outbreak of the war.

Eusebius' source placed the outbreak of hostilities between Lesbos

---

[36] 250 F 4.
[37] On the interpretation of 'Epainetos the basileus' in the Athenian archon-list as replacing Megakles the Accursed for 636/5.

and Sigeion before 607/6, where he dates the duel between Pittakos and Phrynon: *Kastor* may have agreed. Most historians must have agreed that Periandros' arbitration was before 597/6 when Pittakos became aisymnetes, for if the arbitration had occurred under his government, we should probably have heard of it—it would, for example, have provided a splendid occasion for the symposium of the Seven Sages, among whom both Pittakos and Periandros were numbered.

The Samian colonists of Perinthos (dated by Eusebius to 601/0) were despatched by their governing Geomoroi to the Propontis, where they were heavily attacked by the Megarians of Kalchedon and Byzantium. Both the Samians and the Megarians received reinforcements from their metropoleis, and in the ensuing battles the Samians were victorious; the metropolitan fleet returned home with 600 captives. But the fleet was mutinous, and engaged to free the captives if they would massacre the Geomoric Council: which was done.[38]

The outstanding point in this story for our purposes is the total absence of Lesbos: her fleet was either neutral or ineffective throughout the incident. Megara, so prompt in defence of her noble colonists, was presumably no longer under Theagenes; and when the Samians offered citizenship to their captives, they may have been acting in the knowledge that many of them did not wish to return home—the Megarian fleet may in fact have been as mutinous as the Samian.[39] Whether the Lesbian fleet was immobilized for the same reason is not stated, but some historians at least dated a stasis in Lesbos about this time.[40]

It seems likely therefore that *Kastor*'s thalassocracy of Lesbos began with an alliance with the nobles of Megara fleeing from Theagenes, and ended with a revolution in Mitylene and failure to support the Megarians at the time of Perinthos. The function of the thalassocracy, in *Kastor*'s view, would certainly be that of commanding the approaches to the Propontis, and, in the early years of the thalassocracy assisting the Megarians, Athenians, and Milesians in founding their colonies. By the last ten years of the thalassocracy however there was war with the Athenians of Sigeion.

---

[38] Plt. QG 57.

[39] It may be suggested that the Megarian colony at Astypalaia, near Samian Amorgos, was descended from these captives who preferred not to go home.

[40] e.g. the Parian Marble has Sappho in Sicily in exile around 600.

The problem of *Kastor*'s historiography in this thalassocracy is plainly the view he took of the relations between thalassocratic Lesbos and the Corinth of Periandros. In considering this, it is fair to start (at least) with the assumption that *Kastor* used the orthodox dates for both: Periandros tyrant of Corinth 627/6–588/7, and Pittakos aisymnetes of Mitylene 597/6–588/7. These dates, together with the Eusebian 607/6 for the duel of Pittakos and Phrynon (which probably belongs to the same orthodox system) place the arbitration of Sigeion by Periandros in the years 606/5–598/7. When the Greeks chose arbitrators, they naturally agreed upon a person, or a group of people, who was equally distant from, or equally friendly to, both sides: and Periandros' judgement in this case, restoring the status quo ante bellum, suggest that this normal rule applied. There is certainly no reason to doubt that official Athens and Corinth were on good terms at this time; and the status quo in the Troad seems to have been a resumption of Lesbian policy earlier pursued during their thalassocracy.[41]

Our ignorance makes it difficult to see the sequence of governments in Mitylene at this time, in relation to Sigeion and Perinthos. The series begins with the Penthilidai still in power: and it is to them that we should ascribe the friendship with the Megarian and Athenian enemies of Theagenes and Kylon. Their rule was ended by the revolution of Megakles, succeeded in turn by the tyranny of Melanchros, under whom Pittakos joined the noble rebels. These nobles in due course succeeded in setting up a factious oligarchy: this was presumably the time when Pittakos duelled with Phrynon—at least, the duel cannot presumably be ascribed to the time when Pittakos was in rebellion to his government. The oligarchy passed into the tyranny of Myrsilos, also supported by Pittakos; Myrsilos in turn was killed and the oligarchy restored until Pittakos emerged from the factions as aisymnetes: on the orthodox dating from the duel to the aisymnetia is no more than ten years. The arbitration of Sigeion therefore probably occurred either under Myrsilos, or in the time of

[41] We gain exactly the same impression from the arguments attributed to the two sides at the trial: the Lesbians claimed the Troad in virtue of the victory over Troy of Agamemnon, ancestor of their Penthilidai: this singular ineptitude (for, as the Athenians immediately and forseeably riposted, their ancestors had been at Troy too) suggests that the argument was a matter of form only, permitting the arbitrator to recommend a return to recent Penthilid policy.

the succeeding oligarchy. We must also suppose that the Samian foundation of Perinthos coincided with one of the rebellions.

e. Diodorus' LESBOS 645/4–578/7

The earlier part of Diodorus' Lesbos covers the same years, with probably much the same historiography, as that which we have so far attributed to *Kastor*; the later part extends from 601/0 (perhaps also for Diodorus the year of Perinthos) over the rest of Pittakos' lifetime, the ten years of his aisymnetia 597/6–588/7, and the ten years of his retirement 587/6–578/7: it is not until Lesbos sinks into obscurity at his death that Phokaia achieves thalassocracy.

We have ascribed 44 years to *Kastor*'s Lesbos on the strength of Pliny's reference to 'free Mitylene', and suggested that an explanation of the discrepancy between this figure and Diodorus' 68 years could be a deliberate alteration of his original by Diodorus. We have now however evidence of two kinds: that Diodorus used (and transmitted to Eusebius) some of *Kastor*'s colony dates—that is, was open to *Kastor*'s influence in his historiography;[42] and that some of *Kastor*'s thalassocratic periods include interregna. The probability that Diodorus altered *Kastor* is thus sharply diminished at the same time as another explanation of Pliny's 44 years becomes possible: that *Kastor*'s Lesbian period comprised 44 years of thalassocracy and 24 years of interregnum down to the death of Pittakos, during which no single power, in *Kastor*'s view, possessed the concentration of force and purpose adequate to the predication of thalassocracy.

This general view – that Mitylene for a time controlled access to the Propontis, but that her power declined from the time of Perinthos onwards, though not sufficiently in the lifetime of Pittakos for another power to be granted 'thalassocracy' by the judicious historian—may well be sound; but the dates are open to grave suspicion, especially in that they assume the orthodox dating of Periandros to 627/6–588/7, while his most probable historical dates are 596/5–568/7.[43]

---

[42] The chief example of agreement between Diodorus and Eusebius is of course Selinous in 650/49; and the main source for Eusebius' Sicilian colony dates certainly seems to have much in common with *Kastor*. It is a question, of course, whether this is due to a common source (Apollodoros?) or to Diodoran knowledge of *Kastor*'s own work, or both: the colony dates, and the Register of thalassocracies, together suggests that both causes may have operated.

[43] SCD part VII.

The relevant archaeological evidence is that the earliest pottery from Byzantium suggests a date for the foundation perhaps about 620 or 615;[44] Borysthenes[45] and Istros[46] from Miletos are also still within the seventh century. The early sixth century sees the foundation of Apollonia[47] and Sinope[48] from Miletos, Amisos[49] from Phokaia, and Elaeus[50] from Athens. *Kastor's* date for Byzantium is therefore almost right; the Eusebian dates for Istros in 657/6, Borysthenes in 647/6, and Sinope in 631/0 are considerably too early; Amisos in the 560's according to Skymnos is too late, but Strabo[51] has a mention of 'Milesians first.' The two groups of colonies fall as earlier and later than the Lydian war on Miletos, if this is rightly dateable to the twelve years 607/6–596/5.

If we can argue from these archaeologically-evidenced dates, Kalchedon seventeen years earlier than Byzantium should be dateable around 635, and Sigeion, if contemporary with Elaeus, about 590. Perinthos also lacks archaeological evidence, but as founded $260 = 39 \times 6\frac{2}{3}$ years before the siege in 341/0, the date is certainly too early because the generations are too long. The date 601/0, to have been acceptable generally, must however have been admissible at least to Samian local historians, and for this purpose may have been taken as $54 = 36 \times 1\frac{1}{2}$ years before 547/6. If we recalculate the $6\frac{2}{3}$ generations as cousinly (of the length of 35 ± 1 years), and the $1\frac{1}{2}$ as ithagenic, we obtain the dates 574 and 587, or the period 581 ± 6, as an indication of a probably truer date. So from (say) Kalchedon around 635 to Perinthos around 580 gives Lesbos a thalassocracy of some 55 years, with a fleet and a policy (or succession of policies) about settlements in the Propontis.

The main contribution of the literary evidence is however naturally on the dating of prominent persons. The orthodox dates for Pittakos' aisymnetia in 597/6–588/7 synchronize his rule with the last ten years of Periandros' rule in Corinth. If the synchronism is older than the absolute dates, we can accept it but use the more

[44] Boardman, *op. cit.* pp.249, 254 f., R. M. Cook, JHS 85 (1965) p.219.
[45] Boardman, pp. 260 f.
[46] Boardman, p.258.
[47] Boardman, p.255.
[48] Boardman, p.266.
[49] Boardman, p.266.
[50] Boardman, p.276.
[51] Str. XIII 547.

probably historical dates for Periandros, and Pittakos' aisymnetia then belongs to the year 577/6–568/7: his duel is supposedly ten years earlier, his death ten years later. The duel with Phrynon, thus dated to the neighbourhood of 587, agrees sufficiently with the archaeological evidence from Elaeus and its implication for Sigeion after 600.

A dating of Pittakos' death to something like 558 however raises once more the question of his contemporaneity with Croesus, who is said to have offered him subsidies and, being rejected, to have offered similar subventions to the oligarchs in exile. The historians who dated the aisymnetia to 597/6–588/7 must have mistrusted Alkaios' evidence on this point:[52] and indeed, Alkaios' view of Pittakos is so opposed to that of the prose tradition that it is highly reasonable to infer that the historians in general regarded all Alkaios' statements about his enemy as unworthy of credence, and were prepared to fix Pittakos' dates on their conclusions for Periandros without reserve. Nevertheless, so long as Alkaios' poems survived so also must there have been a residue of doubt; and there were those who spoke of Croesus' principality of Adrammytion in his father's lifetime.[53]

The training of heirs to the throne was naturally a preoccupation in the stabler periods of the ancient empires, and there is no *a priori* reason to doubt that at some stage Alyattes placed Croesus in charge of a province; nor is there any reason to doubt that it was centred on Adrammytion opposite Lesbos. There is also some evidence to be extracted from the Lydian traditions on the likely date of Croesus' appointment.

Herodotus says that Croesus was 35 years of age in 561/0; and when the events of his reign are examined we find that Croesus' elder son was married and died immediately before the 'first year of mourning' which Herodotus dates to 553/2.[54] Croesus' elder son was then married in 554/3 when Croesus himself was 42 years of age: the implication is that Lydian princes came of age and were married when they were 20 or 21 years old. Croesus' son was forbidden to go to war in his marriage year; similarly (but with a different *aition*) Alyattes did not go to war against Miletos in the sixth year of his reign, which appears to have been 596 and this (on Herodotus' figures) was the year of Croesus' birth. The implication may therefore

---

[52] It was probably not easy to interpret clearly.
[53] Nikolaos of Damascus 90 F 65.
[54] *Klio* 41 (1963) pp. 74 ff.

be that Alyattes came of age and married in 596; a later romance[55] on The Influence of a Good Woman speaks of Alyattes' mother, and may suggest that his reign began with his minority and the regency of the queen-mother.[56] There is thus some reason to think that a Lydian prince came of age when he was 20 or 21 years old,[57] and therefore that Croesus may have been appointed to Adrammytion about 575.

On the dating of Pittakos' aisymnetia to 577/6–568/7, his rule overlaps with that of Croesus in Adrammytion dated as beginning about 575/4. In this context what is remarkable is not that Croesus tried to add Lesbos to his domains, but that when Pittakos retired in 568/1 the succeeding republic was unmolested by Croesus or the exiles. This implies that Pittakos had come to a general policy understanding with both: and it is at this point (rather than in the accession narrative of 561/0 where Herodotus puts it) that the anecdote about Lydian policy towards the islanders, and 'Bias or Pittakos' finds its place. The name of Bias (who was not an islander) is probably due to the misdating of the negotiations to 561/0; Pittakos' name, the *difficilior lectio*, was almost certainly that of the original story.

We may summarize these re-datings as follows:

about 635:	Megarian nobles found Kalchedon: beginning of LESBOS
about 630–20:	Theagenes, and Kylon of Athens.
about 620:	Megarian nobles found Byzantium.
about 615:	Milesian colonies at Borysthenes and Istros.
607–596:	Lydian war on Miletos.
596:	Alyattes attains his majority in Lydia. Periandros accedes in Corinth. Thrasyboulos in Miletos.
around 590:	Milesian colonies at Apollonia in Thrace, and Amisos and Sinope in the Lydian empire; Athenian colonies at Elaeus and Sigeion.

---

[55] Xenophilos 767 F1.

[56] The admission of minorities among the Mermnads may also be a reason for Herodotus' ascription to them of the 39-year generation.

[57] The custom of a year's absence from war for Lydian princes, if reasonably ancient, may also have a mythic reflex in the story of Herakles and Omphale.

Revolution in Lesbos; war with Sigeion (probably the policy of the Archaianaktidai, for an Archaianax was the founder of Achilleion: Str. XIII 599).

Tyranny of Myrsilos in Lesbos: arbitration of Periandros?

around 585: Revolution in Lesbos: Samians at Perinthos (and Megarians at Astypalaia?).

577–568: Pittakos aisymnetes.

about 575: Croesus appointed to Adrammytion: negotiations with Lesbos.

573/2: (Solon's archonship in Athens).

572/1–569/8: Periandros in Corcyra, Psammetichos in Corinth; various western wars.

568/7: Pittakos retires, unmolested.
Fall of the Kypselids of Corinth and Corcyra.

f. Kastor's PHOKAIA 577/6–534/3

If *Kastor* placed a thalassocratic interregnum in the years 601/0–578/7, but followed Pittakos' death immediately by the Phokaian thalassocracy, then (it would seem) he regarded Phokaia in Pittakos' time as possessing the enterprise and concentration which Lesbos lacked, but as herself lacking a Sage in whose lifetime Lesbos could not be overlooked.

It is presumably to *Kastor* that we should attribute Eusebius' date of 598/7 for the foundation of Massalia by the Phokaians,[58] $108 = 36 \times 3 = 27 \times 4$ years after 706/5 (the Carian thalassocracy, the foundations of Taras and Corcyra, and the outbreak of the Lelantine War), and 108 years before the destruction of Eretria. *Kastor* therefore seems to have envisaged the Lesbian thalassocracy (and interregnum) as covering the period when a north-east province of the Greek world and its international market was established in the Euxine, and the Phokaian thalassocracy as being similarly the period of the establishment of the far western province, the two together delineating the international market as historically known. Such a view would enable him to relate his whole conception of thalassocracy to the Herodotean: Herodotus is taken as speaking of the historically

---

[58] At about the right date: Boardman *op. cit.* p.224.

known situation when he says that Polykrates is the first thalassocrat since the Heroic Age; *Kastor*'s contention is that, however different their contexts may have been, earlier powers and persons were thalassocratic in terms of those contexts.

Alalia in Corsica and Amisos in the Euxine are two colonies attributed to Phokaia in the 560's, Amisos apparently as a reinforcement of an older Milesian settlement, and certainly with the approval of Lydia. In the west, Phokaia is especially famous for her silver trade with Tartessos, and the benevolence of the Tartessian king Arganthonios who 'reigned for 80 years.'[59] *Kastor* may not have imagined the thalassocracy as affected by the πρώτη καταστροφή of 561/0;[60] and Thucydides thinks of Phokaian thalassocracy in the west in the time of Cyrus, that is, after 547/6 and the fall of metropolitan Phokaia to the Persians. It is a question therefore whether *Kastor* thought of an interregnum between the Phokaian thalassocracy (continued in the west, as a leadership of free Ionians—against Carthage and Etruria) and the Samian: the only evidence we possess (if such it can be called) is the Syriac figure of 34 years for the thalassocracy, which might possibly[61] suggest an interregnum of ten years, from 543/2 to 544/3, presumably from the loss of Corsica onwards.[62]

If *Kastor*'s date for the death of Pittakos in 578/7 should in fact have been about 558/7, then the Phokaian thalassocracy (in his definition) was not as long as *Kastor* believed: the more historical dates would seem to be about 558–543, or some fifteen years.

g. Kephalion's *EGYPT 783/2–750/49*

Kephalion's Egypt is sixteen years shorter than *Kastor*'s, and begins nine years earlier, so that it is exactly $27 \times 11 = 297$ years before Xerxes' reconquest in 486/5. He will have been chiefly moved to improve upon *Kastor* by the development of the Greek legend of Bocchoris, which includes the ascription of a 44-year reign at the

---

[59] Hdt. I 163 (Anakreon, the poetic source, says 150 years); Herodotus' years should represent the period from the 630's to the 550's.

[60] *Klio* 41 (1963) 81 ff.

[61] If for instance Diodorus mentioned it.

[62] Perhaps *Kastor* reckoned Herodotus' five years (I 166) as 547/6, 546/5 545/4, 544/3, and the year of the defeat 543/2: then the interregnum begins with the year of the defeat and abandonment of Corsica.

dates,[63] perhaps, of 790/89–747/6. He will have dropped, therefore, the romance of Petoubatis of Tanis, and ascribed Egypt's thalassocracy wholly to Bocchoris' laws and policies.

h. Kephalion's *MILETOS 749/8–722/1*

This dating of Miletos, as noted above under (i)b, seems at its commencement to be due to a calculation of $126 = 36 \times 3\frac{1}{2}$ years earlier than the Lydian war with Miletos taken at its Herodotean date of 623/2, five generations before the expulsion of the Neleids from Miletos in 443/2. Probably *Kephalion* also used a later oriental source than *Kastor* for events in the Levant under this thalassocracy.[64]

i. Kephalion's *CARIA 721/0–671/0*

We have already seen reason above to suspect that the lower date for *Kephalion*'s Caria is also *Kastor*'s date for the termination of the thalassocracy and beginning of the interregnum. *Kephalion*'s historiography may therefore be quite close to *Kastor*'s for this thalassocracy, and the difference in the initial date may in large part be due to the adoption of the Herodotean dates for Lydia: if Gyges acceded in 716/5, and was put on the throne by Arselis of Caria, then Arselis' rise to power must be placed rather earlier. The fixing of the exact year however was probably due to other considerations.

It was not directly, at least, a synchronism with the outbreak of the Lelantine war, for 721/0 is not a chronographic number of years before either the fall of Eretria in 491/0 or that of Chalkis in 506/5. There may however be an indirect connection.

The third[65] Eusebian date for Hesiod is 767/6, where Jerome's entry is *Hesiodus secundum quosdam clarus habetur*. This is $46 = 23 \times 2$ years before 721/0, and so falls on the series of years from Minos'

---

[63] Taking the Revised Manetho summarized above under *Kastor*'s Egypt, and emending Psammetichos I ⟨5⟩4.

[64] Probably Alexander Polyhistor: see below, PHOENICIA.

[65] The second is Porphyrius' date in 809/8: Eusebius names his authority and the year is confirmed Jac 260 F 19, 20 (in his Komm. on these fragments Jac has the wrong year-count: the right method is given in his Komm. to 260 F 4: πρὸ ἐνιαυτῶν ρλβ′ before the First Olympiad and μετὰ σοέ after Troy means 777/6+132=909/8 and 1184/3−275=909/8 for Homer, and 100 years later, 32 years before Ol.1 means 809/8 for Hesiod). Eusebius' first date entered at 1017/6, *his temporibus*, is perhaps not an exact year date.

thalassocracy in 1250/49 to the Carian, $529 = 23 \times 23$ years later. The year 767/6 is also $261 = 27 \times 9\frac{2}{3} = 36 \times 7\frac{1}{4}$ years before 506/5, the year of the fall of Chalkis to Athens and of the beginning of the Eretrian thalassocracy. This linking of thalassocratic and literary history by *Kephalion* appears even more strongly in the Lesbian thalassocracy.

j. Kephalion's *LESBOS 670/69–578/7*

It seems that *Kephalion* not only accepted *Kastor*'s date for the end of the Carian thalassocracy, but also ignored the subsequent interregnum and attributed the beginning of the Lesbian sea-power to 670/69. So far as our knowledge permits us to speak, the reason for this earlier dating of Lesbos appears to have lain in literary history, and *Kephalion*'s general preference for the older historians.

Kastor's date of 645/4 for Lesbos, is, or is very near, the date given by the Marmor Parium[66] for the musical revolution of Terpandros of Lesbos '381 years since', which should mean $644/3 \pm 1$. The same period for Terpandros' career is given in the Eusebian documents:

(1) Jerome at 642/1: Terpander musicus insignis habetur.

(2) Synkellos 402.11 (between Lampsakos 655/4 and Selinous 650/49): Τέρπανδρος μουσικὸς ἐγνωρίζετο.

(3) Synkellos 403.3 (between Tyrtaios 633/2 and Kyrene 632/1) Ἔτι Τέρπανδρος μελοποιός, ὃς τὴν ἑπτάτονον ἁρμονίαν εὑρεῖν λέγεται, ἤκμαζε.

Some light is thrown on these Eusebian dates by Plutarch's statement[67] that Terpandros won four Pythian victories. In the seventh century, these must have been victories at the old octennial Pythia; but we are nowhere informed in which years these octennial celebrations supposedly fell. The possibilities are two: that the old octennial cycle was directly continued by the quadrennial cycle which was agreed to have begun in 582/1; or that an octennial celebration was due when the quadrennial re-organization was 'proclaimed' in 586/5. The Eusebian dates can only mean octennia beginning in 650/49, 642/1 and 634/3, that is, on the 586/5 series.[68]

---

[66] Epoch 34.
[67] *De Mus.* 1132e.
[68] *Klio* 37 (1959) 46 f. The fact that the octennial celebrations were on this series of years helps to explain the errors of the Parian and of Pausanias X 7.3.

The authority to whom these dates were due is revealed by Clement's report[69] that Phainias of Eresos said Terpandros was junior to Lesches of Mitylene, an author of the *Little Iliad*.[70] Eusebius dates Lesches to 658/7, which is an octennium earlier than the first of the three dates for Terpandros. It appears then that Phainias dated Lesches' authorship of the *Little Iliad* to 658/7 and placed Terpandros' first (and unremarkable) Pythian victory in the same year. Terpandros' own great fame was due to his musical revolution dated to $644/3 \pm 1$, after his second Pythian victory in 650/49 and before his two remaining victories in 642/1 and 634/3.

We also have some evidence on how Phainias found his dates for Terpandros. The musician founded a musical family, of whom Aristokleides was the teacher of Phrynis, who was the teacher of Timotheus.[71] Timotheus' *akme* was attributed to 398/7;[72] the beginning of Terpandros' great fame with his second Pythian victory in 650/49 is $252 = 36 \times 7$ years before Timotheus.

But there was also another dating of Terpandros' career:

(1) Hellanikos 4 F 85; Terpandros was the first victor at the Spartan Karneia, and he was contemporary with Midas.

(2) Sosibios of Lakonia 595 F 3: the Karneia was founded in Ol.26.

(3) Eusebius *Chronographia* p.92 Karst: the Karneia founded Ol.26.

(4) Bekker *Anecdota* I 234: the Gymnopaidia part of the Karneia.

(5) Jerome 668/7 (= Ol.28.1, first ordinary entry on a page which begins at 673/2 = Ol.26.4): foundation of the Gymnopaidia.

(6) Glaukos ap. Plut. *de Mus.* 1132 e: Terpandros senior to Archilochos.

(7) Hieronymos Περὶ Κιθαρῳδῶν (ap. Athen 14.37): Terpandros contemporary with Lykourgos of Sparta.

Hellanikos set out his date in the *Catalogue of Karneian Victors* and, no doubt, in his *Karneian Victors: metrical version*. The first of these works was presumably the hand-book for reading and reference, the second for memorising as part of Spartan education. Sosibios will

---

[69] *Str.* I 131 p.397.
[70] So named by Proclus. But Hellanikos (schol Eur. *Troad* 821 = 4 F —) named Kinaithon of Lakonia as the author, apparently not knowing Lesches. This throws very grave doubt on Lesches' existence.
[71] Schol. Aristoph. *Clouds* 967.
[72] Diod. Sic. 64.4.

then be translating Hellanikos' date into Olympic terms, and giving it a new currency as the 'genuine local tradition' of Sparta. The contemporaneity of Terpandros and Midas is presumably an inference from a poem, but would for later scholars acquire confirmation with the fixing of Midas' suicide to 676/5 ;[73] the seniority of Terpandros to Archilochos is probably an inference from the synchronisms with Midas and Gyges. Hieronymos' synchronism of Terpandros and Lykourgos may be no more than a reflection of the association of both names with the Spartan educational system: apparently Hieronymos gave no date, for Athenaios goes on to say that Lykourgos was by common consent contemporary with the First Olympiad, and he must have known that the Lykourgan Olympiad was often dated to 884/3 rather than to 776/5.

In Phainias' dating, Terpandros' musical revolution is placed between his second and third Pythian victories; when Sosibios and later authorities (Eusebius' immediate sources) worked on the Hellanikan date they probably followed the same general sequence of events, and Terpandros' visit to Sparta was notoriously after his revolution. Taking these indications together, Hellanikos probably had Terpandros' first Pythian victory in ⟨682/1⟩ before the death of Midas; his second Pythian victory in ⟨674/3⟩; his musical revolution; his visit to Sparta in ⟨673/2⟩[74] (01.26.4); his third and fourth Pythian victories in ⟨666/5⟩ and ⟨658/7⟩, the last being the year that Phainias gave to the first victory. It may be some confirmation of these dates that Jerome places the next Lesbian musician, Arion, in 619/8, which is $54 = 27 \times 2 = 36 \times 1\frac{1}{2}$ years after 673/2.

It seems probable therefore that *Kastor* noted the synchronism at about 645/4 between the music and the thalassocracy of Lesbos; and that *Kephalion* (with his general preference for Herodotean—and therefore Hellanikan—dates) kept the synchronism, and consequently placed the thalassocracy where *Kastor* had an interregnum.

Moreover, if the Eusebian dates for Megarian colonies at 711/0 (Astakos), 685/4 (Kalchedon), and 659/8 (Byzantium) are *Kephalion*'s, that historian abandoned *Kastor*'s close association of Lesbos and Megara. It may be however that he emphasized the association of Lesbos and Miletos, for the Eusebian dates for the Milesian colonies

---

[73] If indeed this date for Midas is not an inference from the dating of Terpandros.
[74] The earliest date possible according to Jerome's pagination, but still in O1.26.

111

are: 657/6 (Istros), 13 = $39 \times \frac{1}{3}$ years after 670/69; 647/6 (Borysthenes), 23×1 years after 670/69; and 631/0 (Sinope), 39×1 years after 670/69.

So far as can be seen, *Kephalion* kept in being the Lesbian thalassocracy throughout the lifetime of Pittakos, bringing it to an end where *Kastor* ended the interregnum before Phokaia, in 578/7.

k. Kephalion's *PHOKAIA 577/6–534/3*

Since, apparently, *Kephalion* has the same dates for Phokaia as *Kastor*, he probably agreed with *Kastor* on the historiography. Since this thalassocracy extends into historical times, this is not surprising.

iii. PHOENICIA

We come now to the thalassocracy which is perhaps the most important single entry for our understanding of the problems of historiography which faced *Kastor* and his successors.

Kastor's dates for this thalassocracy are (if our textual discussion was correct in its conclusions) 819/8 to 775/4, and the archival material relevant to this is represented for us by a fragment from Menandros of Ephesos,[1] which contains a—no doubt brief—summary of the information in the *Acts of the Kings* of Tyre on the dynasty of Ithobaal. This may best be set out, with some contextual material from other sources, as follows:

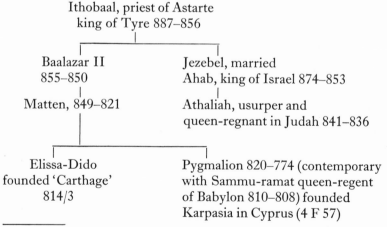

Ithobaal, priest of Astarte
king of Tyre 887–856

Baalazar II
855–850

Matten, 849–821

Jezebel, married
Ahab, king of Israel 874–853

Athaliah, usurper and
queen-regnant in Judah 841–836

Elissa-Dido
founded 'Carthage'
814/3

Pygmalion 820–774 (contemporary
with Sammu-ramat queen-regent
of Babylon 810–808) founded
Karpasia in Cyprus (4 F 57)

[1] Jac 753 F 1. Menandros' translation of the Tyrian archive is parallel to the work of Manetho for Egypt and Berossos for Mesopotamia, but perhaps rather later; apparently he worked at Pergamon.

Pygmalion of Tyre had been known to Greek historiography from Hellanikos' time, and to Greek legend (like his contemporary 'Semiramis') undoubtedly from his own time, which was that of the foundation of Al Mina. In seeking a definitive dating of the rather general and vague Greek notion of Phoenician sea-power therefore, *Kastor* would naturally centre his search on the historical Pygmalion, the conqueror of Cyprus.[2]

The archaeological evidence from Carthage, where the earliest dateable pottery (in the second level) is perhaps a century later than Menandros' foundation-date, gives rise to the suspicion that the Greeks may have mistranslated or misunderstood the name of the colony ascribed to the seventh year of Pygmalion, but since the identity of the city does not affect the dates we may leave the question on one side.[3]

Kastor dates the Phoenician thalassocracy to the middle forty-five years of Pygmalion's 47-year reign. Undoubtedly he conceived of it as ended by Petoubatis of Egypt according to Manetho's account of that hero; and he saw it as in turn ending a thalassocracy of Cyprus: we can assume that the Tyrian archive spoke of Pygmalion's 'conquest of Cyprus' in terms of ending piracy or the like. It does not however follow that the archive dated the conquest to the year 819/8: this is sufficiently explained by *Kastor's* chronographic periodization, in which Phoenicia is the first of the archival thalassocracies. We should probably suppose that *Kastor* began his search for the dating of Phoenician sea-power by looking up the reign of Pygmalion in the archive; that there he found, in Pygmalion's time but (adequately to his concept of thalassocracy) in no other, the necessary concentration of force and purpose to qualify that king as thalassocrat. No doubt this determination did not force *Kastor* to disbelieve in Phoenician activities at other times;[4] but he would regard these as perhaps less a matter of successful policy.

Kephalion re-dated the Phoenician thalassocracy to the years from 837/6 to 784/3, making it both longer and earlier, but losing contact (so far as we can see) with the Phoenician archive. This leads to the suspicion that, although *Kastor* derived his dating directly from the

---

[2] Jac 752 F 1.

[3] The date 814/3 is first ascribed to Carthage by Timaios, probably in correction of the date of 1215/4 given by Eudoxos and Philistos.

[4] As a Rhodian, he will have known the stories of Phoenicians in that island and at the colony of Gela (Zenobius 1.54).

archive, in his exposition he stressed some other contextual element, and that *Kephalion* took this element as the determinant. When we ask what other events the later Greeks ascribed to the year 819/8 or thereabouts, we find in Eusebius that this is the year in which the Median and Chaldaian kingdoms come into existence on the ruins of the Assyrian empire.

a. the synchronism with free Media

For *Kastor*, writing a *Register of Babylon and Thalassocrats* the time when Babylon became Chaldaian and free of Assyria was surely of great concern; and a *Register of Babylon* must mean that he had, or believed himself to have, a list of Babylonian eponyms. No trace of this appears however in our secondary sources, so that we do not know whether *Kastor* copied from Berossos, or had additional information. In this situation we are driven back to consider the Greek historiography of Media, which supposedly began at the same time. Here therefore the question is whether we can show that it is probable or possible that *Kastor* dated the beginnings of Media to 819/8, and *Kephalion* the same event to 837/6.

As we have seen above,[5] *Kastor*'s Sikyon seems to have ended 351 years before 777/6 and begun 962 years earlier still, in (therefore) 2090/89 B.C. It is generally and reasonably assumed that his Assyria began with Ninos I at the same time as Aigialeus became king in Sikyon; and we are told[6] that *Kastor*'s Assyria lasted 1280 years. *Kastor*'s Media should therefore have begun in 810/09, with Arbakes independent of Assyria. But naturally this independence had to be won, and Ἀρβάκης ... ἐστρατήγει Μήδων τῶν κατ' ἐνιαυτὸν ἐκπομπομένων εἰς τὴν Νίνον:[7] that is, we should expect *Kastor*'s Arbakes to accede some years before 810/09, and there is consequently no objection to the possibility that Eusebius took 819/8 from *Kastor*'s *Epitome*. To see if this is the most probable Eusebian source, and that another source was available to *Kephalion* for a Median beginning in 837/6, we have to examine the Greek tradition of Median historiography.

b. Greek documents on Media

The Greek accounts of Media consist, for us, of foundation docu-

---

[5] *Kastor*'s LESBOS: IIB ii(e).
[6] 250 F 1 and Synkellos 318.
[7] Synkellos 312.

ments and their derivatives; from the point of view of ancient scholarship this means reports of material, and critical revaluations.

1. Herodotus

The first of our documents is the list of Median kings and years given by Herodotus, which may be summarized:[8]

(701/0)   Deiokes: ⟨22⟩ years of judgeship
(679/8)   ⟨31⟩ years of kingship
(648/7)   Phraortes: 22 years
(626/5)   Kyaxares: 40 years
                  including 28 years of Skyth empire, before 591/0[9]
(586/5)   Astyages: 35 years ending with 552/1[10]
                  A total of 128 years of kingship, ignoring the Skythic character of 28 of them.

In absolute dates Herodotus misrepresents his source:[11] Media fell in 550/49, so the supposed royal years of Deiokes should be dated as beginning in 677/6. It is more interesting that, in discussing the total,[12] Herodotus speaks as though documents were dated by the royal years throughout the period in Media proper, and in the provinces of the empire as well except during the 'Skyth years'. Such a tone in the report suggests an oriental source, so that Herodotus' account at this point may be nearly a translation of the report he obtained, and that report may have believed itself archivally based.

It is unlikely that such a belief was wholly justified, for the historical original of Deiokes seems to have been Daiakku, an official of the Mannai (not the Medes), who conspired with Urartu against Assyria and was transported to Hamath in 715. However, royal Median years beginning in 677/6 begin in Esarhaddon's reign in Asyria, and that king (reversing previous Assyrian policy) established Median

---

[8] *Klio* 41 (1963) pp. 72 ff.
[9] Hdt. I 73 f. (the Skyth years were surely over by the time of the war with Lydia, occasioned by some Skyth refugees from Media).
[10] *Klio* 41 (1963) pp.72 ff.
[11] By a technical error involving the 'accession year' of Nabonidus: *Klio* 41 (1963) p.74.
[12] Hdt. I 130.

puppet princes. It is possible therefore that he repatriated, among others, the family of Daiakku and that, during the absorption of the Mannai into the Medes, one or two generations in exile were forgotten. In that case, the name and position of Deiokes in the list, as well as the documentary tone of the report, suggest that Herodotus' source was Median and not, for example, an abstract from Assyrian and Babylonian archives like our knowledge of Median history.

It is a question therefore of the origin of the dates in Herodotus' account. Median sources, comparing their traditions with Mesopotamian archives, could arrive at an approximate count of royal years, but hardly at years of judgeship. Herodotus, approaching his Median informants from another point of view, could fairly rapidly recognize some figures as historical and others as calculated or inferred, by reference to other sources of his own. For example, Kyaxares was reigning in Media at the beginning of the war with Lydia but, at the peace concluded after the eclipse battle, the Lydian Aryenis entered the harem of Astyages, who must therefore be supposed to have acceded by that time. It is thus highly probable that Herodotus both believed his own figure for Astyages to be historical, and that he worked it out (himself or with assistance) by comparing his Lydian, Median, and Babylonian material. In such working out he may indeed have 'corrected' any figure given by his Median source.

The earlier Median figures are then the more likely to have been supplemented or 'corrected' by Herodotus himself, with a suitable addition for the years of judgeship. The result is a total of $115 = 23 \times 5$ years from 701/0 to 587/6, which is part of Herodotus' general chronographic scheme for Asiatic history.[13] Whatever the quasi-archival Median bases for these dates therefore, as they emerge in Herodotus' report they have been subjected to a wholly Greek process of chronographic treatment.

2. Ktesias

The second foundation-document is the account of the Median kings reported by Diodorus from Ktesias,[14] who explicitly claimed to use oriental archives for his history. His list is given without absolute dates:

---

[13] *Klio* 46 (1966) pp. 17 ff.
[14] Jac 688 F 5.

Arbakes overthrew Assyria and reigned	28 years
Mandakes	50
Sosarmos	30
Artykas	50
Arbianes	22
Artaios (a generalised ancestor[15])	40
foundation legend of a feud	
between Medes and Kadousioi	
Artynes	22
Astibaras	40
succeeded by Aspandas-Astyiges	

In general it is clear that Ktesias delivers a much more ambitious history than does Herodotus, and that at least some of this material is likely to be due to his informants. That is to say, there was some oriental research into the archives between the time of Herodotus' enquiries and that of Ktesias, and the question is that of the size of Ktesias' own contribution. His desire to correct Herodotus may sufficiently account for the replacement of the names of Deiokes and his successors by other names which are apparently fairly arbitrarily chosen but may rest on a Persian rather than a Median source: the story of the Kadousian feud ends with an undoubtedly Persian statement: ἀεὶ πολεμικῶς ἐσχήκεναι Καδουσίους πρὸς Μήδους καὶ μηδέποτε τοῖς τούτων βασιλεῦσιν ὑπηκόους γεγονέναι, μέχρι οὗ Κῦρος εἰς Πέρσας μετέστησε τὴν ἡγεμονίαν. In this context we may perhaps suppose that the exclusion of the names of Deiokes, Phraortes and Kyaxares from the history of the Medes is a reflection of some controversy and official action in the archives.

However, the figures reported from Ktesias for the kings from Arbianes to Astibaras are identical with the Herodotean, except that the 40 years of Artaios stand instead of the 31 royal years of Deiokes. It is therefore obviously probable that, either in Ktesias' text or that of Diodorus, the figure of ΛΑ has at some stage been misread as Μ.

In that case, Ktesias agreed with Herodotus on the chronographic rendering of these reigns—which is to say that he preferred Greek historiographic method above any values in his sources. His total of Median years before Astyages is, with this emendation, $273 = 39 \times 7$, and a pattern of chronography which omits Astyages agrees with Herodotus that Astyages' years are historical.

---

[15] Jac 4 F 60.

117

This probably means that Ktesias agreed with Herodotus on the absolute dates of the last kings of the Medes; if so, his Arbakes began in 859/8, and Assyria, 1306 years earlier, in 2165/4. Ktesias also made Astyiges survive the loss of his kingdom, and the fall of Sardis in 547/6: so his total of pre-Persian years in Asia was at least the 1619 years beginning in 2165/4 and ending in 547/6. Probably indeed the actual total, for Ktesias, was the chronographic figure of 1620 = 36×45 years; and this seems to be confirmed by Synkellos' report (from Ktesias' Book II) of a total of 45 generations.[16] The last year of Astyiges-Aspendas was then 546/5, the year after the fall of Sardis; and Ktesias has a double chronography, of 36×45 years beginning in 2165/4 and ending in 546/5 for Asia as a whole; and of 39×7 years beginning in 859/8 and ending in 587/6 for Media:

$$
\begin{array}{llll}
859/8 & \text{Arbakes} & 28 \\
831/0 & \text{Mandakes} & 50
\end{array}\left.\right\} \text{years} \qquad 78 = 39 \times 2 \qquad\qquad\quad \left.\begin{array}{l} +2 \\ -2 \end{array}\right\} \quad 0
$$

$$
\begin{array}{llll}
781/0 & \text{Sosarmos} & 30 \\
751/0 & \text{Artykas} & 50 \\
701/0 & \text{Arbianes} & 22
\end{array}\left.\right\} \quad 102 = 39 \times 2 \quad -2 \quad \left.\begin{array}{l} +4 \\ -2 \\ -4 \end{array}\right\} -2
$$

$$
\begin{array}{llll}
679/8 & \text{Artaios} & 31 \\
648/7 & \text{Artynes} & 22 \\
626/5 & \text{Astibaras} & 40
\end{array}\left.\right\} \quad 93 = 39 \times 2 \quad +2 \quad \left.\begin{array}{l} +5 \\ -4 \\ +1 \end{array}\right\} +2
$$

$$
\left.\right\} 0
$$

586/5 Astyiges   41 historical years of kingship and deposition.

The residue pattern of the main periods of Asia as a whole is:

$$
\begin{array}{lll}
1306/5 & \text{chronographic years of Assyria:} & (36 \times 36)+10 \\
273 & \text{chronographic years of Media:} & (36 \times 7)-15 \\
41 & \text{historical years of Media} & (36 \times 1)+ 5
\end{array}\left.\right\} 0
$$

The chronographic constructions are therefore simple in style, and contain several figures which might be regarded, either by ancients or moderns, as implausible.

The Ktesian tradition, speaking loosely, is influential on later writers on Media, in particular in the Christian documents. Two versions are however discernible, differentiated principally by the names and the sequences of the names of the kings: the last four are commonly given their Herodotean names, and Arbianes is omitted: but in one version the Ktesian order is followed for the first four, while in the other the sequence is Arbakes, Sosarmos, Mandakes,

---

[16]Synkellos 313 quoting Diodorus. He takes this for a total for Assyria alone, but this must be wrong.

Artykas. This variation is a matter of documentary fact: either Diodorus misquoted Ktesias and a later influential authority quotes him rightly; or Ktesias misquoted the Persian archive, and a later researcher—such as a Pergamene historian like Menandros of Ephesos—re-examined the archive; or one of the traditions goes back to an ancient and influential error. It is of course impossible to decide on the plausibility of these alternatives without external documentary evidence.

Ktesias' basic claim is that the first of his Medes, Arbakes, was in very close touch with Assyria: and this is probably a more important assertion than the statement that Arbakes was a Mede, for the example of Deiokes-Daiakku shows that the Medes were capable of claiming, or receiving, alien ancestors. The principal enemies of Assyria during the period of Ktesias' early Medes were the kings of Urartu, and there are some correspondences which suggest that they are the originals of Ktesias' early Medes:

Urartu	'Media'
Arame: Assyrian war *c*.859	Arbakes: Ktesian date 859/8
Sarduris I: Assyrian war *c*.831	Sosarmos second name in variant list; 831/0 Ktesian date for second king;
Ispuinis: Assyrian war *c*.821–19	819/8 Eusebian date for Arbakes
Menuas	
Argistis I Assyrian war *c*.781–774 son of Menuas (genitive Menuahi)	Mandakes third name in variant list. 781/0 Ktesian date for third king.
Sarduris II: Assyrian war ends with great defeat at Musasir 743; son of Argistis	(the last Midas accedes 742/1, Eusebius) Artykas: Ktesian date 751/0–702/1
Rusas I, formerly prince of Arbu,[17] ally of Daiakku, kills himself 714	Arbianes 701/0 (= Deiokes)

These correspondences seem to make it inescapable that Ktesias' claim

---

[17] Sayce CAH III 177. For the replacement of the proper name by an epithet, we may perhaps compare Arkeanos, 'the second', for Sargon II in the Ptolemaic Canon.

119

to have used archives was in this case true; the archives also seem to have been at least in part of Assyrian origin, since it is the Assyrian dates which come through to Ktesias before 743, and thereafter the dating is unreliable. The uncertainty about which of a pair of names was the patronymic is found elsewhere in Ktesias.

It seems then that in Ktesias' time there were available versions of a Vannic archive in Susa, and that he used them. It is therefore the more probable that another, later, researcher was also able to consult the archive, which itself may have become more 'Median' and independent of Assyrian records in the meantime.

3. Alexander Polyhistor

The next authority about whose Median history something may be determined was Alexander Polyhistor, who worked in the generation after *Kastor*. He wrote a book 'on the Chaldaeans' and Mesopotamian history, and another περὶ Ἰουδαίων from which[18] we see that he used the Ktesian name Astibaras for Kyaxares. Since he spoke of the Median capture of Babylon,[19] we may suppose that he introduced to historiography from scriptural romance the infinitely troublesome character of Darius the Mede.

Agathias prefaces an account of Alexander's main periods to his own Parthian history, and reports them as follows:[20]

the Assyrians for 1306 years ἢ καὶ ὀλίγῳ πλειόνων.

    (this, like Astibaras, shows Alexander following Ktesias)

the Medes for no less than three centuries

    (the only surviving figure resembling this is to be found in
    Eusebius' *Chronographia* where, after detailing a list totalling
    256 years, Eusebius mentions a total of 298 years, presumably
    from another authority)

the Persians for 228 years;

    (this must mean from 560/59 for Cyrus to 332/1, Alexander king
    in Babylon)

the Macedonians, οὐ λίαν ἐλάττονα χρόνον τῶν Μήδων ὅτι μὴ ἑπτὰ ἔτεσι
δέοντα.

    (this curious expression, if the Medes ruled 298 years, must give

---

[18] Jac 273 F 19(a) 39.
[19] F 79.5.
[20] F 81.

120

the Macedonians 291 years, from Alexander in 332/1 to Pacorus' Parthian occupation of Syria in 41/0 B.C.)

Alexander's history 'of the Chaldaeans' was based on Babylon, where he counted 86 kings from the Flood to the Median conquest, and this Babylonian basis is found in his dating of Alexander. We should expect therefore that (in addition to the universal date of 560/59) he gave the Babylonian date for Cyrus in 539/8. Reckoning from this base-date, 298 years for the Medes begin in 837/6, and the 1306 years of the Assyrians in 2143/2.

Alexander was one of the chief authorities for the Eusebian documents in general, and is therefore a good candidate not only for the 298 years of Medes mentioned in the *Chronographia*, but also as one source of entries in the *Canons*. Eusebius has two entries on the fall of Nineveh to Kyaxares, and two on the war between Astyages and Alyattes of Lydia, and we observe:

  (i) that with the base-date of 539/8, if Alexander's Astyages reigned 38 years as is orthodox in the Eusebian tradition, he acceded in 577/6, which is one of Eusebius' dates for the war with Alyattes: this then corresponds to the year 586/5 (the eclipse battle) in Herodotus and Ktesias;

 (ii) that if Astyages acceded in 577/6, and Kyaxares reigned 32 years as is orthodox in the Eusebian tradition, then he acceded in 609/8, which is one of Eusebius' dates for his capture of Nineveh

(iii) that 577/6 is $1566 = 27 \times 58$ years after Assyria begins in 2143/2 (and this period of $(86 \times 18) + 18$ years comfortably admits the 86 kings of Babylon before Astyages-Darius the Mede);

 (iv) that 609/8 is $1534 = 39 \times 39\frac{1}{3}$ years after Assyria begins in 2143/2;

  (v) that the beginning of Media in 837/6 gives the periodization:
$$1306 = 27 \times 48\frac{1}{3} + 1 \text{ years of Assyria, } 2143/2–838/7 \left.\begin{matrix} \\ \\ \end{matrix}\right\} \quad 1566 =$$
$$260 = 27 \times 9\frac{2}{3} - 1 \text{ years of Media, } 837/6–578/7 \qquad 27 \times 58.$$

It is therefore textually and chronographically legitimate to bring these fragments together under the name of Alexander Polyhistor, and to infer that for him:

1. Assyria and Babylon both began in 2143/2;

2. Assyria existed for 1534 years before the capture of Nineveh by Kyaxares, and Babylon for 1566 years before the accession of Astyages-Darius;

121

3. Media became independent in 837/6, 228 = 36 × 6⅓ years before the fall of Nineveh and 260 = 39 × 6⅔ years before Astyages-Darius in Babylon.

The chronography of the empire of upper Asia thus becomes much more complex in Alexander's treatment than in the hands of Herodotus and Ktesias; and he has two additions: the Babylonian and the Jewish archives and romances. He also has a new chronographic device: for Babylon, where the eponyms who 'took the hands of Marduk' annually often did not succeed παῖς παρά πατρός he uses the length of two-thirds of a generation to approximate or convey the effect of approximating the average length of reign. Alexander's work was clearly erudite and ingenious; it probably made *Kastor*'s *Babylon* obsolete; and it is not surprising that *Kephalion* preferred his Median date of 837/6 to *Kastor*'s 819/8.

4. Thallos(?) and Synkellos

The Median documents in the Christian chronicles fall into two main classes: the representatives of the Ktesian tradition proper follow Ktesias' sequence of names for the early kings. Within this class however there are two variants, a list of 256 years given by the Eusebian *Chronographia* and by the *Chronographeion Syntomon*; and a list with 27 more years added to Phraortes, given by Synkellos.[21] These variants are clearly adaptations of a single original, and the 27 years seems to be the difference between Polyhistor's 837/6 for Media and *Kastor*'s 810/09 for free Media: both versions would then agree on 624/3 for the accession of Kyaxares.

In this earlier part of the list there is, plainly, a chronographic construction:

Arbakes	28 years	⎫	residue over nearest 12 years:	+4 ⎫	0
Mandakes	20	⎭ 48 = 36 × 1⅓ ⎫		−4 ⎭	
Sosarmos	30	⎫	108 = 36 × 3 years	±6 ⎫	0
Artykas	30	⎭ 60 = 36 × 1⅔ ⎭		±6 ⎭	
Deiokes	54	⎫		±6 ⎫	
Phraortes	24	⎭		0 ⎭	

But this construction is not continued with (Phraortes 27 more years), Kyaxares 32 years, Astyages 38 years. We conclude that the last two items are taken from Polyhistor and are not proper to the original of our versions. It is also probable that the extra 27 years (which do not

---

21 372.8 ff., 401.4 ff., 438.3 ff.

show a residue appropriate to the style of this list) indicate that the Synkellan version is secondary.

To judge from the style of the surviving original fragments, (and assuming that Astyages' years were, as usual, taken as historical), the author of this list should have given Kyaxares $12x \times \pm 6$ years to complete his chronographic construction—for example, 30 or 42 years. One of Eusebius' entries for the eclipse battle (which traditionally for the Median lists begins Astyages' reign) is placed at 582/1, which is 42 years after Kyaxares' accession at 624/3. The hypothesis is therefore that this entry in the *Canons* came to Eusebius from the same source as the original of his king-list in the *Chronographia:* and that the original list was:

810/09	Arbakes	28 years	⎫	$+4$ ⎫ 0	
782/1	Mandakes	20	⎬ 108 years: residue pattern:	-4 ⎭	
762/1	Sosarmos	30		± 6 ⎫ 0	
732/1	Artykas	30	⎭	± 6 ⎭	
702/1	Deiokes	54	⎫	± 6 ⎫	
648/7	Phraortes	24	⎬ 120 years: residue pattern:	0 ⎬ 0	
624/3	Kyaxares	⟨42⟩	⎭	± 6 ⎭	
582/1	eclipse battle and beginning of Astyages' historical years				

It is probably to this source also that we should trace Eusebius' entry of the fall of Nineveh to Kyaxares in 622/1.

This document was constructed by a pre-Eusebian orientalist who was clearly of some chronographic originality: the use of the ± 6 residues does not seem to be paralleled in earlier work. The orientalist whom Eusebius and others name next to *Kastor* is Thallos, of whose work there are few named fragments. But we are told[22] that he dated the beginning of Assyria 322 years before Troy, which means 1506/5 or 696 = $36 \times 19\frac{1}{3}$ years before Media in 810/09. This meagre evidence is not sufficient to confirm Thallos' authorship of this Median list, but it makes it probable.

It may be more than a curious coincidence that Thallos chose 582/1 as the years of the eclipse battle; there was in fact an eclipse in that year which some moderns have preferred to that of 586/5 for the fixing of the date. We have no direct evidence that Thallos could have known of this eclipse; but we are certain that he synchronized the Crucifixion with an eclipse;[23] and consequently the possibility remains open.

---

[22] Jac 256 F 3.
[23] F 1.

Eusebius rejected the identification of Astyages and Darius the Mede, and did not use Thallos' Median history in the *fila* of his *Canons*; but the *Syntomon*'s list (which accepts the identification) is shown by a graphic error[24] to have come from a (presumably non-Eusebian) *Canons*; and Synkellos uses the derivative version of Thallos' list.

So far as can be made out therefore Thallos drew upon Ktesias for the sequence of the first three names of the Medes; upon *Kastor* for their initial year, 810/09; upon Alexander Polyhistor for the chronographic period of $228 = 36 \times 6\frac{1}{3}$ years[25] and, probably, for the identification of Astyages and Darius the Mede. The list was probably introduced to the Christian chronicles by Africanus, who may be the source who changed Thallos' years for Kyaxares and Astyages to those of Alexander Polyhistor. As thus edited, Eusebius received the list into his *Chronographia*, though he rejected it for his *Canons*, but it recovered its popularity later among the critics of Eusebius in Byzantium, where it was again edited under the influence of Polyhistor and made to begin in 837/6.

5. Kastor(?) and Porphyry
The anti-Ktesian tradition in the Christian chronicles also appears in two versions, one of 269 years in the *Excerpta Barbari*, and one of 259 years in the Eusebian *Canons* and its derivatives.[26] Eusebius ends his list with the Cyrus base-date 560/59, but Michael contributes a note[27] which suggests that a date nearer 547/6 was also in the tradition Working from this suggestion, we infer that the Barbarian's list is the more original, and should begin in 819/8 and have the base-date of 550/49, Cyrus in Media; Eusebius will then have removed ten years to suit his earlier base-date.

---

[24] The third king is listed as Tyrimeas 38, who is an intruder from a neighbouring Macedonian filum.
[25] Though he changed the base-date to the eclipse battle, while Alexander placed the period before the fall of Nineveh in 609/8.
[26] That is, in the Median filum of years in Jerome; in the list in Jerome's Series Regum; in the list in the Armenian Series Regum (though the filum is missing in the Armenian *Canons*); and in Michael's abstracts: Chabot, pp. 77 (Arbakes, numeral missing), 79 (Sosarmos, 30 years), 81 (Mamycos 40 years), 87 (Qorqos, 13 years), 88 (Dioclemas, 54 years 89 (Aphraotinus, 24 years), 90 (⟨Kyaxares⟩, 32 years); 96 (Astyages, 38 years), 101: 'Cyrus commença à regner seul (i.e. without Darius the Mede) et s'empara de la ville de Sardis'.
[27] p.101 just quoted.

This list, with its sequence of names and terminal dates of 819/8 and 551/0, is archivally based and clearly of a good period: it is the candidate for the representation of *Kastor*'s Media. But as it comes to us it carries Polyhistor's 32 and 38 years for Kyaxares and Astyages, which will not have been original; and there is a considerable corruption of the names common to all our sources: ΜΑΝΔΑΥΚΗΣ has become ΜΑΜΥΚΗΣ, ΜΑΜΥΚΟΣ, for the Syriac and Armenian, ΜΑΜΥΘΗΣ for the Barbarian, and ΜΑΔΥΔΟΣ, ΜΕΔΙΔΟΣ for Jerome; while Cardiceas, Cardyceus, Qorqos, should represent an original καὶ ᾽Αρτύκας, but appear in all sources.

We are therefore led to suppose an editor who replaced *Kastor*'s figures for Kyaxares and Astyages by those of Polyhistor and who gave a new spelling to two of the names. This authority should also be the writer whose arguments in support of *Kastor* moved Eusebius to reject Thallos' list from his *Canons*. So far as we can see, *Kastor* (at least in the *Thalsssocracies* if not in the *Epitome* where his Median list would be found) used the Phoenician archive as well as the Median and others; Thallos depends greatly on Alexander Polyhistor who uses the Jewish archive and, so far as we know, excludes the Tyrian. Among Eusebius' authorities, the person most likely to point out that the Christian use of Thallos neglected the Tyrian archive would be the anti-Christian Porphyry, of Tyre. It is probably therefore Porphyry's edition of *Kastor*'s Medes which was Eusebius' immediate source.

Kastor himself will have counted Astyages as historical and ended Median chronography proper with Kyaxares. Since we have the terminal dates of his list, we can immediately see that his construction was probably:

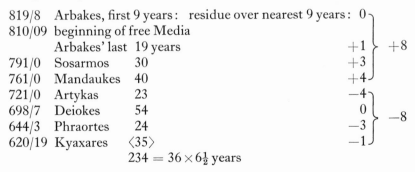

819/8	Arbakes, first 9 years:	residue over nearest 9 years:	0	
810/09	beginning of free Media			
	Arbakes' last 19 years		+1	+8
791/0	Sosarmos	30	+3	
761/0	Mandaukes	40	+4	
721/0	Artykas	23	−4	
698/7	Deiokes	54	0	−8
644/3	Phraortes	24	−3	
620/19	Kyaxares	⟨35⟩	−1	

$$234 = 36 \times 6\tfrac{1}{2} \text{ years}$$

The residue pattern is in *Kastor*'s artificial style, like that of his kings of Lydia:[28] the six generations may explain καὶ ᾿Αρτύκας, as of the same generation as Mandaukes.

This reconstruction makes *Kastor*'s Astyages begin to reign in 585/4, some three months after the eclipse battle, which is soon enough for Herodotus' narrative. Pliny, who gives 585/4 for the eclipse itself,[29] may have been misled by such a departure from the traditional 586/5 for Astyages' accession.

Although *Kastor*, as thus reconstructed, ends his Median regnal chronography with Kyaxares, he has also a period of $260 = 39 \times 6\frac{2}{3}$ years from 810/09 to 551/0: he thus anticipates to some degree the complex Mesopotamian chronography of Alexander Polyhistor.

If we survey the development of the chronography of Media throughout the ancient tradition, as summarized in Table IX, we can

TABLE IX
CHRONOGRAPHY OF MEDIA

Author	Median reigns	Median periods	Assyria	Empire of Asia
Herodotus	$115 = 23 \times 5$ (701/0–587/6)		$520 = 39 \times 13\frac{1}{3}$ (1221/0–702/1)	$675 = 27 \times 25$ (1221/0–547/6)
Ktesias	$273 = 39 \times 7$ (859/8–587/6)		$1306 = (36 \times 36) + 10$ (2165/4–860/59)	$1620 = 36 \times 46$ (2165/4–546/5)
Kastor	$234 = 36 \times 6\frac{1}{2}$ (819/8–586/5)	$260 = 39 \times 6\frac{2}{3}$ (810/09–551/0)	1280^{30} (2090/89)	$1530 = 27 \times 56\frac{2}{3}$ (2090/89–551/0)
Alexander Polyhistor	$260 = 39 \times 6\frac{2}{3}$ (837/6–578/7)	$228 = 36 \times 6\frac{1}{3}$ (837/6–610/09)	$1534 = 39 \times 39\frac{1}{3}$ (2143/2–610/09)	$1566 = 27 \times 58$ (2143/2–578/7)
Thallos	$228 = 36 \times 6\frac{1}{3}$ (810/09–583/2)		$696 = 36 \times 19\frac{1}{3}$ (1506/5–811/0)	
Africanus	combined Thallos and Polyhistor			
Porphyry	edited *Kastor*			
Eusebius	used *Thallos*-Africanus in the *Chronographia*, *Kastor-Porphyry* in *Canons*			
Synkellos	edited *Thallos*-Africanus			

---

[28] See above p.80.

[29] NHII.12.53.

[30] *Kastor*'s chronographic period for Assyria presumably extended to the fall of Nineveh to Kyaxares, his date for which is unknown. If he agreed with Polyhistor, both would presumably be taking 609/8 from Berossos, and *Kastor*'s chronography would include that year to give a total of $1482 = 39 \times 38$ Assyrian years.

126

begin to appreciate some of the difficulties of ancient historiography. Herodotus begins, but only begins, the collection of source material and is much at the mercy of his informants. Ktesias has a remarkably good source, spoiled by over-facile identifications. *Kastor* has a still better version of the same source, but is incredulous about Ktesias' high initial date for 'Media' and his chronographic model belongs to his artificial style. Alexander Polyhistor drifts towards the higher dates at the beginning of his 'Medes', but is fairly ruthless with the tradition of the eclipse battle at the lower end, and accepts romance for history too easily in the 'Median capture of Babylon'. Thallos is severely critical of Assyrian high dates, moderately so of the Median, and may possibly have tried to use astronomical evidence. Africanus, Porphyry and Eusebius in various ways try to re-examine the established stock of information; and so do Eusebius' critics and successors.

c. development of historiography
The history of the synchronism between the beginnings of the Median kingdom and the Pheonician thalassocracy now appears as follows:

1. *Kastor* established the date 819/8 for Media in his *Epitome*.

2. *Kastor* synchronized the Phoenician thalassocracy with Media in his *Thalassocrats*.

3. Diodorus reports Ktesias on Media (859/8) and *Kastor* on Phoenicia.

4. Alexander Polyhistor proposes the date 837/6 for Media.

5. *Kephalion* accepts Alexander's date and *Kastor*'s synchronism.

6. Eusebius reports Thallos-Africanus for Media, *Kastor*-Diodorus for Phoenica, in the *Chronographia*; and accepts *Kastor*-Porphyry for Media, *Kephalion* for Phoenicia, in the *Canons*.

When *Kastor* synchronized the rise of Media-Urartu with the Phoenician thalassocracy and conquest of Cyprus he was certainly doing more than drawing merely arithmetical inferences from his source-material. If we look at the Ithobaal dynasty of Tyre (so far as we know it) and its context, we observe that it held a position somewhere near the storm-centre of its time. The struggle of its daughters with Elisha and Elijah is legendary; it is paralleled to some degree in the struggle within Tyre itself between the priest of Astarte and his

127

sister, wife of the 'priest of Herakles'; and by the difference in the interpretations put upon Pygmalion's cult as on the one hand an abomination, and on the other a source of life-giving love. It seems clear that the west Semitic world into which the power of Urartu and the traders of Al Mina intruded was on the move, and that *Kastor* derived a sense of this from his source-material: he expressed it with the equipment at his disposal, in the synchronism of the freedom of Media and the thalassocracy of Tyre.

We are now in a better position to consider *Kastor*'s division of his later thalassocracies into the archival and historical. It seems clear that, for him, the historical period was that within which both the sequence of events, and their pace—both the relative and the absolute dating—were known. The archival period on the other hand was the period when both these had to be made out by comparison and interpretation of barbarian archives in the first sub-period (Phoenicia, Egypt, Miletos), and Greek poets in the second (Caria, Lesbos, Phokaia): each source, and each kind of source, gave incomplete sequences to be arranged in relation to one another and to be given absolute dates—either accepted from archives, or created by chronography.

iv. the traditional thalassocracies after the migrations

Kastor's major period of the traditional thalassocracies has two sub-periods, the first of which contains the thalassocracies of ⟨Aeneas⟩, the Lydoi-Maiones, the Pelasgoi, and Thrace in Europe. These names are, or are associated with, those of migrants: Aeneas to Italy; the Lydians and the Tyrrhenian migration; the wanderings of the Pelasgoi; the first Thracian thalassocracy which ends with the migration from the Strymon valley to Bebrykia in the Propontis. The second sub-period consists of Thrace in Asia, Rhodes, Phrygia and Cyprus, and these are post-migration communities: the Bebrykes were still in the Propontis when the Phokaians established Lampsakos there, at the chronographic date of 655/4.

a. CYPRUS

Of the Greek items in this sub-period Cyprus was presumably mentioned in the Tyrian archive as giving some offence to Tyre before Pygmalion's conquest, and this offence was no doubt such that it could be interpreted as 'thalassocracy'. At this time, Cyprus should have been welcoming Euboians on their way to Al Mina; and if the

128

Semitic name for Cyprus, Iadnana, has anything to do (as is often suspected) with the Danaans or Dnnym of Kilikia, there may have been offence in this area too. It is likely therefore that *Kastor* derived not only the approximate date, but even the notion of a Cypriote thalassocracy, from the Tyrian archive.

b. RHODES

An indication of date for the Rhodian thalassocracy may also be due to Tyre, for *Kastor* places the thalassocracy at the period when the archaeologists see the arrival of the Dorians,[1] and Dorian piracy based on Rhodes is consequently very probable and if it existed would be mentioned in the Phoenician records.[2] But for *Kastor*, himself of Rhodes, while the date might be archival the content would be native, and was probably similar to that recorded by Strabo:[3] the Rhodians πρὸ τῆς Ὀλυμπικῆς θέσεως συχνοῖς ἔτεσιν ἔπλεον πόρρω τῆς οἰκείας ἐπὶ σωτηρίᾳ τῶν ἀνθρώπων· ἀφ' οὗ καὶ μέχρι Ἰβηρίας ἔπλευσαν, κἀκεῖ μὲν τὴν Ῥόδον ἔκτισαν, ἣν ὕστερον Μασσιλιῶται κατέσχον, ἐν δὲ τοῖς Ὀπικοῖς τὴν Παρθενόπην, ἐν δὲ Δαυνίοις μετὰ Κῴων Ἐλπίας. τινὲς δὲ μετὰ τὴν ἐκ Τροίας ἄφοδον τὰς Γυμνασίας νήσους ὑπ' αὐτῶν κτισθῆναι λέγουσιν . . . τινὲς δὲ τῶν Ῥοδίων καὶ περὶ Σύβαριν ᾤκησαν κατὰ τὴν Χωνίαν. We may compare also :[4] τινες δὲ καὶ Ῥοδίων κτίσμα φασί καὶ Σιρῖτιν καὶ ἐπὶ ⟨Τραεντος⟩ Σύβαριν.

These colonies, in so far as they are archaeologically known, belong to the seventh and sixth centuries, but *Kastor* may have been the readier to accept the Tyrian date (which belonged, if it existed, to quite different events) because by his time the orthodox history of Messenia, by changing the Hyameian into Stenyklarian traditions, will have

---

[1] Boardman, *op. cit.* p.46.
[2] We could compare Sanchuniathon VIII 11, who records piracy to the north of Rhodes in Hiram's time (tenth century).
[3] XIV.2.5. John of Antioch F 30, Mu (οἱ Ῥόδιοι θαλασσακρατήσαντες στήλην ἔστησαν, ἣν διὰ τὸ μέγεθος Κολοσσὸν ἔλεγον, καὶ διὰ τοῦτο ὠνομάσθησαν Κολοσσαεῖς. Ἡ Καρχηδὼν᾽ χωρα ὑπὸ Καρχηδόνος τοῦ Τυρίου ἐκτίσθη) looks like a pair of 'archaeological' abstracts from a history of the time of the colossus and the Punic Wars, irrelevant to *Kastor*'s thalassocracy.
[4] Strabo VI 1.14.
[5] Paus. III 19.9; SCD part VII. Dotadas is the fifth king from Kresphontes, so if Kresphontes becomes king at the Return in 1104/3, he and his three successors occupy at most 39 × 4 years, and Dotadas' schematic date is then 948–910. A slightly later date could be obtained by giving years to the period of anarchy on Kresphontes' death: Dotadas would then be about contemporary with *Kastor*'s Rhodian thalassocracy.

129

carried back (for instance) Dotadas' port at Mothone into the tenth century.[5] *Kastor* probably felt that his native traditions, supported by Messenian history ,were confirmed by the Tyrian archive.

The chronography of the Greek items in both lists is simple. For *Kastor*, Rhodes beginning in 900/899 is 48 $= 36 \times 1\frac{1}{3}$ years before Cyprus, and Cyprus beginning in 852/1 is 156 $= 36 \times 4\frac{1}{3}$ years before Kilikian Tarsos became Assyrian in 696/5; Rhodes is also 81 $= 27 \times 3$ years before Pygmalion's thalassocracy begins in 819/8. The nexus of associations is therefore between Rhodes, Kilikia, Cyprus and Phoenicia, as we might entirely expect. For *Kephalion*, Cyprus in 865/4 is the same number of generations but a different number of years (169 $= 39 \times 4\frac{1}{3}$) before Assyrian Tarsos; the Rhodian date is however simplified to the native reckoning of 225 $= 36 \times 6\frac{1}{4}$ years before Gela in 691/0, in general conformity with *Kephalion's* disuse of the Phoenician archive.

c. THRACE-IN-ASIA and PHRYGIA

The barbarian thalassocracies of this period require more consideration. Thrace in Asia is primarily concerned with the Bebrykes,[6] but no doubt included also 'the Phrygians round Kyzikos, the Thracians round Abydos, the Treres further south'[7] in the Troad and the Edones of Antandros.[8] It is however Mandron king of the Bebrykes who in Charon's story[9] invited the Phokaians to Lampsakos, and the chronography of the thalassocracies followed this tradition: *Kastor's* Thrace in Asia in 979/8 is 324 $= 36 \times 9$ years before Lampsakos in 655/4, while *Kephalion's* in 967/6 is 312 $= 39 \times 8$ years above the same base-date.[10]

---

[6] For the texts see Table II entry 4.

[7] Strabo XIII 1.8.

[8] Aristotle ap Steph Byz s.v. Ἀντανδρος.

[9] Jac 262 F. At the date of 655/4, *Kastor's* Lydian king would be Ardys, and Mandron was presumably his vassal. The story says that Mandron remained loyal to the Greeks even when conspiracy among the Bebrykes led to bloodshed. Perhaps *Kastor* (and his predecessors in Lydian historiography) connected this conspiracy with the Kimmerian devastations, in which the Treres joined: if Mandron in the 640's remained loyal to Ardys, he would merit reward later, and consequently the history of his dynasty and people might be well-known to (for example) Xanthos of Lydia and Charon of Lampsakos.

[10] *Kephalion* uses the nine-generation count for Thrace in Europe in 1006/5, 351 $= 39 \times 9$ years before Lampsakos.

Since the Bebrykes carry the Phrygian name, the question arises of the connection of their migration and thalassocracy with the Phrygian thalassocracy of the ninth century, and the empire of 742/1–676/5. For *Kastor*, the Phrygian thalassocracy and empire are connected by the dating of the thalassocracy $135 = 36 \times 3\frac{3}{4}$ years before 742/1: *Kephalion* expresses the same idea by placing his Phrygian thalassocracy $216 = 36 \times 6$ years before Midas died in 676/5. Also in *Kephalion* a relationship between the arrival of the Bebrykes and the Phrygian thalassocracy is clear: 973/2 is $81 = 36 \times 2\frac{1}{4}$ years before 892/1. *Kastor*'s reasoning seems to be less simple: his Phrygian thalassocracy is not a chronographic number of years after the Bebrykes arrive, but it is $99 = 36 \times 2\frac{3}{4}$ years after Apollodorus' date[11] for the supposed Samian colony on Samothrace in 976/5. *Kastor* probably regarded this colony as the important consequence of the transference of the Thracian thalassocracy from Europe to Asia in 979/8, while *Kephalion* saw it among the causes of the migration in 973/2.

Both chronographers therefore stress the continuity between the Bebrykes and their thalassocracy, the Phrygian thalassocracy, and the Phrygian empire. Since *Kephalion* derives from *Kastor*, and *Kastor* in at least the Samothracian detail draws on Apollodoros, we are brought back once more to Pergamene sources for Asiatic history, and in fact to Menandros, who is quoted on the history of Thrace[12] in an obscure fragment which mentions Aiolic and Ionian Greeks, and probably an embassy. Behind Menandros stands Xanthos of Lydia,[13] with his firm belief that the Phrygians came to Asia after Troy.[14]

It seems therefore that for his Bebrykian and Phrygian thalaso-cracies *Kastor* was drawing on an already well established history,

---

[11] Jac 244 F 178a.

[12] Jac 753 F 8. Menandros is also credited with a history of Phrygia: 753 F 9.

[13] Jac 765 F 14. He thought the Phrygians of the Trojan Catalogue came from a far Askania in Europe; and he will have taken the Phrygian enemies of the Amazons in Priam's youth as Mygdones: they are led by Mygdon and Otreus (Iliad 3.189). Otreus is eponym of Otrous, a town of the 'Phrygian Pentapolis' (W. M. Ramsay, *The Cities and Bishoprics of Phrygia* II 677 ff.) beyond the Sangarios watershed; another was Stekterion, in the mountains near which Mygdon was buried. These immigrants will therefore for Xanthos have had a character of their own, and they do not carry the Phrygian name.

[14] The doctrine is repeated by Strabo XIII 1.8.

which dated the arrival of the Bebrykes in the tenth century, and traced the extension of their name to the Phrygian power which *Kastor* calls thalassocracy in the ninth century, and to the empire of the eight and seventh centuries. Probably if we had more East Greek local history we should see more clearly: there survive only hints and fragments: Pausanias' charming little story of the Thracian women 'bond and free', at Erythrai;[15] romances[16] which mention the Neleid Phrygios of Miletos, who succeeded Neleus' grandson and therefore (on any dating of Neleus near to 1044/3 or 1037/6) must belong to the Bebrykian period; and a report[17] that Midas invented the anchor.

Among the fragments of Phrygian history, one of the oddest survivals is a statement by Justin[18] that when Karanos became king in Macedon he drove out Midas—odd because the dating of Karanos was of course of high importance from Alexander's time onwards. The orthodox view was that Karanos was brother of Pheidon, the seventh Temenid of Argos; and 36×7 years after the Return in 1104/3 brings us to 852/1, *Kastor*'s date for the succession of the Cypriote to the Phrygian thalassocracy. We are bound to suspect that *Kastor* may have connected the fall of Phrygian maritime power with the loss of European dependencies, just as he seems to have connected the Bebrykian migration with the loss of Samothrace.

The period of continuous Phrygian development seems to have been regarded as having begun with the Bebrykian migration: *Kastor*'s Thrace in Asia will have been distinct from his Phrygia in the degree to which the 'Thracians' admitted the Asiatic contribution; and the period when this was most freely admitted will have been the time of great expansion—say, in the two generations which *Kastor* would place on either side of 885. There is as yet no archaeological information on this question, nor on the dating of the arrival of the Bebrykes to the 970's.

The last Phrygian period, that of the empire 742–676, does not as such appear in *Kastor*'s thalassocracies. This is the period of Agamemnon of Kyme and his daughter Demodike or Hermodike, who 'invented coinage',[19] and of her husband Midas, who, as 'roi des

---

[15] Paus. VII 5.5.
[16] Parthenios 14; Aristainetos *Ep.* 1.15.
[17] Paus. I 4.5.
[18] VII 1.
[19] Pollux IX 83.

Phrygiens, fils de Lydios, fît connaître les dinars d'or'.[20] These references are at least to Phrygian metals, and perhaps also to the Phrygian organization of trade and exchange, in the later eighth century, and no doubt *Kastor* mentioned them together with developments under Bocchoris in Egypt.[21]

v. the traditional thalassocracies of the migration period
a. THRACE-IN-EUROPE

The thalassocracy of Thrace in Europe is short and ends with the Bebrykian migration; the only surviving source which seems to throw light on its nature is a passing remark in Orosius,[1] who says that after Aeneas and the death of Kodros *ignoti Thraces nova in bella surgentes, et generalis tunc per totam Asiam Graeciamque commotio.* If this goes back ultimately to Diodorus and *Kastor*, then this first Thracian thalassocracy is probably that, in the whole list, in which the lowest degree of concentration of force and policy was found, and the thalassocracy was only minimally distinguishable from interregnum. It seems likely also that *Kephalion* expressed something of the same idea by his emphasis on the six-year interregnum between the two Thraces—possibly the only interregnum he admitted in his list.[2]

This shadowy thalassocracy is suitably dated by *Kastor* on his most abstract series of numbers, $1092 = 39 \times 28$ years after the beginning of Sikyon and Assyria in 2090/89, and $221 = 39 \times 5\frac{2}{3}$ years before the Olympic era year in 777/6. Presumably the tradition he was following provided practically no evidence; and indeed the existence of the thalassocracy in any sense may be wholly inferential: that the Bebrykian migration implied a period of command of northern waters during which time the expedition was organised. *Kephalion* may be similarly guessing when he dates Thrace in Europe one generation (39×1 years) before Thrace in Asia.

---

[20] Michael of Syria: Chabot p.86.

[21] The mention of a Midakritos, as the first to import tin from Kassiteris, by Pliny NH VII.197, is sometimes quoted in this context also. But this person must be later than the discovery of Tartessos: Cary and Warmington *The Ancient Explorers* (London 1963) p.45.

[1] I 18.2.

[2] We have seen reason to believe that *Kephalion* refused to admit the interregnum placed by *Kastor* between Caria and Lesbos, and instead dated Lesbos' accession to thalassocracy much earlier. This may exemplify a general habit in his criticism of *Kastor*.

The most interesting of the historical questions that can be asked about the thalassocratic Thracians in Europe is whether the East-Greek tradition preserves a truer rendering of the oral traditions of Thracian intruders into the Aegean world than do the mainland stories of the Eumolpidai in Eleusis, Tereus in Phokis, and others, all of whom are placed before the Trojan War, and of the Thracian and Pelasgian invaders of Boiotia whom Ephoros dates from the time of Troy to the Return of the Herakleids.[3] The Eumolpid genealogy unfortunately does not survive: we only know that for some historians it was not long enough, since they spoke of three Eumolpoi in five generations and distinguished the Thracian invader from the first hierophant of Eleusis.[4] Similarly the genealogy of the Thraikidai of Delphi does not survive, if it existed. In fact, the only available material comes from the Dorian side: the ithagenic abstract of the Spartan royal cousinhoods (regarded with a generous eye) goes back to the first half of the tenth century,[5] or contemporary with the thalassocratic Thracians at *Kastor*'s dating. This coincidence is not of course to be crudely taken, for the Spartan settlement may have been relatively late among the Dorian establishments, and all the Dorian settlements may have been later than a Thracian intrusion which set the Dorians on the move; nevertheless it is sufficient to suggest that an examination of the stories of Thracian settlements might be worth while.[6]

b. PELASGOI

We do not know which of the possible Pelasgian theories *Kastor* embraced, nor are we sure that we know all those that were current by his time. For example, Strabo[7] mentions briefly a statement by Menekrates[8] of Pelasgian presence in all the Asiastic coasts and

---

[3] Strabo XIII 3.

[4] Andron 10 F 5. Since the Thracian invader is dated to the time of Ion, grandson of Erechtheus, the first hierophant would accordingly (on the orthodox genealogy of the Athenian kings) fall in the generation of Apheidas, Thymoites and Melanthos. i.e. at the time of the Return.

[5] SCD part V.

[6] For example, Tereus of Phokis is dated to the time of Pandion of Athens, who has no place on the akropolis.

[7] XIII 3.3.

[8] Quoted from his Περὶ Κτίσεων, without date—the period may have, for example, been supposedly before the Trojan War.

islands north of Mykale: but we do not know who these Pelasgoi were or what they did. Similarly, Strabo[9] argues that at the time of the first Aiolic settlements on the Asiatic mainland, the Pelasgian base was at Larisa Phrikonis in the lower Hermos valley; but the form and tone of his argument suggests that this was a conclusion of his own, not representing any established historiographic tradition. If this is correct, then *Kastor* is not likely to have shared Strabo's view. Again, Herodotus states briefly that the Aiolic and Ionic Greeks were Pelasgoi.[10] This is probably a Dorian tradition, and will hardly have survived, in its entirety at least, the development of local historiography in the Asiatic cities: it is therefore also unlikely to have been *Kastor*'s view.

We have in fact two starting-points for an enquiry into *Kastor*'s Pelasgoi: the appearance of the name Pelasgos among his kings of Sikyon, dated to 1179/8–1160/59; and the fact that the Pelasgian thalassocracy dated to 1083/2–999/8 is contemporary with many of the foundation-dates given for the Aiolic and Ionian cities of Asia.

1. Kastor's *Pelasgos*

Pelasgos[11] is the last of the pre-Karneian eponyms of Sikyon, and is succeeded by Zeuxippos, son of Apollo and βασιλεὺς Ἑλλήνων. Nothing is said about him in Eusebius' abstract, but it can scarcely be doubted that *Kastor* intended both Aigialeus, the first of all the eponyms, and Pelasgos, to be connected with the *phyle* of the Aigialeis at Sikyon,[12] who share their name with the Pelasgoi Aigialeis of Achaia,[13] ancestors of (some of) the Ionians. It seems likely that *Kastor* thought of Pelasgos, or some of his subjects, as expelled by Zeuxippos, βασιλεὺς Ἑλλήνων, and consequently arranged the series:

1160/59 last year of Pelasgos in Sikyon

$$65 = 39 \times 1\tfrac{2}{3} \text{ years}$$

1095/4 accession of Charidemos, last Karneian eponym in Sikyon, commemorated in Kyzikos[14]

$$338 = 39 \times 8\tfrac{2}{3} \text{ years}$$

---

[9] XIII 3.2.
[10] VII 94 f.
[11] 250 F 2.
[12] Hdt. V 68.
[13] Hdt. VII 94 f.
[14] 250 F 2 (a).

757/6   first foundation of Kyzikos[15]

$$78 = 39 \times 2$$

679/8   second foundation of Kyzikos.[16]

It is tempting to try and add to this series the tradition of a much earlier and Pelasgian Kyzikos, visited by the Argonauts,[17] but there is no evidence for a Kastorian date.[18]

When the Aigialeis left Achaia at the time of the Return, they went (according to the tradition followed by Eusebius) first to Athens; and we have already seen[19] that *Kastor* seems to have dated this expulsion to 1092/1, and connected with it the flight of the last Karneian eponym from Sikyon. This should mean that the refugees of 1092/1 were Hellenic Aigialeis, to be distinguished at least in Sikyon from the Pelasgoi Aigialeis whose last year in that city was 1160/59. It is clearly a question whether *Kastor* brought some Pelasgoi Aigialeis to Athens in or after 1160/59 (thus retaining a part of the Herodotean tradition), and had the feud with the Hellenic Aigialeis continue after they in turn arrived in Athens in 1092/1, with the consequence that the Pelasgoi were driven out of Attika. This would mean that the Pelasgoi whose thalassocracy began in 1083/2 were Pelasgoi expelled in 1092/1 or later, that is, the traditional Pelasgoi of Lemnos.

The only means of checking this guess about the identity of *Kastor*'s Pelasgoi is through the participation by the Minyai they expelled from Lemnos in the Spartan colony at Thera. No date for this foundation survives, but since it was synchronized[20] with the

---

[15] Eusebius: see SCD Index of Years.
[16] The same.
[17] Konon 41; schol. Ap. Rh. I 1040; Apd. I 9.18; Hyg. *Fab.* 16.
[18] The derivatives of the Eusebian *Canons* have a foundation of Kyzikos just before the voyage of the Argonauts, and date it to 1271/0 (Jerome, a bad text), 1273/2 (Dionysius of Tell Mahre), and 1277/6 (Arm.). The *Chronicon Paschale* says that Kyzikos was founded 34 years after Troy, and Jerome and the Armenian agree on 1308/7 for Troy (Dionysius says 1306/5). The Eusebian date for Pelasgian Kyzikos should then be 1274/3, which is not a chronographic number of years before 757/6 or 679/8, and so presumably does not come from *Kastor*.
[19] See above p.99.
[20] Hdt. IV 147.

establishment of the dyarchy at Sparta, its orthodox date must have been very well known.[21]

Eusebius (and apparently Diodorus before him) does not quote *Kastor* for the Spartan kings: we must therefore assume that *Kastor* accepted the Apollodoran dates which Diodorus used.[22] The terminal dates given in the quotation[23] are 1104/3 and 777/6, but the details of the list give 298 instead of the required 328 years. The missing thirty years may in principle be found in one of two ways: the first and generally preferred is by changing figures or adding names within the list.[24] The alternative is to assign thirty years to the rule of Aristodemos[25] and the regency of Theras before the twins achieve their majority. It is generally taken as fatal to this alternative that in all other cases the years of minority are naturally counted as part of the reign concerned; but the minority of the twins is unique for, until they actually attained their majority, Sparta was a monarchy under king Aristodemos or the regent Theras: only at the majority of the twins does the peculiar Spartan institution of the dyarchy appear. All Greek historians, we may be sure, regarded the institution of the dyarchy as much more important than consistency in counting the years of the minority of the twins into their reigns: and if this is so, then we find the missing thirty years before the majority of the twins,[26] and the absolute dates are:

1104/3: Return of the Herakleidai. Aristodemos is king, then Theras regent, in Sparta for 30 years.

1074/3: Institution of the dyarchy at the majority of the twins. Theras colonizes Thera with some of the Minyai previously arrived from Lemnos: $312 = 39 \times 8$ years before Eusebius' first colonization of Kyrene in 762/1, and $442 = 39 \times 11\frac{1}{3}$

---

[21] The omission of a date for the Dorian emigration in Eusebius may be accounted for by the attachment of the beginning of the movement to a much more important Spartan event (the accession of the twins) in the ancestral annalist.

[22] This in turn should illuminate the composition of Eusebius' chapter on Greek Dates in the *Chronographia*.

[23] 244 F 62.

[24] So Jacoby adds king Menelaos from the Barbarian.

[25] Hdt. VI 52.

[26] We should also note that the numbers of years given to the twins, their sons and grandsons, are biologically improbable if the count is from the infancy of the twins.

years before its reinforcement in 632/1 by Battos of Thera.[27]

Thus *Kastor*'s Pelasgian thalassocracy, beginning in 1083/2, appears to have expelled the Minyai nine years before these refugees joined in the colonization of Thera; if our previous guesswork is right, it was also nine years after the Hellenic Aigialeis arrived in Attika and expelled the Pelasgoi—in each case, the expelled population establishes itself anew in nine years. It seems therefore in general a reasonable guess that *Kastor*'s Pelasgic thalassocrats were the traditional Pelasgoi of Lemnos, whose command of the sea was illustrated by the raid on Brauron.

2. Kastor's *Asiatic Greeks*

The second approach to an understanding of *Kastor*'s Pelasgian thalassocracy is through the dates given to the contemporary Greek foundations in Asia. For these, absolute dates of a scattered kind are available from Eusebius; and for some Aiolic foundations also from the pseudo-Herodotean *Life of Homer*.

The *Life* gives the absolute dates:

1141/0: Lesbos founded κατὰ πόλεις 20 years before Kyme;

1121/0: Kyme founded 18 years before Smyrna;

1113/2: Neonteichos founded 8 years after Kyme (chapter 9);

1103/2: Smyrna founded 622 years before the Diabasis of Xerxes.

The *Life* is written as by Herodotus, but is a product of late antiquity:[28] it thus belongs to same general archaising trend in historiography as *Kephalion*'s work and, for example, the use of years of Priestesses of Hera for dating events as in the inscriptions on the foundation-legends on Magnesia.[29] We can probably safely assume therefore that the author of the *Life* used genuinely Hellanikan dates (since only these would be available to Herodotus), but—since on the whole he is writing for schoolboys—expressed them in a simpler

---

[27] For these Eusebian dates see SCD Index of Years.
[28] T. W. Allen (*Homer: The Origins . . .*) ascribed it to *Kephalion*, but though he imitated Herodotus, *Kephalion* did not write in Herodotus' name.
[29] Jac 483 F3.

form than years of Priestesses. It is therefore not surprising that the date for Lesbos κατὰ πόλεις is chronographically connected with two other dates which we have already ascribed to *Kephalion* and Hellanikos: it is $104 = 39 \times 2\frac{2}{3}$ years before the Ionian Migration in 1037/6, and $468 = 39 \times 12 = 36 \times 13$ years before Terpandros at Sparta in 673/2.

The Eusebian dates are:

1052/1: Μαγνησία δὲ πόλις κτίξεται ⟨in Asia⟩.
  Text: Cramer *AP* ii 228.29; ⟨in Asia⟩ in Jerome, Dionysius, Arm.
  Date: Jerome, Dionysius 1055/4, Arm. 1053/2.

  Text: ibid; Jerome: Mycena in Italia condita: *SA/B/D* add uel Cumae, *T* adds quae nunc Cumae.
  edition: Synk 340.13 Κύμη ἐκτίσθη ἐν ᾽Ιταλίᾳ.
  Date: the Greek shows the entry was connected with the Magnesia item, although Jerome divides between 1052/1 and 1050/49, Dionysius between 1055/4 and 1052/1.

1046/5: Μυρίνα ἡ παρά τισι Σμύρνα λεγομένη ἐκτίσθη ἐν ᾽Ασίᾳ.
  Text: Synk. 340.11; Jerome: Myrena condita; Dionysius: Murina urbs condita est.
  Date: Jerome in a good text, Dionysius 1050/49.

1045/4: ῎Εφεσος ᾽εκτίσθη ἐν ᾽Ασίᾳ ὑπὸ ᾽Ανδρονίκου.
  Text: Synk. 340.12; ἐν ᾽Ασίᾳ omitted by Jerome, Dionysius.
  Date: Jerome, Dionysius 1049/8.

1037/6: Ionica emigratio, in qua quidam Homerum fuisse scribunt.
  Text: Jerome, translated in Armenian.
  Date: Jerome and Armenian agree.

1036/5: Samos urbs condita est.
  Text: Dionysius, Armenian translates.
  Date: Dionysius and Armenian agree.

  986/5: Samus condita et Smyrna in urbis modum ampliata.
  Text: Jerome; Dionysius: Samos condita est et Smyrna condita est.
  Date: at the titulus or first year of Doryssus of Sparta, Jerome *M/SA/XC/F/L*, others later; Dionysius: Samos at 987/6 and Smyrna at 983/2.

139

We may consider these dates in relation to the Pelasgian thalassocracies of *Kastor* (1083/2–999/8) and *Kephalion* (1057/6–1007/6).

α. *the Dorian emigration*

The date of 1074/3 for Thera is likely to have been accepted by both *Kastor* and *Kephalion*, and to have been recognized as that for the first of the Dorian colonies—certainly from Sparta and probably also from Argos. For *Kastor* it is within the period, but presumably outside the territorial waters, of the Pelasgian thalassocracy; for *Kephalion* it is outside the period also.

The double foundation of Kyrene, Thera's colony, in Eusebius (probably from *Kastor*) may have originated in attempts to reconcile genealogical data and a 'known' absolute date. It is obvious from Herodotus' excursus on the history of Kyrene that the dating of Battos and his descendants was known: the Eusebian 632/1 will express this in terms of later learning, and there seems to be no reason to doubt its approximate historicity. Above this, the alleged $11\frac{1}{3}$ generations in Thera take us back to the synchronism with the Spartan dyarchy; but above the 'first' foundation of Thera there are only eight generations. Probably local Theraian tradition knew of eight generations only: the expansion to $11\frac{1}{3}$ generations will modify the local genealogical data to fit the requirements of the Spartan part of the story— to bring Theraian local tradition into conformity with universal history. This accommodation would certainly be older than *Kastor*: one naturally thinks of the Alexandria of Kallimachos and Eratosthenes.

But if we calculated eight generations before Kyrene in 632/1, at the cousinly value of 35 ± 1 years, we arrive at the date of 912 ± 8. This would make Dorian Thera approximately contemporary with the archaeological date for Dorian Rhodes, which seems likely enough.

β. *the Ionian emigration*

Neleid Miletos will have been 1044/3 (Eratosthenes) for *Kastor*, and 1037/6 (Hellanikos) for *Kephalion*: for both, therefore, within the period of the Pelasgian thalassocracy. Since Miletos is south of Mykale however, even for Menekrates this foundation would be outside Pelasgian territorial waters.

Ephesos in 1045/4 is one year senior to *Kastor*'s Miletos (and this seniority is known to the tradition in Pherekydes' version of it). For *Kastor*, 1045/4 is $99 = 27 \times 3\frac{2}{3} = 36 \times 2\frac{3}{4}$ years after:

1144/3 :   τὸν ἐν Ἐφέσῳ ναὸν ἐνέπρησαν Ἀμαξόνες.

> *Text*: Exc. Eus. 137.5; *Kastor*'s Athenian king-list, note to Oxyntes; Synk. 334.18
>
> *Date:* Dionysius and Armenian; Jerome 1146/5

and $9 = 27 \times \frac{1}{3} = 36 \times \frac{1}{4}$ years before the foundation of Samos in 1036/5. All these entries are therefore attributable to *Kastor*: and Samos is $279 = 27 \times 10\frac{1}{3} = 36 \times 7\frac{3}{4}$ years before Kyzikos in 757/6.

Ephesos and Samos were closely associated in the foundation legends. Although they are north of Mykale, it seems unlikely that *Kastor* supposed them to be Pelasgian dependencies; and therefore for him either the Pelasgians did not command the Lydian coast, or the settlers drove them off before establishing their colonies: see below on the Magnesians.

Eusebius' entry of *Samos condita* in 986/5 does not seem readily explicable. It is much too late for Samos, and rather too early for Samothrace, for which both *Kastor* and *Kephalion*, as we have seen (in connection with Thrace in Asia), probably accepted Apollodoros' date of 976/5, and associated it variously with the end of the thalassocracy of Thrace in Europe. It is possible that *condita* is wrong, and that the date belongs to another event.

γ. *the Aiolic emigration*

Smyrna was destroyed by Alyattes of Lydia, who for *Kephalion* acceded in 617/6. This is $369 = 36 \times 10\frac{1}{4}$ years after *Smyrna in urbis modum ampliata* in 986/5, and $429 = 39 \times 11$ years after Myrine-Smyrna was founded in 1046/5. These two generation-counts seem to be really the same, and to contrast with the arithmetical fact that the date for Smyrna in the *Life of Homer*, at 1103/2, is $486 = 36 \times 13\frac{1}{2}$ years before 617/6. These arithmetical relationships seem to mean (1) that there were two important generation-counts in the foundation and establishment of Smyrna; and (2) that *Kephalion*, accepting no doubt the Eratosthenic years for Troy in 1184/3 and the Return in 1104/3 could not also accept the Hellanikan 1103/2 for Smyrna: he therefore abandoned the $13\frac{1}{2}$ generations, and instead adopted two versions of the 11-generation count.

We should expect Hellanikos to have secured the best available genealogical evidence for his calculation, and $13\frac{1}{2}$ generations at the cousinly value of 35 ± 1 years give us about 470 years (± 13). With Alyattes' accession about 605, we thus have a foundation-date for Smyrna around 1075—which would be rather early in the Proto-Geometric period, but is perhaps not at variance with the archaeological evidence. On the other hand, if we apply to this generation-count the ithagenic value of 27 years, we have a period of some 365 years, and therefore (calculating again from Alyattes in 605) the date of about 970, still Proto-Geometric, which is perhaps preferable. On this reckoning, the 10–11 generations used by *Kephalion* would give some 270 or more years back to Smyrna's establishment as a city, or a date about 875 or a little earlier, and this might then be recognised as the traditional counterpart to the archaeological epoch of the first fortification, in the ninth century.[30]

It is interesting to note that all the calculations use Alyattes' accession for their base-date. This should mean that the year of the fall of Smyrna was not known.

The Hellanikan Kyme in 1121/0 is $36 \times \frac{1}{2}$ years earlier than Smyrna, which suggests that in dating both cities Hellanikos was using foundation-narratives relating the two, and taking the count of 14 generations from Kyme. The Eusebian Mykene in Italy in 1052/1 must be the remnant of an annal which spoke, at this date, not only of Aiolic Kyme but also of her daughter-city Cumae, and emphasized in Cumae the inheritance of the Agamemnonid tradition of Kyme. The chronography agrees: 1052/1 is $528 = 36 \times 14\frac{2}{3}$ years before 524/3, the year in which Aristodemos of Cumae emerged to fame,[31] and $132 = 36 \times 3\frac{2}{3}$ years after 1184/3, the year when Agamemnon captured Troy. The dating is no doubt orthodox, going back to Apollodoros and accepted by *Kastor* if not also by *Kephalion*.[32] Strabo's

---

[30] Boardman, *op. cit.* 49 f.

[31] Dion. Hal, VII 2.

[32] If there was genuine genealogical material for Cumae, we must suppose that the Aiolic element in that city was, socially and politically, strong enough to make it an exception to the general rule of the 'Euboian lacuna' in the traditions. We should also note (1) that there is as yet no archaeological evidence of substance for the foundation-date of Kyme; and (2) that Eusebius' source(s) dated Cumae either before the first Olympiad, after which his colony entries begin, presumably because he then began to use *Olympiades* books which used Appollodoros-*Kastor* as much as he did himself; or at 776/5 ($252 = 36 \times 7$ years before 524/3), in which case the notes on the First Olympiad have extruded the notice of Cumae. The second is perhaps the more probable.

story of the founding of Kyme and Neonteichos includes hostilities with the Pelasgoi, and *Kastor* may well have shared this tradition, since the date 1052/1 is used also for the foundation of Magnesia.

δ. *the Magnetes*

The Magnetes, coming immediately from Crete and ultimately from Thessaly, claimed to have been 'the first Hellenes to cross into Asia,[33] and to have arrived at the time of the Aiolic and Ionian migrations and assisted both.[34] The use of the same year for the foundations of Magnesia and Kyme by Eusebius probably means that *Kastor* accepted this account at least in so far as Kyme was concerned, and probably for Ephesos also, since the Magnetes claimed that their first settlement was at Kretinaion in Ephesia.

The oecist of Magnesia was Leukippos son of Kar,[35] a descendant of Glaukos son of Hippolochos son of Bellerophon.[36] The great importance attached to Glaukos and his ancestors and kinsmen in the *Iliad* show that there was interest in this kinship unit and its genealogy and history in Homer's time, and undoubtedly this epic treatment would be continued and enlarged in Magnes' *Amazonia*, which seems to have been written after Gyges' first Kimmerian war (when he was Ashurbanipal's ally) and before the second (when he was killed) so in the years 655 ± 5.

Eusebius seems to preserve parts both of *Kastor*'s and of *Kephalion*'s history of the Magnetes:

1078/7: Ἀμαζόνες τῇ Ἀσίᾳ ἐπῆλθον ἅμα Κιμμερίοις[37]
$$26 = 39 \times \tfrac{2}{3} \text{ years}$$

1052/1: Magnesia founded; Kyme founded
$$390 = 39 \times 10 \text{ years}$$

662/1: *Kastor*'s date for the accession of Ardys, who fought the Kimmerian incursion in which Magnesia was sacked, and in which Ashurbanipal says that Gyges was killed.

---

[33] Jac 483 F 3.
[34] Konon 26 F 1 (xxix): the *Life of Homer* makes Theseus the oecist of Smyrna a Magnesian, and this is presumbly a variant of the more general tradition.
[35] Schol. Ap. Rh. I 583/4.
[36] Jac 483 F 3; Hdt. I 147; *Iliad* VI 197.
[37] *Text*: Synk. 334.17; *Date*: Jerome and Armenian.

This series, attributable to *Kastor*, may be compared and contrasted with a series similarly attributable to *Kephalion*:

1341/0: Bellerophon's career (including his killing of the Amazons);
$91 = 39 \times 2\frac{1}{3}$ years

1250/49: Minos of Crete, thalassocrat[38] ($529 = 23 \times 23$ years before Caria becomes thalassocrat in 721/0)
$572 = 39 \times 14\frac{2}{3}$ years

678/7   *Kephalion*'s Herodotean date for the accession of Ardys.

Kastor's ten generations before Ardys for Kyme contrasts with Hellanikos' fourteen generations before Alyattes, but is comparable with *Kephalion*'s 10–11 generations before Alyattes for Smyrna; and enables us to guess that the double epoch of Smyrna had to do with the existence of 'Aiolic-Pelasgian' and 'Magnesian' epochs of foundation and establishment; and that these variations also reflected back into the treatments of Kyme. Hellanikos' 14 generations before Alyattes, if given an ithagenic value, yield a date about 983; *Kastor*'s ten generations before Ardys acceding about 645, if similarly valued, yield a date about 915, for epochs in Kyme parallel to those in Smyrna. For Kyme however we still await archaeological evidence.

Kephalion's series gives us the generation-count for Bellerophon, seventeen generations before Ardys. No doubt the Glaukid kings of Ionia, like the Neleids, formed a cousinhood, so the correct value to give to these generations is that of 35 ± 1 years. Taking Ardys' accession as about 645, this gives us the date of 1240 ± 17 for Bellerophon. At this date he is contemporary with the reign of the Hittite emperor Tudhaliyas IV (1265–1235) and his son and successor Arnuwandas III (1235–1215), in whose times the activities of Attarissiyas of Ahhiya[39] in Asia Minor and Cyprus provide a historical parallel to the traditions of Bellerophon in Caria-Lykia and the Aleian plain. The Magnesian generation-count is therefore very acceptable.

The date of 1250/49 for the beginning of the thalassocracy of Minos was important to *Kephalion*: apparently on the strength of Minos' Carian seamen he placed his Carian thalassocracy $529 = 23 \times 23$ years later in 721/0. Also the date satisfied his archaistic

---

[38] The Magnetes came to Asia immediately from Crete.
[39] O. R. Gurney, *The Hittites* pp.38, 51 f.

historiographic tastes, for it is $46 = 23 \times 2$ years before Antiochos' date in 1204/3 for the death of Minos in Sicily.[40] As part of the tradition of the Magnetes however we should recalculate the date to $(35 \pm 1) \times 2$ or about 70 years after Bellerophon in 1240 ± 17, which yields 1170 ± 15. At this date Minos the thalassocrat is to be identified with the traditional Minos who founded Gaza of the Philistines,[41] and who seems to represent the Cherethite or Cretan element in the Philistine settlement. This generation-count from the Magnesian traditions is therefore also acceptable.

So far as we can tell therefore the genealogical records both of the Neleid[42] and of the Glaukid kings of Ionia show a high degree of accuracy back to the middle of the thirteenth century. In the Glaukid case, Homer's story of Bellerophon[43] remembers the time when kings east and west of the Aegean were in correspondence, and society was stable if warlike; but nevertheless the character of the tradition is oral: the possibility of an ultimate written source for these generation-counts does not arise. In the Glaukid case, nevertheless, the seventeen generations from Bellerophon probably derive from Magnes' *Amazonia*, which is an exceptionally early historiographic source of about 655, and would be unaffected by considerations of Universal History.

Of the two Amazon events dated by *Kastor*, the incursion in alliance with the Kimmerioi dated to 1078/7 probably interprets a story in, or the story of, the *Amazonia* in relation to the Magnetes and Kyme, where the Magnesian Theseus married the Amazon Smyrna and named his new city after her.[44] The burning of Ephesos dated to 1144/3 may come from the same ultimate source, even though it is given to us in a rather different context.

---

40 SCD Index of Years.
41 Steph. Byz. s.v. Gaza. This late Minos may represent the brief twelfth century *Koine* in the Aegean: V. R. d'A. Desborough, *The Last Myceanaeans and their successors* (Oxford 1966) p.282.
42 SCD Part V.
43 Whose name may be in part 'Hittite': personal names beginning with Pall- or Ball-, including Ballara- and Balluwaru- are not uncommon (Forrer, *Syria* XVIII p.158); and even for the Greeks Bellerophon was 'originally' called Hipponoos.
44 This Amazon marriage of Theseus of Kyme may very well be the original upon which the story of the Amazon marriage of Theseus of Athens was built.

ε. *Lesbos*

Eusebius has no mention of the settlement of Lesbos, which in the *Life of Homer* (and probably in other accounts also, so far as the fragments enable us to judge) is the earliest of the Aiolic settlements. Possibly, as in the case of Thera, we should suppose that in the ancestral annalist this settlement was attached to some other event and therefore came to be omitted: it is of course not impossible that this other event has also been omitted by the time Eusebius came to make his abstracts.

The only guidance we have, therefore, to *Kastor*'s date for Lesbos is the Hellanikan date and generation-count: 1141/0 and 104 $=$ $39 \times 2\frac{2}{3}$ years before Miletos in 1037/6 and 468 $= 39 \times 12 = 36 \times 13\frac{2}{3}$ years before Terpandros in Sparta in 673/2. If this second generation-count was accepted by the Pergamenes, they could obtain a date for Lesbos by calculating 432 $= 36 \times 12$ years before Terpandros in 645/4, that is, about 1077 B.C. Then the original Lesbos entry could have been attached to the Amazons and Kimmerians of 1078/7 by the ancestral annalist.

The extraordinary tale of the Aiolic settlement in Lesbos must have been narrated and explained very many times, but we possess only Strabo's version, which is probably based on Ephoros. In this account, Orestes organised the emigrants, and they were assembled at Aulis when he died. His son Penthilos arrived to take over the leadership at the time when the returning Boiotians (60 years after Troy) were driving out the Thracians and Pelasgoi who had occupied Boiotia after the Theban and during the Trojan war. Some of their refugees joined Penthilos. Even with this reinforcement however Penthilos journeyed no further than Thrace: apparently the boats were lost, and perhaps the sojourn in Thrace was made possible by the Thracian refugees in Penthilos' force. Under Penthilos' son Echelas or Archelaos, the expedition reached Kyzikos and Daskylion. The sojourn in this old Pelasgian country was perhaps made possible by the Pelasgoi in Echelas' force. Finally, Echelas' son Gras led a dash across the Troad to Lesbos, leaving his name to the river Granikos on the way.

According to this story, the settlers of Lesbos were mixed, being a part (under Echelas' youngest son) of an Achaio-Thrako-Pelasgian population on the move. The earliest relevant pottery from Lesbos includes 'trifling finds of Protogeometric' but consists largely of silver-grey bucchero. This archaeological evidence therefore bears out

146

the traditional statements about the culturally mixed nature of the settlement, though it does not fix the date within the two centuries 1100–900, nor (at least as yet) confirm that the non-Greek elements were Thracian and Pelasgian.

By *Kastor*, this mixed settlement, coming immediately from the Pelasgic Propontis and dating certainly before 1052/1 when Magnesia and Kyme were settled, and either early in the Pelasgian thalasso-cracy or not long before, must—it would seem—have been regarded as a reinforcement of the Pelasgian thalassocracy based on Lemnos. That is to say, there survives some part of the old view that the Aiolic and Ionian Greeks were Pelasgoi:[45] settlements (pre-eminently Les-bos) before the appearance of the Magnetes in eastern waters are Pelasgic rather than Greek. From 1052/1 onwards however, for *Kastor*, the Greek element is continually reinforced: by the Magnesian oecist Theseus at Smyrna; by the Neleids at Miletos; and, no doubt, the Dorians further south.

* * *

Thus so far as can be made out, *Kastor*'s Pelasgian thalassocracy was a conservative and moderate construct, offering no startling alternative to the Lemnos story, and rejecting the very wide extent of Pelasgian power or character supported by, for example, Menekrates. It seems likely also that there were periods within the thalassocracy: the first from 1083/2 to 1053/2 when Pelasgian rule of northern waters is unchallenged; the second from 1052/1 onwards when the Magnetes set a limit which is backed by Kyme, Smyrna, Ephesos, Miletos and Samos; it seems quite probable also that there was an interregnum, or perhaps the function of such a power-vacuum was fulfilled by the thalassocracy of Thrace in Europe.

The date of the beginning of the Pelasgian thalassocracy is, for *Kastor*, one generation before the establishment of Neleid Miletos. The Milesian genealogies point to a date, just before 1000 B.C. for the arrival of Neleus at Miletos,[46] but the archaeological evidence from

---

[45] If *Kastor* related Gras' departure from Kyzikos and Daskylion to the Amazon and Kimmerian incursion five years after the beginning of the Pelasgian thalassocracy, it is possible that *Kephalion*'s date for the beginning of the Pelasgian thalassocracy was also his date for the founda-tion of Lesbos: 1057/6 is $384 = 36 \times 10\frac{2}{3}$ years before Terpandros in 673/2.
[46] SCD Part V: archaeological evidence for the forcible change of govern-ment at Miletos is not yet available.

Lemnos shows nothing 'obviously earlier than the eighth century'.[47] The historicity of a pre-Neleid Pelasgian thalassocracy based on Lemnos remains therefore an open question until the archaeologists are sufficiently sure that there is no gap in their record in the island.[48]

c. LYDO-MAIONES or LYDOI

This is the only thalassocracy of which the name varies in our documents: Jerome (presumably following Eusebius and *Kephalion*) speaks of the Lydians; the Register and other documents (presumably following *Kastor*) speak of the Λνδοὶ οἱ καὶ Μαίονες. These variations seem to be connected with other Eusebian entries: Tantalos of Phrygia or Maionia in 1350/59 is 690 = 23 × 30 years before *Kephalion*'s Lesbian thalassocracy in 670/69; while Midas of Phrygia in 1310/09 belongs to a different ethnography although he is 135 = 27 × 5 = 36 × 3¾ years before both the Lydian and the Lydo-Maionian thalassocracy in 1175/4. He is recognizable as *Kastor*'s because 1310/09 is 780 = 39 × 20 years after the beginning of Assyria and Sikyon in 2090/89, 312 = 39 × 8 years before the thalassocracy of Thrace in Europe in 998/7, and 612 = 27 × 17 years before *Kastor*'s Gyges in 698/7. We seem therefore to have the fragments of an ethnographic controversy about the Maiones: *Kephalion* regards them as contributing to the Phrygians but not to the Lydians, while *Kastor* apparently sees them as giving the Phrygians the name and function of Midas, but also making an important contribution both in thalassocracy and the Mermnad dynasty[1] to Lydia. This controversy no doubt was linked with other ethnographic problems in western Asia of which we have occasional traces: Xanthos of Lydia, for example, seems to have recognized two elements in Lydia, the Lydoi proper and the Torrheboi, and it is not clear how he regarded the Maiones. Xanthos also, as we have seen, distinguished the Phrygians proper (who came to Asia after Troy) from the Mygdones who arrived in Priam's youth. Although we cannot follow these controversies in detail, it seems certain that when *Kastor* named the

---

[47] Boardman, *op. cit.* p.103.

[48] The increase in the density of population in Attika in the ninth century seems to preclude any non-Greek emigration from that area as late as the eighth.

[1] The chronographic connection between Midas of 1310/09 and *Kastor*'s Gyges may mean that there was some propaganda to this effect about the new Mermnad dynasty as early as Gyges' time.

Λυδοὶ οἱ καὶ Μαίονες he was emphasizing the composite nature of this entity.

The same or a similar view appears in Strabo's account of the history of the plain of Thebe or Adrammytion opposite Lesbos, for he says that this was often fought over, in earlier times between the Maiones and Mysoi, and later between the Lesbian and (other) Aiolic Greeks.[2] The far northward appearance of the Maionian name[3] may possibly go back to Xanthos, who mentioned a Lydian king Adramyttes,[4] perhaps the eponym of Adramyttion; and a town Ardynion,[5] presumably named after a Lydian Ardys.

Thus the suggestion appears to be that before Lydia or Phrygia (in the historical senses of those names) came into being, the Maiones were an important people of western Asia whose rulers provided dynastic patterns or ancestors for various later political groupings— from the Penthilid descendants of Tantalos in Lesbos to the Midas of Phrygia. The area within which the Maionian name is found extends from the Plain of Thebe southwards to the Hermos valley, or in general north of the territory apparently occupied by Arzawa in Hittite times, and it would be interesting to know how *Kastor* related his Maiones to the Amazon sack of Ephesos dated to 1144/3, especially if Ephesos is Apesas, the capital of Arzawa.

The problem of Maionian relations with or contributions to Phrygia is now complicated by a Hittite document concerned apparently with a vassal named Midas.[6] The document is an indictment, probably by Arnuwandas III (1235–1215), of a disloyal vassal or subject-ally or mercenary named Mita, who had been posted to Tephrike in Armenia Minor. The name of Mita's place of origin, or of his people, is not given or at least does not survive.

The Assyrians from the twelfth century onwards intermittently refer to Mita of Mushki, in which name the Moschoi or Meshech of Armenia are recognized but (at least in the eighth century) Phrygia is clearly meant. The Moschoi known to the Greeks lived between the

---

[2] Strabo XIII 1.8, 61, 65.

[3] In Homer's Trojan Catalogue, the Maiones live in the Hermos valley under Mt. Tmolos.

[4] Jac 765 F 4.

[5] F 5.

[6] O. R. Gurney, 'Mita of Pahhuwas' and J. Garstang, 'The Location of Pahhuwa' in *Liverpool Annals of Archaeology and Anthropology* XXVIII (1948) pp.32 ff. and 48 ff.

upper Euphrates and the Euxine, and their country is said to be connected by a natural route to Tephrike. This Armenian locale is decidely distant from Maionia, even if *Kastor* and Arnuwandas agree on the existence of the name of Midas in the Bronze Age.

Herodotus[7] in his account of the Persian army mentions that the Armenians were ἄποικοι of the Phrygians. The term ἄποικοι implies a separation from the mother-country, either by sea (as usually for Greek colonies) or perhaps in this case by lands inhabited by other peoples.

It is therefore a hypothesis that the Mita of Arnuwandas in the thirteenth century had separated from his people or place of origin and entered Hittite service, whereupon he was appointed to govern or garrison Tephrike, apparently as a consequence of the final conquest and dissolution of the kingdom of Hyasa north of Tephrike. *Kastor's* Midas of Phrygia in 1310/09 then points to Maionia as the place of origin, and Herodotus' story of a 'Phrygian colony' in Armenia may, at many removes, be an attempt to explain the transference. If Arnuwandas' attack on Mita, prepared in the indictment, was successful and Mita and his followers established themselves beyond the Hittite frontier as rulers of the Moschoi, we should similarly have an explanation of Mita of Mushki as known to the Assyrians. The hypothesis has however the great weakness of treating evidence which, for us at least, is of very different sources and periods, as equal throughout: we should expect quite an element of inference and construction in our Greek sources, though they may basically have been good. The most we can really say about the Midas of 1310/09 is that (while his date is likely to be inflated) he cannot be dismissed as apocryphal.

*   *   *

1. Mopsos

At the year 1184/3 (which is $9 = 27 \times \frac{1}{3} = 36 \times \frac{1}{4}$ years before the beginning of the Lydian or Lydo-Maionian thalassocracy in 1175/4) Jerome has the entry *Mopsus regnauit in Cilicia, a quo Mopsicrenae et Mopsistiae*. At this date an entry about Mopsos, who took over the leadership of a Greek host abandoned without ships after the fall of Troy, belongs to a source for whom Troy fell in 1184/3, and it has been copied mechanically by Eusebius (whose own Troy fell in 1182/1). The general chronographic tradition was that Troy fell in

---

[7] VII 73.

the last months or month of 1184/*3*; the original historian presumably dated Mopsos' departure for, rather than his arrival in, Kilikia in the same year.

Mopsos or Moxos the Lydian has become of recent years a fairly solid figure: the evidence is both Greek and Asiatic, and the Asiatic evidence is literary, toponymic, and epigraphic.

To the Greeks, Mopsos is a μάντις, grandson of the μάντις Teiresias of Thebes, whose daughter bore him to Apollo, or to Rhakios, a Cretan settler in Kolophon. After the fall of Troy, and a contest with another μάντις. (Kalchas or Amphilochos), Mopsos took the leadership of those Greeks who had no boats, and led this mixed host to Pamphylia or over the Taurus to Kilikia. His mingled band gave the name of 'all tribes' to Pamphylia,[8] or that region was named after Mopsos' wife, Pamphyle the daughter of Kabderos;[9] or after his daughter Pamphylia: his other daughters were Rhode eponym of Rhode in Lykia, and Μηλίας who was apparently not eponymous.[10] Mopsos himself died in Kilikia and was buried at Megarsos;[11] he left his name in Mopsouhestia and Mopsoukrene, and founded Mallos,[11] Aspendos[12] and Phaselis.[13] The name of Mopsos apparently did not occur in the cyclic epics, but was certainly mentioned by Kallinos about 645, as (presumably) a superior parallel to the land-treks of the Kimmerioi of his time.[14]

The toponymic evidence consists of Mopsouhestia and Mopsoukrene in Kilikia; there is also Moxoupolis[15] in the upper Indus valley on the eastern road which proceeds to Kibyra (the site of a Lydian settlement[16]) and thence to Pamphylia and Kilikia. Also in Phrygia,

---

[8] Kallinos F 7, writing at the time of the Kimmerioi *c.* 645, calls Pamphylia Mopsopia.
[9] Schol. Dion. Perieg, 850. Kabderos may be a Graecisation of Kaphtor: Barnett JHS 73 (1953) pp. 141 ff.
[10] Theopompos of Chios 115 F 103.
[11] Strabo XIV 5.16: the statement implies an ancestor cult.
[12] Schol. Dion. Perieg. 852.
[13] Pomp. Mela I 14.
[14] Proclus' summary of the Nostoi says that the (Lapith) followers of Leonteus and Polypoites went with Kalchas to Kolophon, where Tiiresias died. This may in fact imply a mention of Mopsos, but it is not reported. 'Hesiod' apparently knew of Mopsos (F 278 MW, see the *Melampodia*).
[15] Ramsay, *Cities and Bishoprics* II pp.256, 258, 260.
[16] Strabo XIII 4.17.

but considerably further north, were a people named the Moxeanoi[17]. It seems doubtful whether this people have anything to do with Moxos or Mopsos, though their territory came down to the Royal Road on the south: they may be a northward eddy of a generally eastward movement.

The epigraphic evidence covers a very wide span of time. Mopsos has long been known from the Roman coins of Hierapolis-Kidrara[18] in the Lykos valley, where the main eastward roads from Sardis and Kolophon-Ephesos-Magnesia join. More recently, the Phoenician and Hieroglyphic-Hittite bilingual inscription from Karatepe in Kilikia, dated 750–700 B.C., has been shown to mention Bt Mps, Mopsouhestia, the house or dynasty of Mopsos: and this dynasty ruled the Dnnym of Adana.[19] The fact that the dynasty of Mopsos ruled Dnnym or Danaoi is sufficient to explain Greek statements about Greek troops after Troy, whether the identification is acceptable to moderns or not. Finally for the epigraphic evidence, the name Moxos appears as Muksas in the Madduwattas document of the Hittite king Arnuwandas III (1235–1215). The name appears in an extremely mutilated portion of the text, which reports on the mission of Mulliyaras who was sent to negotiate with Madduwattas on a number of differences between him and Arnuwandas. These included questions of extradition and restitution, to some of which Maddu-wattas apparently agreed, then began to explain his position on others: 'because Muksas . . .',[20] and a little later the land of Karkisa (Caria) is mentioned.

The Asiatic literary Moxos is a military and cultic personage. He first appears briefly in Xanthos of Lydia[21] as Moxos the Lydian who drowned Atargatis and her son Ichthys in the lake at Philistine Askalon. Some light is thrown on this by another fragment [22] which

---

[17] North-west of the Phyrygian (Mygdonian) Pentapolis: Ramsay *op.cit.* II 631 ff.

[18] Head HN^2 675.

[19] R. D. Barnett *Anatolian Studies* III pp. 87 f.

[20] Reverse line 75 of the document transcribed and translated by Goetze Madduwattas' in *Mitteilungen der Vorderasiatisch-Aegyptischen Gesellschaft* 32 (1927) pp. 1 ff. There is now the possibility of a much earlier dating of this document, in which case of course Muksas is not the same man as Mopsos.

[21] Jac 765 F 17.

[22] F 8.

tells us that Askalos and Tantalos were the sons of Hymenaios:[23] Askalos was appointed by king Akiamos of Lydia to march against Syria, where he founded the city of which he was eponym. Nikolaos of Damascus adds to this meagre record:[24] Moxos the Lydian accomplished many great deeds, and having removed Μήλης from his tyranny he summoned the Lydians to pay the tithe to the gods, as they had promised: they obeyed, counted out their possessions, took the tithe and sacrificed it. In his time a great dearth seized Lydia, and the people had recourse to the oracle.. ⟨. . . .⟩ This man is said to have made many campaigns, and his fame for courage and justice was very great in Lydia. In the course of these actions he prepared an attack on Krabos and after a long siege captured and sacked it: he took the inhabitants to the nearby lake and drowned them as atheists.

From these fragments it has generally been agreed that the overland march of Mopsos-Moxos is the traditional expression of the events otherwise known to us from Egyptian archive-propaganda, the migrations which destroyed the Hittite empire and such city-states as Ugarit, and ended with the settlement of the Philistines on the border of Egypt. The peoples recorded[25] as participating in this migration, which reached Egypt in the 1190's or so, are the Danuna or Danaoi, the Pelesata or Philistines, the Tjikar (Tjikal), the Shardana of the Sea, the Washasha of the Sea, the Shakarusha, and the Turusha of the Sea. The Danuna are represented in the literary tradition by Mopsos-Moxos, and the Pelesata presumably by Askalos, an eponym who has, apparently, replaced the historical name of the Philistine leader. The details in the literary tradition seem on the whole to agree: the great dearth, for example, may be the historical famine mentioned by Merneptah of Egypt (around 1220), when he sent corn-ships to the Hittites. The oracle mentioned by Nikolaos may be the same as that which, according to Herodotus,[26] established the Herakleid dynasty in Lydia. Krabos, where Moxos

---

[23] This name is sometimes emended to ⟨T⟩ymenaios, on the assumptions that the unlocated Phrygian mountain Tymenaion (Steph. Byz. s.v.) had an eponym, and was relevant. But if the evidence (Laroche, 'Recherches sur les noms divins hittites' in *Revue hittite et asianique* VII (1945) p.109) is confirmed that the chief Hittite god was Humunna, the name Hymenaios will stand.
[24] Jac 90 F 16.
[25] Papyrus Harris and Medinet Habu: Breasted *Anc. Rec.* IV.
[26] I 7.

drowned the atheists, has been taken as an error for Nerabos, a 'city of Syria' also mentioned by Nikolaos,[27] but this is unnecessary: the name may be found in that of the Καρβοκομηταί,[28] a community in Roman times at the north-east corner of the Limnai near Antioch in Pisidia, on the horse-road to the east.

It thus appears that the Egyptian records tell us of the final episodes in the migrations from the fall of the Hittite empire on-wards; the Greek traditions come to a halt with the main Danaan settlement, in Kilikia; the Asiatic toponyms and literary tradition trace the route from Moxoupolis and Hierapolis-Kerara to Karbo-kome, but dissolve into cultic myth in Palestine; the Hittites give us the beginning of Moxos' career and, probably, the starting-point of his operations in Karkisa. From the report of Arnuwandas III we gather that Mopsos had begun his career before 1215 B.C.; from the fact that his tomb was shown in Megarsos, we gather that he did not reach Palestine in the 1180's. His career should thus fall, approxi-mately, within the years 1220–1185, and the date 1184/3 given by Jerome is as accurate as any non-archival date can hope to be.

It is $23 \times 26 = 598 = 39 \times 15\frac{1}{3}$ years before 586/5, the year of the eclipse battle between Lydia and Media, after which Syennesis of Kilikia and Nebuchadnezzar of Babylon arranged the peace terms. It is also $442 = 39 \times 11\frac{1}{3}$ years before 'the accession of Midas' (after the battle of Musasir in which Urartian power was fatally weakened) in 742/1 B.C. It would appear that Hellenistic research in Kilikia was able to discover archives back to 742/1, and a reliable oriental poly-gamous genealogy for the house of Mopsos; and to construct a chronographic equation upon this information.

2. Herakleid Lydia

The date of Mopsos' departure from Lydia provides a *terminus ante* for the fall of Troy, and a *terminus post* for the accession of the Herakleid dynasty. It seems possible, and perhaps likely, that Eratos-thenes fixed the date of Troy with the Mopsos evidence in mind. So far as can be seen however he did not discuss Lydian dates:[29] and their inclusion in the general Eratosthenic system was probably due to *Kastor*. It is a question therefore what date *Kastor* gave to the acces-sion of the Herakleids.

---

[27] Jac 90 F 17.
[28] Ramsay, *Classical Review* XIX (1905) pp.417 f.
[29] *Klio* 41 (1963) p.67.

Hellanikos' date of 1221 B.C. is much too early for those who dated Troy to 1184/3, and the Eusebian documents preserve only the last part of *Kastor's* Lydian list, from 777/6 onwards: not counting Croesus (because he is historical) this gives a period of $216 = 27 \times 8$ years for eight kings. *Kastor's* date for the first Herakleid therefore would have to provide for 22 kings before Gyges, παῖς παρὰ πατρός, and was probably $27x$ years before 777/6.

The most intractable part of the material would be the genealogical, and Hellanikos-Herodotus had assigned to these 22 kings the total of $(23 \times 22) -1$ years from 1221 to 717, with Gyges beginning his 38-year reign in 716. This implies that Gyges was a generation younger than his predecessor: the implication is unnecessary, and contrary to the spirit of the story of Candaules' queen. *Kastor* was therefore free to assign to the Herakleids a generation less than Hellanikos had done, above his own accession date for Gyges in 698/7. The generation thus excluded might either be one of the full 23-year generations or the odd 22-year 'generation': the accession-date for the Herakleids would then be ⟨1182/1⟩ or ⟨1181/0⟩, and the former is more likely as being $405 = 27 \times 15$ years before the beginning of the surviving fragment of *Kastor's* list in 777/6. We then have:

1184/3:   fall of Troy and departure of Mopsos with the Danaans; Akiamos of Lydia (presumably the successor of the tyrant Meles) orders Askalos to Syria.

⟨1182/1⟩:   accession of the Herakleid dynasty by appointment of the oracle, $621 = 27 \times 23$ years before Croesus' accession in 561/0; $99 = 27 \times 3\frac{2}{3}$ years before the beginning of the Pelasgian thalassocracy in 1083/2; $104 = 39 \times 2\frac{2}{3}$ years before the Amazon-Kimmerian devastation of 1078/7, and $130 = 39 \times 3\frac{1}{3}$ years before Magnesia and Kyme in 1052/1.

1175/4:   beginning of the Lydo-Maionian thalassocracy with the disappearance of Aeneas' fleet from the historical scene.

The large remaining question of *Kastor's* historiography of Lydia in Mopsos' time is his treatment of the Maionian entry in Homer's Trojan Catalogue. It is not necessary to take for granted that such rulers of the Lydians as Meles and Akiamos were also, for *Kastor*, rulers of the Maiones; and conversely it is not necessary to suppose that he thought of Homer's Maionian leaders (Mesthles and Antiphos, sons of Talaimenes and the Gygaian lake) as rulers of the Lydians.

There are some hints that the Lydian, as distinct from the Maionian, homeland lay south of the Hermos, in the Morsynos valley. On the road up that valley was Aphrodisias, formerly Ninoe,[30] where there was a cult of Zeus Nineudios:[31] this name is no doubt in some way connected with that of Ninos father of Agron, the first of the Herakleid kings. The coins[32] of Aphrodisias-Ninoe sometimes bear the device of the double-axe, and this device also appears over the hills eastwards at Herakleia-Salbake,[33] sometimes also with a goddess, reminiscent of Herakles' gift of the Amazon double-axe to Omphale.[34] It is thus quite likely that *Kastor* (no doubt anticipated to some degree by Xanthos and the Pergamenes) brought the Herakleids from the Morsynos-Salbakon area[35] to Maionia under Mt. Tmolos, and that his Lydo-Maionian kingdom, founded in ⟨1182/1⟩, was a composite entity.

*   *   *

3. thalassocracy and the Tyrrhenes

Within this kingdom, we are to assume, there was an element which exercised the thalassocracy that *Kastor* names Lydo-Maionian, What immediately leaps to the mind in this connection is of course the Herodotean story[36] of the Tyrrhenian emigration from Lydia through the port of Smyrna. There are however difficulties: the emigration is a single event, not a period of thalassocracy; it is dated to pre-Herakleid times which means certainly not later than Mopsos and probably earlier than Troy; it was not mentioned by Xanthos of Lydia,[37] but is apparently a discovery of Herodotus' own.

The use of Smyrna as the port of emigration implies that the people who emigrated came chiefly from the Hermos valley, especially its lower reaches round Mt. Sipylos. Consequently, we receive no help from Homer, who does not mention this area: his Maiones live higher up the valley, under Mt. Tmolos. Xanthos himself

---

[30] Ramsay, *Cities and Bishoprics* I 187 f.
[31] *op. cit.* p.154 f.: another form of the name, Zeus Noneuleus, is found at Dionysopolis to the north (for the site see Calder and Bean, *Classical Map of Asia Minor*, supplement to *Anatolian Studies* VII (1957).
[32] Head HN² 609.
[33] Head HN² 609.
[34] Halliday *Plutarch's Greek Questions* 185 ff.
[35] Which is not far from the Indos valley and Moxoupolis.
[36] I 94.
[37] Jac 765 F 16.

however[38] is quoted for an important correction of the usual Greek tales of Mt. Sipylos (which were concerned with Tantalos, his daughter Niobe, and her husband Amphion). Xanthos' story is a variant of this tale, but about Assaon, his daughter Elyme, and her husband Philottos of Assyria. Xanthos' story is probably quoted from the version given by his editor Menippos, and is certainly Graecised;[39] like the Niobe story it probably began as a cultic myth, and the divinity of Mt. Sipylos was the Meter Plastene.[40] Xanthos certainly therefore had something to say about the people of the Sipylos area, and this included a connection with 'Assyria': as the name Assaon looks like a rendering of the Hittite Assuwa, so Plastene and Philottos look like renderings of the name of the Philistines or Pelethites of Palestine, who were in the Assyrian empire and sphere of influence for some time. It seems therefore that Herodotus discovered a story about the sea-borne part of the Philistine migration and identified it with the Tyrrhenian: Xanthos treated of the landward part of this migration in his stories of Mopsos and Askalos[41] and did not recognize a Tyrrhenian migration from this area. It seems clear that the Sipylos area and the port of Smyrna cannot in Lydian—and consequently in Pergamene or derivative—tradition have been regarded as Tyrrhenian.

Nevertheless, it seems entirely likely that *Kastor's* Lydo-Maionian thalassocracy names the same entity or activity as in our other sources is called the period of Tyrrhenian piracy, the most effective piratical regime in the history of the Aegean.[42] If this is so, we must suppose that by using the name Λύδοι οἱ καὶ Μαίονες, *Kastor* meant to emphasize not only the composite nature of the old Lydo-Maionian kingdoms, but also that, in his view, the Tyrrhenians (at least in the period 1175/4–1084/3) were distinct from the Pelasgoi.

Apart from Herodotus, the Greek tradition about the Tyrrhenians knows of the Herakleid Telephos and his sons Tyrsenos and Tarchon in the Kaikos valley and the port of Gryneion. The stories begin in the

---

[38] Jac 765 F 20.
[39] In addition to the motifs of the Niobe story, there is the frequent late Greek motif of incest.
[40] Paus. V 13.7 and the inscriptions quoted in Frazer's commentary. It will be the Meter Plastene who is replaced by Leto in the Greek version.
[41] Whether he also treated of the sea-borne part of the migration is not clear. Tantalos, as brother of Askalos should also be a Philistine: it is obscure whether this is derived from the Greek or the Lydian story.
[42] Strabo X 4.9.

Odyssey,[43] where Odysseus tells the ghost of Achilles how his son killed Eurypylos son of Telephos, and many of his Keteioi. In the *Kypria*,[44] the Greeks landed by mistake in Teuthrania instead of the Troad, Telephos killed Thersandros of Thebes and was wounded by Achilles: after the Greeks withdrew, Telephos had to go to Greece to be healed of his wound by Achilles. Probably the *Kypria* made Telephos (like the Cypriote ancestors Agapenor and Kepheus) of Arcadian descent: in the Hesiodic Catalogue[45] this is accepted, together with Telephos' affiliation to Herakles, the adoption of his mother as a daughter by Teuthras, and the kingship of Telephos over the Mysians who replace Homer's Keteioi. Hekataios[46] is the earliest surviving source for the name of Telphos' mother Auge (sister of Kepheus), the *larnax* story, and the localization in the Kaikos valley, but these were probably all in the *Kypria*. Later sources add that Achilles fought Telephos at Gryneion,[47] and wounded him because Dionysus caused him to trip or become entangled in a vine; and various genealogical details may be conveniently tabulated:

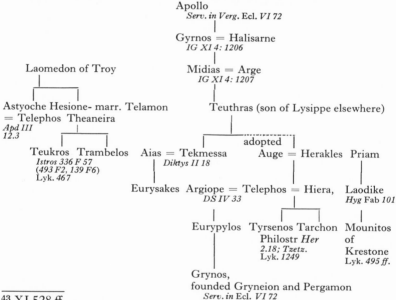

Apollo
Serv. in Verg. Ecl. VI 72

Gyrnos = Halisarne
IG XI 4: 1206

Laomedon of Troy

Midias = Arge
IG XI 4: 1207

Astyoche Hesione- marr. Telamon
= Telephos Theaneira
Apd III 12.3

Teuthras (son of Lysippe elsewhere)

adopted

Teukros Trambelos Aias = Tekmessa
Istros 336 F 57
(493 F2, 139 F6)
Lyk. 467

Diktys II 18

Auge = Herakles Priam

Eurysakes Argiope = Telephos = Hiera, Laodike
DS IV 33

Hyg Fab 101

Eurypylos Tyrsenos Tarchon Mounitos
Philostr Her
2.18; Tzetz.
Lyk. 1249

of

Krestone
Lyk. 495 ff.

Grynos,
founded Gryneion and Pergamon
Serv. in Ecl. VI 72

---

[43] XI 528 ff.
[44] According to Proclus' summary.
[45] Pap. Oxy XI 1359 = Hesiod F 165 MW.
[46] Jac 1 F 29.
[47] Steph. Byz. s.v. Grynoi, Scylax 98.

Leaving aside the various elaborations of Telephos' biography by the Attic tragedians, the main body of the material here is probably Pergamene, as is shown by the termination of the genealogy in Grynos (of whom the earlier Gyrnos is presumably a variant[48]). Halisarne and Teuthras are also eponyms of places; Arge and Argiope were probably suggested by the meaning of the name of Auge, who should be a derivative of the Sun-goddess known in Hittite times: Herakles similarly here should represent the weather-god. Telephos' own name has frequently been derived from that of Telipinu or Telipi,[49] an agricultural[50] god of the Hittites, who was a son of the Sun-goddess and the Weather-god. Hiera should, by her name, represent another goddess: her story was that when the Greeks arrived she mobilised the 'Mysian' women and led them, herself riding a horse: she was killed by Nireus.[51] Of her sons, Tyrsenos is the Tyrrhenian eponym, and Tarchon is Tarhun, the Weather-god particularly worshipped by the neo-Hittite states.[52] Mounitos of Krestone apparently represents the Tyrrhenes reported there by Herodotus.[53] Teukros is Homeric, but Trambelos of Lesbos and Miletos is, for us at least, Hellenistic and interesting: his name seems to be a version of that of the Trm̃mili of Lykia (which the Greeks usually rendered as Tremilai or Termilai) and who claimed, like the Teukroi, Cretan origins.[54] Trojan princesses are of course natural choices for wives for Telephos the ally of Troy, but Hesione's name makes her originally the daughter of Asia or Asios, and perhaps in origin she belonged to Assuwa rather than to Troy.

The Tyrrhenes of the Kaikos valley have therefore, in the Greek sources, an epic origin and a continuously growing history worked up in Cyprus, Athens, and Pergamon: that is, a general acceptance in the literary tradition, quite unlike the Herodotean Tyrrhenes of the

---

[48] And in the table above identified with Grynos father of Midias.

[49] First by Hrozny and Kretschmer: not disallowed by Laroche op.cit. p.34.

[50] Which suits the story of Dionysus and the vine.

[51] Since he ἀλάπαδνος ἔην, he was apparently thought a suitable victor over a women warrior.

[52] M. Kalac, 'Das Pantheon der Hieroglyphischen-luwischen Inschriften' in Orientalia 34 (1965) 401 ff. Tarhun, 'the hero', was also known in the Hittite empire: Laroche, op. cit. p.89.

[53] I 57.

[54] Hdt. I 173.

Hermos Valley. We should suppose that *Kastor* shared this view: the Kaikos valley is well within the territory of the Maiones, being south of the plain of Thebe.

This tradition provides three names of populations: Keteioi, Tyrsenoi or Tyrrhenes, and Mysians. The name Keteioi appears only in the Odyssey, and may be the Greek rendering of the name of Hatti, though whether in this remote north-western corner of Asia the name would refer to a Hattic or a Hittite population is not clear. The Mysians are the historical population: the name is held by Strabo to be of Thracian origin, and the Mysians succeeded the Maiones on the Plain of Thebe. The name of the Tyrrhenes themselves is known to us first in the later thirteenth century, when Merneptah of Egypt reports a contingent of Tursha among the Peoples of the Sea:[55] he records that over seven hundred were killed. In the 1180/70's, Rameses III barely mentions Tursha among the Philistines:[56] it seems that by this time the Tyrrhenes had lost interest in the Levant, and the stories of Tyrrhenian piracy and Lydo-Maionian thalassocracy, suggest that they were busy in the Aegean.[57] Thus in the three names of populations in the Greek traditions we seem in fact to have three periods: the first is that of the Keteioi, Hatti or Hittites (down to the time of Eurypylos); the second is that of the Tyrrhenes as part of Lydo-Maionia; and the third that of the Mysians. If the Tursha of Merneptah about 1220 are rightly identified with the Tyrrhenes, then perhaps there was no change of population, but only of political allegiance, between the first and second periods; the arrival of the Mysians is undated, but was before about 750, when they are mentioned by Araras of Carchemish.[58]

Most of the Greek stories about the most effective period of piracy in the Aegean will have been told in the east-Greek and island local histories, which are lost to us. Their character may however be

---

[55] Breasted, *Ancient Records* III 574 ff. The other contingents were Achaian, Lykian, Shakrusha and Shardana.

[56] Rameses III at the Medinet Habu: Breasted IV 129. Vocalization of the name of the Tursha: W. F. Albright, 'Some oriental glosses on the Homeric problem' AJA 54 (1950) p. 162 ff.

[57] So also (but with different inferences) G. A. Wainwright, 'The Teresh, The Etruscans, and Asia Minor' in *Anatolian Studies* IX (1959), 197 ff.

[58] H. T. Bossert, 'Zur Geschichte von Karkamis' in *Studi Classici et Orientali* (Pisa 1951).

illustrated in one which survives:[59] Eurystheus, the last Perseid (Danaan) king of Mycenae had a daughter Admete, who was priestess of Hera Argeia. When she fled to Samos she took with her the ancient xoanon of the goddess, and the Argives, wishing to recover it, asked the Tyrrhenes to attack Samos. The story shows a situation in which the Danaans themselves (one of the Peoples of the Sea) have lost command of the sea, and perhaps also the means of sea-borne communications, to the Tyrrhenes.

The oldest surviving document on Tyrrhenian piracy is the Homeric hymn to Dionysus, where the god is kidnapped for sale in Egypt, Cyprus, or to the Hyperboreans. This seems to reflect, with some wilful exaggeration, a situation in which the sale of a single personable youth would pay for the longest voyage, and so belongs presumably to the period when the piractical regime was dying of the poverty it had helped to create. The hymn continues with the story of how the god turned the ship's mast into a vine, and the pirates threw themselves overboard and became dolphins. We are reminded of the stories that Mopsos drowned Fish and his mother in the lake at Askalon, and that he drowned the atheists of Krabos in the nearby lake: it would seem that among the Peoples of the Sea there was a belief that the dead—or at least the drowned—became fish or dolphins.

Another variant of this connection between Dionysus, death, and deep waters appears at Lerna in the Argolid. In this story,[60] Dionysus is Cretan and leader of the Pelagiai, the Women of the Sea. We may suspect that the Pelegiai are feminine only because they follow in Dionysus' rout, and their legend is used as the *aition* for the ritual at Lerna, where Dionysus dived through the lake to Hades, to bring his mother to immortality in Olympos.

Also in the Argolid, the cultic myth of Athena Salpinx specifically names Tyrrhenes and Lydians. The *salpinx* from which this Athena takes her surname is said to have been Tyrrhenian,[61] introduced by

---

[59] Menedotos Jac 541 F 1. This story should mean that the period of Tyrrhenian piracy, or Lydo-Maionian thalassocracy, should correspond in its beginning to the archaeological date for the end of Mycenaean pottery in Samos.
[60] Paus. II 20.4; 22.1; 23.7; 37.5. In the Argive version of the story Perseus the Danaan of Mycenae beat off the Dionysiac horde; in the Kilikian version, Perseus fled from Mycenae and founded Tarsos.
[61] Paus. II 21.3.

Hegesileos son of Tyrrhenos, or by Archondas,[62] or by Μήλας son of Herakles and Omphale of Lydia, who ἐν τῇ καθόδῳ τῶν Ἡρακλειδῶν σαλπίζων κατέπληξε τοὺς πολεμίους,[63] much as the trumpets dealt with Jericho near the Philistine country.

In the Argolid therefore it appears that tales of the period of the Peoples of the Sea, and of Tyrrhenian piracy, were firmly attached to certain cults, including even that of Hera Argeia and her priestess Admete.[64] The connection with the Return of the Herakleids or the Dorian invasion is on the other hand rather loose: Hegesileos-Archondas is a great-grandson of Herakles and ally of Herakles's grandson's grandson Temenos, which is orthodox; but Μήλας is Herakles's son and was presumably therefore active in the 'first' Return, during which Tlepolemos was expelled to Rhodes,[65] and which was ended by dearth and plague. We gain the strong impression that these stories were originally quite independent of the Dorian cycle of traditions, and refer to the last period of Mycenae, say 1250–1150.

The name of Μήλης is particularly important, since it is the personal name which Greek tradition regarded as typically Tyrrhenian or Lydian. Hipponax (F 40) knew a Lydian god Malis. In Attika, the ritual of the Dionysiac Aiora finds its *aition* in the story of the Tyrrhenian Maleos or Maleotes and his daughter Aletis.[66] Malis was the slave of Omphale who bore Akeles to Herakles;[67] Μήλης of Sardis had a concubine who bore him a lion child that guaranteed the

---

[62] Schol. Soph. Ajax 17; Suidas s.v. κώδων. Radke in Roscher s.v. Tyrsenos emends Archondas to ⟨T⟩ archondas (which would represent the Hittite genitive Tarhuntas, while Tarchon represents the accusative Tarhun): but Hegesileos looks like a 'translation' of Archondas.

[63] Schol. Hom *Iliad* 18.219.

[64] The period of rule by the Danaans at Mycenae, universally recognized as of outstanding importance in Greek historiography (apart from Homer's use of the name, Herodotus in expounding his Pelasgian theory makes the *Danaans* introduce cults and divine names generally), is not necessarily placed rightly when it is made earlier than the rule of the Pelopids. If Agamemnon's Trojan War is to be dated before the middle of the thirteenth century, the Danaan kings of Mycenae should perhaps be later.

[65] Apd. *Epitome*.

[66] Hesych. s.v. Aiora; *Et. Mag.* 62.7. Strabo V 225 goes so far as to bring this Tyrrhenian from Regisvilla near Volci in Italian Etruria. Other accounts called the hero Ikarios of the deme Ikarieis.

[67] Hellanikos 4 F 112: Akeles is Herodotus' Alkaios.

impregnability of his citadel;[68] Μήλης of Lydia was a tyrant put down by Moxos;[69] a Herakleid Μήλης, perhaps the same as the lion's father, ruled at Sardis;[70] Μηλιας was a daughter of Mopsos the Lydian;[71] Apollo Maloeis was worshipped in Lesbos,[72] where Metas the Tyrrhenian was eponym of Metaon;[73] Malaos was synoecist with Kleues son of Doros the Agamemnonid at Kyme, and a Malaos was oecist of Temnos in Aiolis;[74] Μᾶλος was ancestor of Asklepios,[75] whose cult-centres in Caria and the islands were notable. It can hardly be doubted that in the name thus rendered by the Greeks we have a reflection of some typical Tyrrhenian and Lydian cult-figures to whom human stories (as in the case of Telipinu-Telephos) could readily be attributed.

The Hittite evidence provides the name Maliya and its derivatives, which have not yet been thoroughly analysed, and which therefore are difficult to compare with the Greek stories. The name is chiefly known from toponymics: these include the river Maliya, which was both divine itself, and had gods. Other gods, the Maliyannas, may have been gods of the vine,[76] which would accord well with the Dionysus and Telephos of the Tyrrhenian stories. The river Maliya appears in a closely-knit divine company, composed of Pirwa the Lady, a goddess represented by the allogram ISTAR, and the goddesses Kamrusepa and Asgasepa, both of whom are connected with horses,[77] like Hiera the wife of Telephos. Maliya was apparently also the name of a goddess, who like Asgasepa and Pirwa, was the Queen.[78] Kamrusepa, the goddess of health and horses, was the mother of Aruna, the sea,[79] who in turn was the mother of Hatepinu, the wife of Telepinu-Telipi.[80] When further work has been done on

---

[68] Hdt. I 84.
[69] Nikolaos of Damascus 90 F 16.
[70] 90 F 45.
[71] Theopompos 115 F 111.
[72] Hellanikos 4 F 34.
[73] Steph. Byz. s.v.
[74] Steph. Byz. s.v. Temnos.
[75] Isyllos of Epidauros: *Anth. Lyr.* VI 284 Diehl.
[76] Laroche *op. cit.* p. 85.
[77] Laroche pp.87, 68. Asgasepa's name may mean 'goddess of the entry' and so is reminiscent of Eurypylos.
[78] Laroche p.104.
[79] Laroche p.72.
[80] Laroche p.24.

this divine complex, we shall perhaps be able to speak more surely on Telephos, Hiera, and the names Meles-Malaos-Melias. The appearance of oecists of this name at Kyme and Temnos suggests that these settlements were not Greek innovations, but that groups of Greeks settled with the population on sites already occupied. In Lesbos especially, the name of Mytilene seems to be derived from that of Mu(wa)tila, one of the principal epithets of the Hittite Weather-god[81] as the god of the 'strength of life'.

Such Greek stories as survive therefore speak not only of intense Tyrrhenian piracy, but also of strong religious influence in Attika and the Argolid, connected especially with Dionysus but also involving Athena Salpinx and Hera Argeia. The archaeological evidence from the Aegean shows, in the twelfth and earlier eleventh centuries, 'the sort of cultural break which betokens either complete abandonment or considerable depopulation'.[82] In some places, notably Karphi in Crete, there were refugee settlements almost inaccessible to the inhabitants and certainly so to alien marauders. But Mycenae survived, in a dwindled way, to about 1150; Knossos in Crete, an open city, continued to be inhabited; Athens and Salamis were apparently never conquered either by pirates or by Dorians. It may not be coincidence that Attika and the Argolid are credited with some Tyrrhenian inhabitants, and that Crete was the home of the Teukroi and Termilai, 'kinsmen' of the Tyrrhenes. Looked at from another point of view, this means that the Tyrrhenes and allied peoples ended the seaborne communications of the Achaians and Danaans in the Aegean, and themselves ruled the seas with a network from Crete to the Argolid, Salamis and Athens, but based mainly in Lydo-Maionia and the offshore islands.

Greek historiography in general (especially perhaps in Hellanikos and Herodotus) notoriously identifies or confuses the Tyrrhenes and the Pelasgoi. *Kastor*, if we have understood him aright, clearly distinguished them: for him the Tyrrhenes were Asiatic (though with Achaian admixture in Telephos son of the Arcadian Auge, and with Cretan 'kinsmen') while the Pelasgoi come from Greece (though

---

[81] Laroche p.110; Kalac s.v. It has frequently been supposed that the god of Lazpa who was summoned to heal the sick Mursilis II (1345–1315) was from Lesbos, and Muwatila would be very suitable to such a function.
[82] Boardman p.43.

through Attika where some Tyrrhenes lived): the Pelasgoi thus represent the beginnings of the movement which, through the Magnetes, the Dorians, the Neleids and the Aioleis of Kyme and Smyrna, led to the restoration of the Aegean as a Greek sea. Such a view would not prevent an admission by Kastor that the Pelasgoi of the thalassocratic period included some Tyrrhenes or persons of Tyrrhenian descent, and he may have conceded as much to the older theories.

Although the Tyrrhenian detail in the Greek traditions is scattered and inconclusive, and often from very late sources, there is not only more of it than might be expected, but also it tends to be coherent and informative in itself, and to have apparently excellent connections with our growing knowledge of the Anatolian cultures. Tentatively, and while awaiting further knowledge, it seems reasonable to accord a degree of historicity to *Kastor*'s first thalassocracy, at, approximately, the dates he gives – that is, from the time of Mopsos to about the beginning of the Protogeometric period. That period itself then corresponds to the much more dubious thalassocracies of the Pelasgoi, Thrace in Europe, and Thrace in Asia.

PART 3

GENERAL HISTORIOGRAPHY OF THE THALASSOCRACIES

BOTH *Kephalion* AND *Kastor*, in their chronographic constructions, show a major periodization in the ninth century. In *Kephalion*'s version, this appears in the 39-year reckoning between Phrygia and Cyprus: the period is not also represented in the 27-year construction. In *Kastor*'s calculation however, where the second 39-year reckoning begins with Phoenicia, a 27-year reckoning sub-period also begins at the same point, so that the date of 819/8 and the periodization are emphatic. We have traced this back to a synchronism between the rise of Phoenicia to thalassocracy, and the fall of Assyria which liberated Media and Babylon from The Empire of Upper Asia. That is to say, Phoenicia in 819/8 is a major point at which *Kastor* brought together the two parts of his Ἀναγραφὴ Βαβυλῶνος καὶ Θαλασσοκρατη-σάντων. We should therefore expect *Kephalion*'s ninth-century periodization with Cyprus in 865/4 to have a similar meaning for his general historiographic view, though no evidence survives for what this might have been. Only if we believe that *Kastor* thought of Cyprus succeeding a Phrygia which was losing its European posses-sions to Karanos of Macedon; and that *Kephalion* followed him in this synchronism and made it central to his construction and historio-graphy, should we have a possible explanation. But it is a tempting explanation, for it seems clear that *Kephalion* abandoned not only Babylon but other close associations with oriental archives: and the Greek mainland tradition of Herakleid (and so Temenid and Mace-donian) genealogies is the obvious alternative, to partner the thalas-socracies in a general historiographic scaffolding.

Kastor's periodization (and so, derivatively, *Kephalion*'s) looks to the modern eye as though its main effect is to distinguish between the Dark and later Ages: and there is probably some truth in this, in spite of the fact that *Kastor*'s periodization is certainly in another aspect more sophisticated, distinguishing between the Traditional, Archival (and poetically contemporarily witnessed), and the Historical periods. *Kephalion* shares the simpler modern view, which shows that it is a possible way to understand *Kastor*, even if the witness is not impressive.

A. The Traditional Thalassocracies

It seems therefore worth while to set out *Kastor*'s Traditional thalassocracies together with events which he seems to have dated in their times, and with the modern archaeologists' periods by pottery sequences:

LH III C

1184/3 MOPSOS   Fall of Troy
(1183/2 Aeneas)

1175/4 LYDO-MAIONES

1160/59	last year of Pelasgos in Sikyon
1144/3	Amazons burn Ephesos
⟨1124/3	Boiotian Return⟩
⟨1104/3	Herakleid Return⟩
⟨1092/1⟩	Ionian Aigialeis flee to Attika (?and expel the Pelasgoi?)

PROTO-GEOMETRIC

1083/2 PELASGOI

⟨1083/2	Pelasgoi succeed Minyai in Lemnos⟩
1078/7	Amazons and Kimmerioi devastate Asia
⟨?1077	foundation of the cities of Lesbos?⟩
⟨1074/3	Dorian Thera⟩
1052/1	Kyme and Magnesia founded
1045/4	Ionian Ephesos founded
1044/3	Neleid Miletos founded
1036/5	Ionian Samos founded

998/7 THRACE IN EUROPE

979/8 THRACE IN ASIA 979/8 Bebrykes from the Strymon Valley arrive in Asia

⟨976/5 Samians in Samothrace⟩

167

900/899 RHODES   ⟨Rhode, Parthenope, Elpiai etc founded⟩

GEOMETRIC

877/6 PHRYGIA

852/1 CYPRUS   (? Karanos takes the European
possessions of Phrygia?)

As soon as such a tabulation is made, *Kastor*'s difficulties, and ours are clear. The first three entries are of Mopsos, Troy and Aeneas. The first is archaeologically (and epigraphically?) confirmed; the archaeological evidence for the second puts its date some eighty or more years earlier; the story of Aeneas has a long constructive and poetic development which—whatever its original roots—really takes it out of the ambit of history altogether. Consequently, we are informed by this that *Kastor* drew (necessarily) upon very unequal sources, and nothing can be trusted without archaeological confirmation.

One of the modern questions is therefore the possibilities of archaeological confirmation, apart from the epigraphical which is hardly to be expected for some centuries after Mopsos' time. Direct archaeological evidence for any thalassocracy of this period is scarcely to be looked for, unless a pirate's hoard of Mycenaean heirlooms is found at Gryneion (for the Lydo-Maionian Tyrrhenes), or in other places for the Pelasgoi and their successors. The kind of event which might be archaeologically evidenced is the burning of Ephesos (though this would probably tell us nothing of the Amazons) or a devastation of Asia, or the foundations of Greek settlements, though the Proto-Geometric period is long, and exact dates within it scarcely available. Perhaps the most interesting single confirmation or rejection would be that of the arrival of the Bebrykes (at Lampsakos and its neighbourhood), carrying the Phrygian name in the tenth century and no earlier—for now that Mita of Pahhuwa is known in the thirteenth century, Assyrian mentions of Mita of Muski no longer mean, necessarily, that the Phrygians arrived as the Hittites fell. In fact, in contrast to this recently modern view, *Kastor* envisages first, a Lydo-Maionian parallel to the neo-Hittite states of Syria; then an ill-defined and (apparently) ill-organized Pelasgian period based on islands, arising from or during devastations of the Lydo-Maionian area and leading to extensive Greek settlements; and only after this the appearance, and arrival in Asia, of the Thracian peoples, Bebrykes and Phrygians. Any tendency to reliance on this, without archaeological confirmation, is however abruptly checked by the 'Rhodian

168

thalassocracy', the date for which (as we have seen) might have been provided by the Tyrian archive, while the probable content of it is some two to three centuries too early.

B. The Eastern Adventure

The thalassocracies of Phrygia and Cyprus form a sub-period in *Kastor*'s 27-year calculation for the Eastern Adventure, and it is natural to ask how he connected these two powers in particular. Between Rhodes and Cyprus, 'Phrygia' presumably means especially Kilikia and the Danaans there, who share their name with Adana in Kilikia and Iadnana or Cyprus. Much remains to be discovered about these Danaans, apart from Asitawandas' inscription in the eighth century, and occasional mentions elsewhere, such as the Assyrian record of assistance to the Hittites of Sam'al against the Dnnym about 841.[1] Greek historiography and mythography—after Homer— had much to say of the Danaans, and some of these statements are more naturally to be connected with the Levantine than with the Argive representatives of the name: their importance, for example in the Heroic age of Rhodian Lindos and connection with the cult of Athena Lindia,[2] or the statement that Bebryke was a daughter of Danaos,[3] and the connection of the eponymous names of Danaos and Danae with such mythical persons as Akrisios (who shares his name with Akrisias: Kronos among the Phrygians[4]) and Proitos, who seems to share his name with Phrygians called Proitavos.[5] The importance of some of these apparently Asiatic stories to the (reconstructed) history of heroic Mycenae suggests an Asiatic-Danaan contribution of some substance to Ionian and Hesiodic epic—and this is supported, to some degree, by the appearance of the *Kypria*, presumably at the time when Euboian trade to Al Mina brought some close associations between oral literatures. If we are right therefore in thinking that

---

[1] Barnett, *Anatolian Studies* III pp. 87 ff.
[2] Jac. 239 A9.
[3] Dion. Perieg. 805.
[4] Hesych. s.v. Ἀκρίσιας.
[5] A. H. Sayce in JHS 46 (1926) pp. 31 ff. The famous story of the purification of the Proitides by Melampous, whose name is 'black foot', who threw the off-scourings into a river, and married one of the Proitides, seems also to be Asiatic in origin, for a Hittite magical text tells of a magic for restoring sexuality, in which the patient is dressed in a black shirt and black gaiters etc., and these are afterwards thrown into a river: O. R. Gurney, *The Hittites* p.161.

Kastor may have derived his dates for Rhodes, Phrygia, and Cyprus from the Tyrian archive, then it seems likely that the archive was speaking of Dorians and Danaans in Rhodes, and Danaans in 'Phrygia' and Cyprus: and something of this, reinforced by Greek tradition, may be reflected in *Kastor*'s sub-periodization.

If therefore we look at *Kastor*'s Dark Age historiography as a whole we observe that his Asiatic and island thalassocracies are indeed dovetailed into a single structure with such orthodoxies as the Herakleid Return and the Ionian Migration, but also that this dovetailing was necessary: there seems to have been a largely independent Asiatic tradition. What we cannot tell is how much this apparently independent tradition has been treated to fit in with the orthodoxies: the seeming examples of Rhodes—where we can guess that the date is the date of Dorian piracy at the beginning of the settlement, though the content (because of the orthodoxies) is misplaced—suggests that the independent history might be recoverable with enough archaeological evidence. In other words, the treatment of the Asatic tradition to fit the orthodoxies has probably not hopelessly destroyed that tradition, and we should probably take *Kastor*'s form seriously enough to enquire into it.[5a]

[5a] *Kastor*'s ninth-century thalassocracies in particular are beginning to have some interesting archaeological correlations, as may be seen from J. N. Coldstream's *Greek Geometric Pottery* (London 1968). The arrival of the Dorians in the Dodecanese in the late tenth century is accompanied by some connections with the north Cyclades (p.337) and with Cyprus (p.339): The Cypriote connections continue into the ninth century (p.342). These agree with the traditions of the Dodecanesian Triopas and Phorbas from Thessaly, and with the probability that *Kastor* combined Rhodian material with indications of date from the Phoenician archives. The period which *Kastor* assigns to Phrygia is the time when Assyria devastated the Levant (884–844) and the Thessalo-Cycladic potteries were exported to Macedon and Israel (p.341). The Cypriote thalassocracy correlates not only with the approach of the Euboians to Al Mina, but also with the latest time allowed by the archaeologists to the establishment of the Phoenicians at Kition, so that the suggestion that *Kastor* was here also drawing on the Tyrian archives is supported. *Kastor*'s Phoenician thalassocracy itself correlates with the period when Phoenican black-on-red cosmetic flasks were being imported to the Dodecanese (p.346) and ivories were being dedicated in the Idaian cave in Crete (p.347).

Thus by contrast with the 'Egyptian thalassocracy' in the eighth century, *Kastor*'s ninth-century history appears to contain information of historical value from an excellent source in the Tyrian archives.

170

C. Thalassocracies and Colonies

With the second half of the thalassocracy lists, we come to the questions of the relationship with the colony foundation dates. In *The Sicilian Colony Dates* we recorded the suspicion that they had passed through the hands of a 'sea-power historian,'[6] and emerged as a tripartite system set out in Table VIII of that book. In the preceding chapters of the present work, we have been able to identify some of the the entries as *Kastor*'s and some not: it is now clear that Table VIII represents *Kephalion*'s system, which includes a very substantial inheritance from *Kastor*. In relation to his thalassocracy dates, we can tabulate *Kephalion*'s remnants as follows:

			from *Kastor*	
865/4	CYPRUS	(?Karanos in Macedon)		
837/6	PHOENICIA			
783/2	EGYPT (?780 Bocchoris)			
			771/0	Pandosia-Metapontion
			762/1	Kyrene I
			758/7	Trotilon-Zankle-Sinope I
			757/6	Kaulonia-Makalla-Kyzikos I
749/8	MILETOS	749/8 Naukratis		
			741/0	Naxos
			736/5	Syracuse-Katane
			732/1	Leontinoi-Maroneia
721/0	CARIA			
		(717/6 Chersonesos)		
	(716/5 Gyges)			
		711/0 Astakos		
			709/8	Kroton-Parion-Sybaris

---

[6] Part I C iii b–c.

		706/5 Taras-Corcyra
		691/0 Gela-Phaselis
	685/4 Chalkedon	
		679/8 Kyzikos II—
		Lokroi
(678/7 Ardys)		
670/69 LESBOS		
	659/8 Byzantium	
	657/6 Istros	
		655/4 Akanthos-
		Stageira-
		Kardia-
		Lampsakos
	(652/1 Akragas)	
		650/49 Selinous
	647/6 Borysthenes	
		632/1 Kyrene II
	631/0 Sinope II	
	(630/29 Lipara)	
		627/6 Epidamnos—
		Kios
(623–611 Lydo-		601/0 Kamarina-
Milesian War)		Perinthos
		598/7 Massilia
		⟨583/2 Akragas⟩

It is certain that Eusebius' date for Byzantium is not from *Kastor*, and most of the other entries in the centre column are highly probable, for reasons already discussed. The most doubtful are the three Sicilian dates, which Eusebius may well have taken from one of his *Olympiades* rather than from *Kephalion*.

It appears that *Kephalion* revised *Kastor* especially in the dates of the Megarian and Milesian colonies in the Propontis and Euxine, placing all the former earlier than Theagenes, and the latter than the Lydo-Milesian War. That the Megarian colonies were earlier than Theagenes probably means that *Kephalion* accepted *Kastor*'s view that the colonists were descendants of the Megarian nobility, and drew from this inferences as to dates which a greater knowledge of Asiatic synchronisms denied to *Kastor*; and something similar has probably happened in the Milesian case. *Kephalion*, that is to say, appears to be working from a greater ignorance than *Kastor*, and combining this with archaism and orthodoxies. In no case does he seem to use *Kastor*'s convention of the east-west pairs of colonies.

These pairings, so prominent and *a priori* inexplicable in the Eusebian entries, now fall into place as an expression, in the details, of the same tendency as is seen in *Kastor*'s pairing of Sikyon and Assyrian in the remote past, and of Babylon and the thalassocrats after Troy. We cannot doubt that *Kastor* deliberately adopted this convention to express a double-edged historiographic conviction: that Greek history was as old, and could be made as exact, as Mesopotamian; and that barbarian traditions and archives could be made to yield as much history as Greek. Within this conviction, the employment of a transparent convention is useful as a constant reminder of the model, non-archival nature of the absolute dates.[7]

Kastor's own synchronisms of thalassocracies and colonies may be tabulated as follows:

819/8 PHOENICIA   Pygmalion conquers Cyprus

        814/3   Carthage

      ⟨?? 776/5 Cumae??⟩

774/3 EGYPT

  –752 Petoubatis

        771/0   Pandosia-Metapontion

        762/1   Kyrene I

        758/7   Trotilon-Zankle-Sinope I

        757/6   Kaulonia-Makalla-Kyzikos I

  751/0 Osorcho

  742/1 Psammous   742/1 Midas

        741/0   Naxos

        736/5   Syracuse-Katane

  732/1 Bocchoris   Leontinoi-Maroneia

  726/5 Ethiopians

---

[7] It is only because of the long barbarizing period which intervenes that we suppose *Kastor* (or Eusebius) to have been unable to compile any composite lists of the kinds we ourselves take for granted. An example to hand is the Table of Hittite Kings on page 216 of Gurney's *The Hittites*, from 1740 to after 1215; a note on page 217 informs us that 'the dates for the Old Kingdom (1740–1460) have to be entirely reconstructed in accordance with the average length for a generation' from that of the death of Mursilis I (1590). We should regard *Kastor*'s dates in the same way.

724/3 MILETOS ⟨724/3 Naukratis⟩
709/8 Kroton-Parion-Sybaris

706/5 CARIA 706/5 Taras-Corcyra⟨-Methone⟩
Lelantine War

698/7 Gyges

696/5 Tarsos
691/0 Gela-Phaselis
679/8 Kyzikos II-Lokroi
676/5 Kimmerians in
670 interregnum? Phrygia
War of Corinth and
662/1 Ardys Corcyra?
655/4 Akanthos, Stageira,
Kardia, Lampsakos
650/49 Selinous
⟨?? 649/8 Kimmerioi
in Lydia and Ionia??⟩

645/4 LESBOS ⟨645/4 Kalchedon⟩
632/1 Kyrene II
628/7 Byzantium
627/6 Epidamnos-Kios
616/5–605/4 War of
Miletos and Lydia
615/4 Panaitios tyrant
in Leontinoi
601/0 ?? interregnum
601/0 Perinthos-Kamarina
598/7 Massilia
⟨583/2 Akragas⟩

577/6 PHOKAIA (Amisos, Alalia) 547/6 fall of Sardis

We have already discussed the sources of *Kastor's* error in ascribing a thalassocracy to Egypt in the eighth century, and the importance of this error in confirming the existence of the 'Euboean lacuna' in Greek tradition. The omission in the Eusebian chronicle of a date for Cumae is of course of quite a different kind, but the general omission of any mention of Al Mina is probably also due to the paucity of the Euboian tradition.

One of the historiographic questions to which we should most

174

like an answer is that of how, in view of the Euboian lacuna, *Kastor* treated of the Lelantine War. He seems to have placed it after the rise of Naxos (first appearing in the name of Sicilian Naxos), Chios (the foundation of Maroneia, Paros and Erythrai (the foundation of Parion), and of course Miletos (the thalassocracy). It is difficult to suppose, with the local histories of all these states before him, that *Kastor* misplaced the *relative* date of the Lelantine War, even though in the same period he dates Naukratis a century too early, and Taras a considerable part of a generation too late. It is obviously conceivable that he misapprehended the relationship between the Lelantine War in the Aegean, and the Greek emigration northwards and eastwards out of which he made the Milesian thalassocracy: they may well have been contemporary, partly as cause and effect. But such a misapprehension would not change the placing of the outbreak of the Lelantine War between, on the one hand, the Chalkidian colonies in Sicily around 730, and on the other the Greek defeats in Kilikia in 696. It remains therefore a question whether the occasions or the causes of the Lelantine War included the removal from the Old Eretria to the New in the period 750–25. The suggestion is rather that this removal was insufficient, and that despite it Chalkis and Eretria came to war in the next generation. This question might be settled if Macedonian Methone were explored and found to date to the same period as Taras, or if the archaeological history of Corcyra were known.

The remnants of *Kastor*'s colony dates have a gap of some fifty years in the Ionian record from the beginning of the Lelantine War, and geographically omit the foundations in Chalkidike. It is not clear that these two gaps are the same, nor what dates *Kastor* gave to the war between Corinth and Corcyra which Thucydides dates about 664: the acceptance of the high date for Selinous may have required a higher date for this war, approximately contemporary with the foundation of Lokroi,[8] and causally connected with a general interregnum in the succession of thalassocratic powers between Caria and Lesbos.

A fairly close connection between the Megarian foundations in the Propontis and the thalassocracy of Lesbos seems clear, and probably also *Kastor* did not carry Milesian colonization (apart from Sinope I, witnessed by Eumelos of Corinth) beyond Kios-Prousias before the war with Lydia. Here again, it seems likely that the relative dating

---

[8] Konon 26 F 1.3.

may be reliable—if only because (archaeologically) the foundation of Naukratis *c.*620 suggests that Milesian interests were not yet mainly directed northwards.

D. Thalassocratic and Orthodox Historiography

It is interesting, important, and informative that *Kastor*'s periodization shows that he did not begin his historical period at the end of the interregnum after the last barbarian thalassocracy, Caria: the late beginning of history in the thalassocracy list is consistent with the Lydian king-list, where only Croesus is historical. When we recognize *Kastor*'s caution in this respect, and nevertheless see how he erred in the Thalassocracy of Egypt, we have full warning about the necessity for understanding the nature of his assertions before accepting any of them.

Nevertheless, the conception of constructing a history of Greece as a history of sea-power, its implications and developments, rather than as a history of polis-organization or a sum of local histories κατὰ γενός, was, and was recognized as, of the highest importance, down to the time of Eusebius with his emphases on his thalassocracy entries by special placings or colours of ink. Diodorus certainly reported the doctrine, whether or not he used its results in his narrative; Strabo and Pliny seem to have *Kastor*'s work as one of the histories to be referred to from time to time; *Kephalion* plainly knew it as thoroughly as his notion of historiography permitted; for Eusebius the thalassocracy doctrine was probably one of the great products of higher learning towards which popular handbooks should direct their readers. But unfortunately for *Kastor*, he produced (it would seem) a work of professional historiography at the beginning of a period of popularization, which itself developed into a process of barbarization; and it is only with the modern development of archaeology, historiography, and the allied social sciences that it is possible to envisage the purposes and scope of his endeavour.

* * *

At the end of the *Sicilian Colony Dates*, we discussed the possibility of considering Greek archaic history with the unifying theme of the history of the international market over this two centuries 760–560 B.C. The thalassocracies should add to our equipment in this respect, but very much more work, from the point of view, needs to be done. The Euboian period 760–695 clearly continues a development already under way: it may be most useful to consider it as the third period in the development of a Greek province of the international market, of which the first two periods would then be those from *c*.900–*c*.819, when Iron-age Greeks made contact with the organization of trade in Phoenicia, Cyprus, Kilikia, Rhodes and Crete, and Athens (about 850) begins to import small luxury goods; and the period *c*.819–*c*.760, when Phoenician influence is paramount, the Danaans adopt Phoenician side by side with their use of Hieroglyphic Hittite, and the Greeks import the alphabet and the mina.

The preceding two centuries of the Proto-Geometric period are divided into the thalassocracies of the Pelasgoi and the Thracians. Archaeologically, this is a period of recovery and technological reconstruction: thalassocratic history concentrates this aspect in the roster of foundations—Dorian, Ionian, Aiolic and Magnesian— while keeping the rule of the sea out of Greek hands. In this respect, thalassocratic history sees the proto-geometric period rather as a consequence of its predecessor than as preparing for the geometric period, when the Dorians of Rhodes break through to the organization of which the Danaans are a part. It is obviously possible that in this view *Kastor* was over-patriotic and gave too much weight to the traditions of his own island: but possibly also final judgement should be reserved until we have evidence of Greek imports and exports in the eleventh and tenth centuries, and until we have much more evidence of how the reconstruction was actually organized.

The latest Mycenaean period corresponds to the thalassocratic Lydo-Maiones or Tyrrhenes, from the expedition of Mopsos onwards. In thalassocratic history this is par excellence the age of piracy; in the archaeological record it is the age of the final devastations in Attika and the Argolid. We have however to remember that as long as late Mycenaean painted pottery continued to be made (however badly) and used, so long did at least a portion of the diminished populations continue to eat off something other than their kitchen ware: there was something left to plunder if it was accessible.

Thus the thalassocratic history, on the whole, follows the same contours as the archaeological history, but often with different senses of direction. The latest Mycenaean period is the great age of piracy, and leads into the less organised proto-Geometric, first under the Pelasgoi and finally under the Thracians, in whose time there seems to be the minimum of organization, Greek or other. The beginning of the new age in thalassocratic history corresponds to the beginning of the Geometric period in archaeology, and proceeds through the Danaans and Phoenicians to the Euboians. Taken at the level of degree of organization (and ignoring questions of the historicity of detail), it is clear that for *Kastor* the Thracian century was the real Dark Age, the second half of the Proto-Geometric period. Why this should be the case for a historian who accepted the orthodox dates for the return in 1104/3 and Ionian in 1044/3, is something of a mystery: it would seem to imply a certain reserve, on *Kastor*'s part, about the alleged Dorian histories and Herakleid genealogies for the period.

BIBLIOGRAPHY

W. F. Albright: 'Some oriental glosses on the Homeric problem'
in AJA 54 (1950) pp. 162 ff.

T. W. Allen: *Homer: The Origins and Transmission* (Oxford 1924)

W. Aly: 'Kastor als quelle Diodors im 7 buch'
in *Rheinisches Museum* 66 (1911) 585 ff.

R. D. Barnett: 'Mopsos' in JHS 73 (1953) pp. 140 ff.
'Karatepe, the key to the Hittite hieroglyphs'
in *Anatolian Studies* III (1953) 87 f.

J. P. Barron: 'Ibycus: *To Polykrates*'
in *Bulletin of the Institute of Classical Studies* 16 (1969) pp. 119 ff.

J. Boardman: 'Tarsus, Al Mina, and Greek Chronology'
in JHS 85 (1965) pp. 5 f.
The Greeks Overseas (London 1964)

H. T. Bossert: 'Zur Geschichte von Karkamis'
in *Studi Classici et Orientali* (Pisa 1951)

J. H. Breasted: *Ancient Records of Egypt* III and IV (Chicago 1906–7)

A. R. Burn: *The Lyric Age of Greece* (London 1960)
'Greek Sea-power 776–540 B.C.' in JHS 47 (1927) 165 ff.

W. M. Calder and G. E. Bean: *Classical Map of Asia Minor:*
Supplement to *Anatolian Studies* VII (1957)

M. Cary and E. H. Warmington: *The Ancient Explorers* (London 1963)

J. B. Chabot: *Chronique de Michel le Syrien* Vol. I Fasc. i (Paris 1899)

J. N. Coldstream: *Greek Geometric Pottery* (London 1968)

V. R. d'A. Desborough: *The Last Mycenaeans and their Successors*
(Oxford 1966)

J. K. Fotheringham: 'On the list of thalassocracies in Eusebius'
in JHS 27 (1907) 75 ff.

J. Garstang: 'The Location of Pahhuwa' in *Liverpool Annals of
Anthropology and Archaeology* XXVIII (1948) pp. 48 ff.

A. Goetze: 'Madduwattas'
in *Mitteilungen der Vorderasiatisch-Aegyptischen Gesellschaft* 32
(1927) pp. 1 ff.

O. R. Gurney: *The Hittites* (Baltimore 1966)
   'Mita of Pahhuvas' in *Liverpool Annals of Anthropology and Archaeology* XXVIII (1948) pp. 32 ff.
H. R. Hall: 'The Restoration of Egypt' in CAH III¹ 290
R. Helm: 'Liste der Thalassocratien in Eusebius' Chronik'
   in *Hermes* 61 (1926) 241 ff.
L. H. Jeffery: *The Local Scripts of Archaic Greece* (Oxford 1963)
M. Kalac: 'Das Pantheon der Hieroglyphischen-luwischen Inschriften'
   in *Orientalia* 34 (1965) 401 ff.
C. M. Kraay: 'Hoards, Small change, and the origin of coinage'
   in JHS 74 (1964) 86 ff.
E. Laroche: Recherches sur les noms divins hittites'
   in *Révue hittite et asianique* VII (1945) pp.7 ff.
J. L. Myres: 'The list of thalassocracies in Eusebius'
   in JHS 26 (1906) 84 ff. and 27 (1907) 123 ff.
H. W. Parke: 'Polykrates and Delos' in *Classical Quarterly* 40 (1946) 105 ff.
W. M. Ramsay: *Cities and Bishoprics of Phrygia* (Oxford 1895–7)
M. Richter: *Archaic Greek Art against its historical background*
   (New York 1949)
A. H. Sayce: 'The new neo-Phrygian inscriptions'
   in JHS 46 (1926) 29 ff.
R. Campbell Thomson and M. E. L. Mallowan:
   '*British Museum* Excavations at Nineveh'
   in *Liverpool Annals of Anthropology and Archaeology* XX
   (1933) pp. 79 ff.
G. A. Wainwright: 'The Teresh, the Etruscans, and Asia Minor'
   in *Anatolian Studies* IX (1959) 197 ff.
M. White: 'The Duration of the Samian tyranny'
   in JHS 74 (1954) pp. 38 ff.
H. Winckler: 'Die Euphratlaender und das Mittelmeer'
   in *Der Alte Orient* Vol. VII part 2 (1905) pp. 3 ff.

ANCIENT SOURCES

Abydenos
Aethlios of Samos(?) 544 F 3
Africanus, ap. Cramer *Anec. Gr.* II 264.6
    ap. Malalas, Migne XCVII 260
Agathias (see Alexander Polyhistor)
Aglaosthenes of Naxos 499 F 7
Alexander Polyhistor 273 F 19a, 39, 79.5, 81
Alexis of Samos 539 F 2
Alkaios
Andron of Halikarnassos
Apollodoros of Athens 244 F 21, 62, 178a
(Apollodoros) *Bibliotheke* I 9.18, III 12.3
    Epitome
Archemachos 424 F 5, 8
Aristainetos Ep 1.15
Aristotle F Rose
    Oeconomica II 2
    Politics 1313b and *ad fin.*
Arrianos 156 F 92
Athenaios XII 540
Bekker, *Anecdota Graeca* I 234
Berosos
Cedrenus 252b (442.15)
      243
Charon of Lampsakos 262 F 6
Chronicon Paschale 265 b (494.15)
Chronographeion Syntomon
Clement of Alexandria, *Stromata* I 131 p. 397
Diktys of Crete II 18
Diodorus Siculus I 79
        IV 33
          64.4

Dionysius of Halikarnassos VII 2
Dionysius of Tell Mahre
Douris of Samos 76 F 63
Etymologicum Magnum 62.7
Eusebius, *Chronika*
Excerpta Barbari
Glaukos, ap. Plutarch *de Mus.* 1132 e
Herodotus I 56
        I 57
        I 64
        I 73 f.
        I 84
        I 94
        I 130
        I 147
        I 163
        I 165 f.
        I 171
        I 173
      II 39, 47
      II 178
    III 59
    III 122
    III 139
    III 148
    IV 144
    IV 147
    IV 166
     V 30
     V 41, 43
     V 68
     V 80
     V 92
     V 99
    VI 52
    VI 65
    VI 108
   VII 73
   VII 94 f.
   VII 235
    IX 97
[Herodotus] *Life of Homer*
Hekataios Jac 1 F 29

Orosius I 18.2
Pankrates: *Bokchoreis* 625 F 1
Parthenios 14
Pausanias   I 4.5
          II 6.7
          II 20.4; 22.1; 23.7; 37,5
          II 21.31
         III 4
         III 19.9
         IV 7.8
          V 13.7
        VII 5.5
          X 7.3
Phainias of Eresos ap. Clem. Alex. *Str.* I 131
Philostratos Her 2.18
Pliny N.H. II 12.53
        VI 31.39
       VII 197
Plutarch   *de defect. orac.* 21
         de Mal. Her. 21
         de Mus. 1132 e
         QG 11. 45, 57
Pollux IX 83
Polyainos I 23
Polycharmos of Naukratis 640 F 1
Pomponius Mela I 14
Porphyrius of Tyre 260 F 4
Promathidas 430 F 1 and 3
[Pythagoras] of Samos
Rylands Papyrus Jac. 105 F 1
Sanchuniathon VIII 11
Scholia to:
    Aischines II 7
    Apollonius Rhodius I 583/4, 1040
    Aristophanes *Plutus*   1005
               Clouds   967
    Dionysios Periegetes 850, 852
    Homer *Iliad* 18.219
    Sophocles *Ajax* 17
Servius in Verg. *Ecl.* VI 72
Skylax 98
Skymnos 715
Sosibios of Lakonia 595 F 3

Strabo I 127.1
    VI 1.14
    X 4.9
    XIII 1.8, 2.5, 3.2 f., 4.17
    XIV 1.35, 5.16
    XVII 1.18
Suda s.v. Ἴβυκος
    s.v. κώδων
    s.v. ταῦτα σοι καὶ Πύθια καὶ Δήλια
Synkellos (see Bibliography, Dindorf)
Stephanus of Byzantium s.v. Ἄντανδρος
                s.v. Γάζα
                s.v. Γρύνοι
                s.v. Δικαιαρχία
                s.v. Μέταον
                s.v. Τῆμνος
Thucydides I 13.6, III 68
Xanthos of Lydia 765 F 4, 5,8, 14, 15, 16, 17, 26.
Xenophilos 767 F 1
Zenobius I 54